RESHAPING THE WORLD

for the 21st CENTURY

D1481644

RESHAPING THE WORLD

for the 21st CENTURY

Society and Growth

Virginia R. Smith

BLACK
ROSE
BOOKS

Montréal/New York/London

Black Rose Books No. EE 307
Hardcover ISBN: 1-55164-195-X (bound) Paperback ISBN: 1-55164-194-1 (pbk.)

Canadian Cataloguing in Publication Data
Smith, Virginia R.
Reshaping the world for the 21st century : society and growth

Includes bibliographical references and index.
Hardcover ISBN: 1-55164-195-X (bound) Paperback ISBN: 1-55164-194-1 (pbk.)

1. North America—Economic conditions. 2. Latin America—Economic conditions—1945-
3. America—Economic policy. 4. Social justice. I. Title.

HC94.S63 2001   338.97   C2001-901165-2

Cover design by Associés libres, Montréal

C.P. 1258	2250 Military Road	99 Wallis Road
Succ. Place du Parc	Tonawanda, NY	London, E9 5LN
Montréal, H2W 2R3	14150	England
Canada	USA	UK

To order books in North America:

In Canada: (phone) 1-800-565-9523 (fax) 1-800-221-9985
email: utpbooks@utpress.utoronto.ca

In United States: (phone) 1-800-283-3572 (fax) 1-651-917-6406

In the UK & Europe: (phone) London 44 (0)20 8986-4854 (fax) 44 (0)20 8533-5821
email: order@centralbooks.com

Our Web Site address: http://www.web.net/blackrosebooks

A publication of the Institute of Policy Alternatives of Montréal (IPAM)

Printed in Canada

The Canada Council | Le Conseil des Arts
for the Arts | du Canada

CONTENTS

For my dear daughter, Kerry

Bliss was it in that dawn to be alive,
But to be young was very heaven!
—William Wordsworth

PREFACE

I wrote this book in order to help develop economic development practices that are different from both the modern pursuit of growth and the postmodern drive to deconstruct. My approach is rooted in a belief in human rights, in the experience of leftist thinkers and activists, and in the knowledge that people generate in their daily lives.

The book depicts how the roads and buildings of the New York City area became quintessential manifestations of the 20th century faith in capitalist growth. I watched in horror on 11 Sept. 2001, as the World Trade Center, the hub of New York's financial activity, was levelled. Grief and terror overwhelmed me as a I realized that thousands had been cruelly murdered, and that my continent is now subject to the kind of violence that has long been unsurprising to many of the world's less fortunate people.

President George W. Bush called what happened in New York a "war." "Now that war has been declared on us, we will lead the world to victory," he said. CNN adopted the banner "America's New War." Other paradigms were also invoked. A few pundits compared the terrorists' deadly accuracy to just-in-time industrial production. Many observers talked instead about the need for fairness in the distribution of the world's power and resources. Real inequities may be at the root of this and other violent outbursts around this world, they said, though unfairness does not justify such mayhem. This book is about the 21st century quest for fairness among nations, a quest that need not include war among its methods.

War seldom achieves fairness, and neither does summary dismissal of the claims made by the peoples of the less affluent world. A week before the attack, the U.S. walked out of a UN sponsored conference on racism. Canada showed its displeasure with the conference by not sending a senior minister. The justification for these actions was that the issues at the forum were contentious. I am not suggesting that there was any link between the conference and the attack. I am proposing that action to eliminate poverty and racism, which adversely affect both human rights and economic development, could go a long way toward reducing the amount of intense hatred in the world. Let's hope that people can move in that direction soon.

Virginia Smith, September 2001

ACKNOWLEDGMENTS

Many people in the Canada, Mexico, Brazil, and the United States provided the encouragement and the critical reading of drafts that made this book possible. Some of them are quoted in the text. Special thanks go (in no particular order) to John Dillon, Fred Flahiff, Bob Jeffcott, Gabrielle Labelle, and Louise Casselman.

I want to thank people at the Department of Canadian Heritage for providing the grant that enabled me to do research for the book. Helpful financial support was also provided by the United Church of Canada, the Canadian Catholic Organization for Development and Peace, the Presbyterian Church of Canada, and David Walsh.

A hearty thank you also goes to Black Rose Books, to Dimitri Roussopoulos, and to Linda Barton, who handled the manuscript. I am happy to be associated with their publishing tradition.

1
◆ ◆ ◆

A REVOLTING DEVELOPMENT

"What a revolting development this is!" railed my mother as she surveyed the walls of traffic hemming in our 1955 Ford on all sides. It seemed to us that there would be no end to our painful crawling along the Long Island Expressway (LIE) toward our home in Roslyn Heights. Most people remember their mothers' favourite expressions as the signposts of their youth, and I am no exception. "What a revolting development this is," was a line taken from the mouth of William Bendix, hero of the TV sitcom "The Life of Riley." Riley would clap his hand to his head and loudly remonstrate about the latest "revolting development" in his life. "What a revolting development this is" was my mother's response to mini-crises such as traffic jams or the cat pooping on the floor. At really horribly moments, such as my father's readmission to one of Long Island's mental hospitals, she usually said nothing at all; instead her face froze into an expression of grim resignation. Some of my mother's other sayings were "That and ten cents will get you a cup of coffee," and "Love many, trust few, always paddle your own canoe."

Like many New Yorkers, my mother has had a deep sense of grievance about everything, which has been constantly strengthened by events in her life and by the people she has encountered. The daughter of Irish Catholic immigrants who came to New York via Ellis Island in the late nineteenth century, my mother was born in what is now Spanish Harlem, moved to Brooklyn, and many years later to Nassau County, Long Island, where I grew up. In a family of four girls and two boys, she was the only one who graduated from university. She never got to work at teaching, her chosen profession, however, because she emerged from college in 1931, at the height of the great depression. She married my father, a handsome, ambitious young man, but he disappointed her by plunging into the first of many psychotic episodes some years later, after the birth of my sister at the beginning of World War II and mine at the end. According to my mother, my father's first paranoid delusion—in the late 1940s—was that he was being chased by the FBI. This curious idea, labeled "insane" by the doctors who examined my dad, has always struck me as being a logical thought to harbour during those early years of the Cold War.

For my mother, the most revolting development of all was the fact that our family was shut out of the bountiful economic development that seemed to be catching nearly all other Americans in a round of lawn mowing, commuting, and country clubbing. We lived in "garden apartments," not a house during an era when there were very few apartment units in Nassau County, which was fast becoming one of the wealthiest areas in the country. A 1974 book celebrating Nassau County's first seventy-five years noted that "the area attracted...energetic and rapidly rising middle-income families...by 1960, the median income of $8,155 was the highest recorded anywhere in New York State."[1] In this environment, there was little demand for apartments; during the postwar years up to 1956, only 6,900 units were constructed.[2]

Instead of spending her Sundays golfing, my mother often spent them driving to visit my father in Pilgrim or Kings Park, two of the state hospitals that made Long Island the "global capital of psychiatric hospitals," according to *The New York Times*.[3] I soon caught on to the idea that Long Island was an all round "revolting" development. I was a mournful, frightened, and overweight girl, but I was also an avid reader who collected a wide array of information. By the time I went to my Catholic high school, I was skeptical of most political and religious authorities, but I was still frightened of their power. I discovered that lots of other people did not fit in with suburban life and that these subversive souls were in fact mounting a critique of it. When I discovered that there were beatnik writers in my universe, I thought "Wow, how cool!" There was a chapter of the right-wing Young Americans for Freedom in my high school, but I and some other eggheads eschewed it. When I first heard that there were people call "freedom riders," I knew immediately that I wanted to ride with them, though I never did so literally; I was more of a couch sitter than a freedom rider.

After high school, I chose the University of Toronto in Ontario because it contained a Catholic school, St. Michael's College. The Vietnam War became a major conflagration during my university years, and many of my friends were drafted. I became an opponent of U.S. imperialism and developed the habit of criticizing imperialist development wherever I detected it, either close at hand or in the just then emerging sphere which called itself "the third world." I took up permanent residence in Canada after graduation because it had become my home, not because it was so different from Long Island.

There were numerous grounds for criticism of the economic development model adopted by the U.S. after World War II. The chief of these was that the postwar model was geared to promotion of the economic sectors which were already the strongest: defense, energy, automotive, and finance. Growth in these and the other strongest productive sectors was considered the engine which would bring peacetime prosperity to the nation and redress economic inequalities. It was hoped that continuous growth would dampen down social unrest and keep at bay contractions like the great depression, which had soured, at least temporarily, the prospects for my parents and so many others of their generation. "The concept of growth as a surrogate for redistribution appears, in retrospect, as the great conservative idea of the last generation," wrote Charles Meyer in 1978, when the great postwar growth spurt had ground to a halt.[4]

The tenet that economic growth was a tonic that would both strengthen capitalism and prove its essential soundness was eventually transferred to the countries of the third world, which was said to have problems of underdevelopment which the U.S. and its allies had the prescription to solve. Developing a model for how growth could occur in underdeveloped countries became the task of U.S. economists such as the Yale educated economist Walt Whitman Rostow.

Over the long term and even from the start, the growth oriented economic model favoured by U.S. policy makers contained deficiencies, which by the 1970s had discredited it among critical analysts in both the most highly industrialized nations and those of the third world. The model's principle deficiency—its failure to eradicate poverty and overcome extreme economic inequalities within societies—was the one communist and socialist systems tried to overcome. Its other biggest shortcomings—its excessive simplicity, its disregard for the rights of underprivileged groups, and its inability to offer a rationale for protecting the environment—were also apparent in one way or another in the communist and other redistributive regimes that surfaced after World War II.

A principle contention of this book is that the formula of growth oriented development was inappropriately applied in both the developed and underdeveloped nations of the world after World War II, despite the very great differences among them. The failures of development in the most prosperous countries, including the U.S., turned out to be quite similar to those experienced in the poorest.

Reshaping the World for the 21st Century tries to overcome the inordinate simplicity and abstraction of growth oriented development theories by telling some stories about how postwar development affected some specific people, communities, and nations. From the tale of our slow creeping along the LIE to our garden apartment in Roslyn, much can be gleaned about the trajectory of development in the New York metropolitan area during the 1950s.

Cars, Cars, Cars

In the 1950s, the northland gave birth, not to the blues, but to cars, cars, and more cars. Production of automobiles for U.S. consumers took off rapidly right after the war's end. Robert Moses's biographer and critic, Robert A. Caro, describes the speedy transformation at the Ford Motor Company's River Rouge Plant. "Within the month, River Rouge and a dozen other giant assembly lines were debouching 25,000 cars per day onto the nations' highways."[5] In Long Island, a huge increase in the car population was necessitated by the patterns of residential construction and transportation development. Nassau auto registrations jumped from 210,000 in 1950 to 700,000 in 1970.[6] Caro characterizes Long Island's postwar configuration as "communities that were not communities, that had no 'downtowns,' none of the focal points that alone make community development possible and that were so spread out that a trip to anywhere—store, church, school, movie, business—generally required a car, so that the lives of its residents were eaten up by the difficulties in getting from one place to another."[7] I remember how my mother clung to our 1955 Ford, even as the odometer climbed above 100,000 miles, because there seemed to be no other way to get around the island.

The boom in car production produced a need for roads and places to go just as, in turn, high speed, multilane highways pushed car production. In the New York area, much of the mid-century road and bridge building was directed by Moses, who, as New York's unelected Park Commissioner and Construction Coordinator, wielded virtually uncontested power as a shaper of the urban landscape for 44 years. In Long Island, Moses added the Long Island Expressway to the network of parkways already completed before the war. It didn't take long for the expressway to become known as the "world's longest parking lot," a description which "was often the kindest epithet uttered by frustrated motorists,"[8] according to *An Illustrated History of Long Island*. Suffocatingly overcrowded conditions became the highway's trademark: "Year by year, the huge road bulled its way eastward." It reached central Nassau in 1958, the Suffolk border in 1962, and ended further east at Riverhead in 1972. "And as each section opened, as each piece of Moses' largest road-building achievement fell into place, the congestion worsened. The Long Island Expressway's designed daily capacity was 80,000 vehicles. By 1963, it carried 132,000 vehicles per day, a load that jammed the expressway even at 'off' hours."[9] Moses' refusal to make provision for rapid transit or at least a bus lane on the LIE is described by Caro as an unmitigated misfortune for island residents.

The LIE was by no means the island's only postwar traffic problem. The Long Island newspaper, *Newsday*, in a recent history of the island community Levittown, provided this account of the town's degreening: "…residents watched as other developers lined what was once a dusty one-lane road with strip malls and asphalt meadows that siphoned business from village greens and created the need to expand the Hempstead Turnpike into the six-lane highway that now bisects their communities."[10]

The highways Moses built to ring the New York area were not always through territory as relatively open as could be found in Long Island. In cases where roads were ploughed through already existing developments, there was often irreparable loss of housing, damage to local commerce, and trauma to the community as a whole. Caro's recounts how the Bronx, a New York City borough across the Sound from Long Island, had its East Tremont neighbourhood ripped apart by the 1950s coming of the Cross Bronx Expressway. The total quantifiable loss in bricks and mortar alone was 54 apartment buildings including 1,530 units.

The residents of those 54 buildings were at first shocked and incredulous at the calamity which had come their way. The bad news, i.e., a notice to move in 90 days signed by Robert Moses, arrived silently in their mailboxes on a Tuesday morning, 4 December 1952. East Tremont residents, spurred on by the leadership of housewife Lillian Edelstein, battled to have the expressway rerouted just slightly so that they could retain their irreplaceable low cost units. There were moments when they seemed close to their objective, but they later saw themselves as never having had much of a chance. Years afterwards, Lillian Edelstein recalled the vote at the decisive board meeting. "It was so fast...I was positive at that last hearing we would win."[11] A big problem was that Mayor Robert F. Wagner, who had seemed to favour their cause, decided not to buck Moses on this issue.

The building of the Cross-Bronx expressway and other New York expressways did ultimately produce some constructive fallout. In the late 1960s, community activists in Toronto, Canada, pointed to the shambles on New York roads in their successful campaign to stop the building of the Spadina Expressway on the west side of the city. The Toronto based ex-New Yorker Jane Jacobs wrote of the Spadina-building folly that:

> Toronto's political leaders must certainly, we thought, have reflected on the lesson of Los Angeles where at rush hour the cars on the great freeway crawl 10 miles an hour, the same speed the horse and buggies used to achieve, where the poor have no practicable way to reach jobs, where the exhausts have turned the air into a crisis, where expressways, interchanges and parking lots occupy some two-third of the drained and vacuous downtown.[12]

After the success of the Stop Spadina movement, it seemed that North American governments might start to learn the lesson that "small is beautiful" in urban development, but, alas, it was not so. In the 1990s, widening roads was still the preferred method of dealing with traffic problems on Long Island; the building of new roads is no longer an option in the most heavily developed areas.

Road building facilitated a large increase in the population of the New York metropolitan area as a whole. The population of the New York area was 9 million in 1920; 11 million in 1930; 12 million in 1940. In also facilitated the transfer of many upwardly mobile young white families to the city's suburbs, including Long Island. At the same time nonwhite immigrants from the American south, Puerto Rico, and Latin American nations moved in great numbers to the poorest areas of upper Manhattan and the Bronx. In 1940, there were 485,000 Negroes in New York City and most of them lived in Harlem, which was an African-American neighbourhood for decades before it became a poverty stricken ghetto. Conditions in Harlem started to worsen after rioting there in 1943. "From that time on, conditions in Harlem continued to deteriorate as ever larger numbers of poor Negroes moved in and more fortunate Negros left."[13]

Puerto Ricans and other Latin Americans moving to New York gravitated toward Harlem's low rents. They moved into East Harlem, which became known as Spanish Harlem, then began moving across the Harlem River into the South Bronx when "the housing in Harlem and East Harlem surpassed the bursting point."[14]

Most white South Bronx residents fled the newcomers. "The old middle class white residents of the South Bronx, in what has become a classic pattern, kept moving further north and east to avoid what they considered the horrors of living among the darker-skinned newcomers."

Overcrowding became a chronic blight of the South Bronx and of one neighbourhood in particular—Hunt's Point, site of the drug raid chronicled in *The French Connection*. It has been estimated that, between 1960 and 1970, about one half million blacks and Puerto Ricans entered New York and about the same number of whites left. In the early 1970s, there were about 84,000 Puerto Ricans in Hunt's Point and 55,000 African-Americans. Just two decades earlier, in the early 1950s, the area housed mainly white middle class residents.[15]

By the 1970s, the population of New York City had levelled off, but population expansion continued inexorably in the New York area, which includes New York City, northern New Jersey, and Long Island. By 1994, the total was nearly 20 million.[16] (From 1990 to 1994, the population of New York City grew just .1 percent; the increase was 1.3 percent for the New York City area as a whole.)

This was the culmination of the mid-century growth spurt which made New York one of the world's first modern megacities or what Riccardo Petrella, head of the European Community's forecasting and assessment of science and technology division, calls a "world city state."[17] An important trigger for this growth was the poverty of nonwhite and other marginalized people in the U.S. hinterlands which spurred them to seek better prospects in a big city. (The U.S. hinterland in its broad sense includes not just the southern states and the U.S. protectorate Puerto Rico, but also whole Latin American countries such as the Dominican Republic.)

The massive transfer of population from hinterland to metropolis has occurred repeatedly during the second half of the twentieth century in the U.S. and other industrialized nations as well as in Latin America and other countries of the less developed world. Through this process, New York developed a "third world" within its borders which its elected leaders were unable or unwilling to care for adequately. (Modern megacities like New York, Sao Paulo, and Mexico are gigantic but in many ways helpless and unsustainable.)

The failure of governments in the U.S. and elsewhere to integrate people who arrived in the world's cities during the post-World War II years was criticized by many commentators, including Canada's Stewart Chrysdale, who, in a book published by the United Church of Canada, concluded that "governments and private enterprise between them have not provided at all adequately for the essential, material conditions of community in the inner city."[18] The lack of happiness and fulfillment even among people who had escaped to the suburbs was a less widely acknowledged or studied failure of the era's economic development. Colin Williams of the National Council of Churches, for instance, charged that the suburb "furnished a welcome escape from the harsh realities of the market place...The painful struggle against poverty, sub-standard housing, inadequate health services and discrimination in employment that is the lot of minority groups and those with inadequate education is left behind when the privileged suburbanite drives home in the afternoon." Williams may never have experienced the pain of those who had to drive on the LIE at 600 p.m.

With the great population bulge, the roads, and the automobile boom came the need to create new housing units. There was a very large amount of rental housing in New York City; it was also available in small pockets like our garden apartments in Roslyn Heights. Even the Levittown houses produced by Long Island developer William Levitt were at first rented rather than sold. Home ownership was, however, the nearly universal goal for postwar American families—to such an extent that if you did not set it as a goal, you might be considered odd or even anti-social. In New York and many other U.S. centres, the creation of large numbers of saleable homes seemed to require the development of large tracts of agricultural and other vacant land near the city. The great suburban development drive of the 1950s and 1960s was launched. The federal government agreed to help provide the financing needed to provide houses for returning veterans.

> The Servicemen's Readjustment Act of 1944, better known as the GI Bill, was piggybacked with housing legislation that had created the Federal Housing Administration a decade earlier...It pumped $20 billion into the industry in its first four years and was the closet thing to free money the housing trades had ever seen.[19]

Levitt wanted to be able to sell his houses to both veterans and non-veterans. On frequent trips to Capitol Hill to promote his cause he adopted the rhetoric of anti-communism, "repeating slogans like, 'No man who owns his house can be a communist. He's got too much to do.' "[20] He developed a relationship with the famous (and now notorious) anti-communist crusader, Senator Joseph McCarthy. "Levitt led McCarthy, the American Legion National Housing Committee, and top FHA officials on a tour of his project in August, 1947. He was photographed with McCarthy peering into one of the Bendix automatic washers that were standard equipment."[21] In 1948, Levitt got the legislation he wanted. A bill written by Joseph McCarthy liberalized lending by lengthening the mortgage term and by extending financing to anyone who could put five percent down.

By 1951, Levitt's Long Island houses, all built on flat farmland, totaled 18,000. They were simple homes with few amenities on almost treeless streets. Yet their owners, many of whom had fled from overcrowded situations in the city, loved their homes. Pat Daniels, one of Levittown's first residents told *Newsday* that "I was so happy to get out of Flushing I would have taken anything that was clean and neat."[22]

Levittown was never a favourite of architects or social critics—though it had a distinctive style that can be detected in the songs of the Levittown raised warbler Billy Joel. It was a sprawling, unfocused community of the type criticized by Robert Caro in his account of Long Island development, Robert Moses style. Levittown was not well liked by Lewis Mumford, who commented that "it's a suburb, and suburbs are just an expansion of a mistaken policy to build without industry...We have to build complete, well integrated 'new towns,' not monotonous suburbs with great picture windows that look out onto clotheslines."

The construction of Levittown launched a dramatic change in the eastern part of the island's Hempstead Plains. West of Levittown, Uniondale and East Meadow rose from former farms. The older communities of Hicksville and Farmingdale expanded onto farmland surrounding them.

A visit to a Long Island community such as Roslyn, East Meadow, or Levittown any day in the mid-1950s might have convinced the onlooker that Long Island was an area where the American dream was being lived to its fullest; a community where no one was poor or left out of postwar prosperity; the engine of economic growth was perking along nicely. I always knew that this patina of cozy domesticity was an illusion because my family was left out and not at all contented. The full extent of our alienation from Long Island society did not become clear to me until much later when I was an adult. That was because my family blended in well with people around us; in other words, we weren't black or Puerto Rican. We had a car—albeit an old one most of the time—and we had new clothes bought at "doorbuster" sales in cheap department stores like Lane's.

To find poverty stricken and visibly marginalized people all that was needed was a drive back along the Long Island Expressway into the nonwhite sections of New York City. The poor could be found in Harlem and during the years after the middle 1950s, in the Bronx too. One of the poorest areas of the South Bronx was Hunt's Point, which Michael Dorman termed in the 1970s "perhaps the nation's worst ghetto." He speculated that Hunt's Point situation was so bad because "the deterioration occurred there much more quickly and completely than elsewhere."[23] Hunt's Point changed from a middle class to a very low income community so rapidly because it was bordered on two sides by water—the Bronx River and the East River. White residents had to "stay where they were and coexist with newcomers, or move completely out of the neighbourhood. Most chose to flee."[24]

A New York City Planning Commission report described Hunt's Point conditions in these terms:

> Bleak tenements line block after block. The teeming district is peppered with shabby warehouses, lofts, garages, marginal businesses, and trash strewn lots. Schools are extremely overcrowded, and green space is all but non-existent. The welfare load is twice the city average. The district is more crime ridden than any other. Rapid social change in recent years has left few stable social or political organizations.

The post-Cross Bronx Expressway condition of Bronx's East Tremont district, as described by Robert Caro, seemed little better than Hunt's Point.

> After seven o'clock, the residential streets of East Tremont are deserted, roamed by narcotics addicts in gangs like packs of wolves. Even on East

Tremont Avenue, by nine o'clock most of the stores are closed, the lights out, huddled behind steel gates and iron bars. The streets of East Tremont are carpeted so thickly with pieces of shattered glass that they shine in the sun. Garbage, soaked mattresses, bits of broken furniture and, everywhere, small pieces of jagged steel fill the gutters.[25]

The Mentally Ill

Nonwhite immigrants to the city were not the only poor, marginalized people in the New York area in the 1950s. There were some homeless people, but their presence was not widespread. "In the 1950s and 1960s, flop-houses and missions in the skid row districts provided shelter largely to single, unattached, middle-aged, or older men. At least one third were identified as chronic alcoholics."[26] Homelessness was not conspicuous, partly because of the era's real prosperity and partly because mentally ill people like my father were kept in hospitals.

During the 1950's, a large portion of New York City's psychiatric patients were housed in three very large Long Island hospitals—Kings Park, Central Islip, and Pilgrim State. The island was considered a good location for the mentally ill because parts of it were semi-rural. "Western Suffolk County, with an abundance of cheap land and a steady supply of patients from New York City" may in fact have merited the *Times'* naming of it as the world capital of mental hospitals.[27] In 1960, Kings Park had almost 10,000 patients; Central Islip had 11,000; Pilgrim had almost 16,000. (The totals for the three in 1997 were 763, 0, and 613.)

Kings Park, which took its name from the old Kings County asylum in Flatbush, Brooklyn, had the best campus of the three hospitals: a total of 630 verdant acres on both Long Island Sound and the Nissequogue River. Nissequogue, one of scores of Indian place names on Long Island, was a branch of the Matinnecock tribe which lived in the area in the seventeenth century. The word seems to mean "mud," "clay," or "mire."[28] A "mire" King's Park certainly was for the thousands of unhappy social misfits detained there, including my father, who was a patient there for some years in the 1950s. Though the grounds are lush, the Kings Park buildings are formidably big, barred, and forbidding. Many patients were subjected to frontal lobotomies or to shock treatment—an intrusive procedure which leaves patients forgetful and may erase some of their memories. During just one year in the hospital, 1949, my father received a total of 77 shock and insulin shock treatments.[29] Lots of patients were chronically disturbed or elderly people who were destined to be permanent residents.

The money, time, and therapeutic energy devoted to most state hospital patients were minimal. A 1964 royal commission on psychiatric care in Canada reported this about the care of psychiatric patients in the U.S. "More than half the [psychiatric] patients are judged to be receiving custody rather than treatment. Twenty-nine state hospitals have no psychiatrists on staff. The average daily cost in 1961 was said to be $3.61 for a day patient; in three states the daily cost was less than $2."[30] Another shocking statistic was that "although there are 12,000 specialists in psychiatry in the United States, less than 2,000 of these are in state hospitals, even though the state hospitals look after nearly 700,000 mentally disordered."[31]

The drug revolution, which eased the symptoms of schizophrenia, depression and other disorders, greatly altered the treatment of emotionally disturbed people in the U.S. and other developed countries. It enabled my father to leave Kings Park for the last time in 1961. He was able work again and to live the rest of his life outside a hospital. Drugs also launched the era of widespread deinstitutionalization which continued and intensified during the 1980s and 1990s. The liberation brought by drugs has been described by Dr. Harvey Stancer of Toronto's Clark Institute of Psychiatry. "I had the opportunity, both in Toronto and New York, to observe these very sick human beings freed by this medication from their physical control by straight jackets, cold wet packs or continuous water baths."[32]

The scope of the liberation provided by drugs was extremely limited. The truism is true—that drugs tend to keep people quiet and docile instead of curing them. My father was never a really free or happy person in his later years, but he was able to function outside hospital walls (a great benefit to be sure). Still, can't a person hope to be really free in the land of the free? During the decades after the 1960s, it became apparent that one very strong motivation for the drug revolution was unwillingness to expend money and human resources on the mentally ill. Freedom for disturbed people eventually came to mean freedom to starve and to live on the streets.

The great surge in homelessness during the 1980s and 1990s has made some analysts nostalgic for the 1950s regime, but a realistic look back suggests that incarceration was no better than deinstitutionalization.

> Several prominent psychiatrists have urged a reinvigorated role for psychiatric hospitals…Yet the problems generated by these earlier practices were legion; to return to them is to ignore the insights of previous generations of researchers and the problems that generated new policies.[33]

Like the shunting of the poor to the inner city, the confinement of emotionally disturbed people in institutions during the 1950s was an inauspicious effort to hide the failures of growth oriented capitalist development. Such folks were not wanted on the streets of Levittown because they demonstrated that the growth ethic, which promoted the belief that all could prosper, was in fact niggardly with opportunities for the people who were unable to work, for nonwhites, and for people who were stuck at a subsistence level in U.S. society. Because these people were living examples of the growth ethic's flaws, they had to be brushed under the rug of social discourse or sometimes literally shut away from society. I always wondered whether my family's troubles really existed, because they were unacknowledged by society as a whole.

The failure mid-twentieth century U.S. capitalism to provide adequate material resources and health care for many Americans was only the first of its serious shortcomings. The second was its disregard for the civil and human—not just the economic—rights of visible minorities and especially of African-Americans. I saw very few black people anywhere I went in Long Island during the 1950s. In Roslyn Heights, there was an agency near the railroad station which found jobs for black domestic servants, but I never saw any of them in our community. (We did our own cleaning up after ourselves.) In my girl's Catholic high school in the town of Manhasset, there was just one black student. In the late 1950s, I knew through newscasts that there were millions of black people who were oppressed, who were mad, and who were riding and walking for their freedom. But still, even then, the existence of black people was almost purely notional to me, because there just weren't many around! Statistics bear out my observations; in 1960 there were just 42,132 nonwhite residents of Nassau County or 3.2 percent of the population. By 1970, the percentage had inched up to 5.1 percent.

Levittown history reveals one of the chief reasons why African-Americans were largely absent from Long Island during the years just after World War II. William Levitt did not even try to conceal the fact that black people were not welcome in Levittown, a policy that was tolerated and even recommended by the Federal Housing Administration. The FHA's underwriting manual at the time specified that, to be stable, a neighbourhood should be "occupied by the same social and racial classes" and recommended use of "suitable restrictive covenants." Levitt used this covenant: "The tenant agrees not to permit the premises to be occupied by any person other than members of the Caucasian race." Ann Gilmore told *Newsday* in 1997 about the cold shoulder she and her husband encountered in Levittown. "It was a Sunday, and when we got there sometime in 1948, well, it was strange, because when we finally approached a salesman to ask for an application, well, he didn't say anything, but just walked away from us. It was as if we were invisible."[34] They did find a place in the newly built Long Island community of Ronek Park, which eventually became North Amityville.

In 1948, the Supreme Court declared restrictive convenants unenforeable and contrary to public policy. The next year, the FHA delinked mortgages from racial segregation and Levitt dropped the covenants, but stated that he would continue racial discrimination in his development. Even in the 1990s, Levittown has remained white; only .4 percent of the population was African-American.

Levittown is just one example of informal agreements that kept suburbs largely white and inner cities black in many American cities. Whether the discrimination is economic or racial, the final result has been the same—black communities ringed by more prosperous lily white ones. In the 1950s, African-Americans were supposedly free to live as they liked, but still not able in most cases to claim full civil and political rights.

Another racial minority which was invisible at that time was Long Island's aboriginal people; the island's first nations seemed to be present only through numerous place names: Amagansett, Quogue, Montauk, Shinnecock, Patchogue, Matinnecock, Nissequogue (the river near King's Park Hospital), Nipscop, Noccomack, Massapequa, and many others. All these are Algonquin names.

The seeming absence of First Nations from Long Island was longstanding. Most of the Long Island Algonquins were wiped out by war, disease, malnutrition, or the effects of alcohol within three generations after the arrival of the Europeans.

The 1609 meeting between a member of Henry Hudson's expedition and the chief of the Canarsies was one of the first contacts between settlers and Long Island's aboriginal people. First nations were at a big disadvantage in dealing with colonists who pushed into their territory because, unlike mainland first nations, they had no hinterland where they could resettle themselves. Daniel Denton observed in 1670 that "…it hath been generally observed, that where the English come to settle, a Divine Hand makes way for them, by removing or cutting off the Indians, either by Wars one with the other, or by some raging mortal Disease."[35]

Still there were survivors; a 1785 census counted 765 Indian people on Long Island. They were forced onto smaller and smaller plots of land. Some Montauks were actually deported from the town of East Hampton and made their way to Wisconsin. The building of the Long Island railroad in the mid-nineteenth century forced the government to make a settlement with the Shinnecock nation, which owned land which the railroad needed. In 1859, the Shinnecock were given an 800 acre peninsula reservation in exchange for the 3,000 acre Shinnecock Hills area that the train would traverse. "Indians helped to build the tracks across their land, but local land developers became wealthy through property sales."[36]

By the middle of the twentieth century, the Shinnecock reservation in Southampton and the Possepatuck reservation in Mastic were the only Indian communities left on the island. During the 1950s, we never talked about Long Island's aboriginal people in the classroom or anywhere else. I knew that the Shinnecock reservation existed, but I never thought of finding out anything about it or going there. We just didn't take any notice of them at all.

A final defect of mid-twentieth economic development which will be discussed in this book is its failure to preserve the world's natural resources and environment. In the U.S., this lack was evident in both the consciousness and behaviour of Long Islanders and of many other suburban citizens. Like many other New Yorkers, I had virtually no contact with the undeveloped world beyond expressways and densely populated neighbourhoods. Roslyn Heights did have a nice park that housed a number of plump ducks, and I went there sometimes to feed them. If anyone had asked, I would have said that nature was what stood in the way of progress. Years later, New Yorkers would have to reassess their blithe assumption that the natural world was there for the taking.

Before Levittown and the six lane Hempstead turnpike, Hempstead Plains, the central area of Nassau County, was a huge pasture of about 60,000 acres used to raise livestock. Marsh grass, which grew in abundance along the island's south shore , was used for feed and bedding. During the commercial and residential development boom of the mid-twentieth century, Nassau County's farm land virtually disappeared.Caro laments the destruction of some the island's most valuable assets during this period—"its openness, its spaciousness, its beautiful North Shore hills and South Shore marshes and wetlands, its ocean and bay and sound."[37]

The folly of this unrestrained rush to modernity is evident on any map of the expressways and parkways that now ring New York like a vise. Some might say that U.S. governments and citizens have a right to use their own resources as they like. This outrageous statement does in fact have a grain of truth in it. When U.S. governments and corporations focused their unbridled enthusiasm for growth on other less developed countries such as Brazil, no such right—if indeed there is such a right—to exploit resources could be asserted.

A Canadian Social Critic

I was an alienated social critic from the moment I got a look at the dysfunctional Long Island Expressway and realized that drivers there spent up to one-fifth of their day sitting trapped on it. Marion Best, a Canadian born during the 1930s in the small town of New Westminster, B.C., acquired the role of critic less immediately than I did, but take it on wholeheartedly she eventually did. In the 1950s, as I was putting on pounds produced by excessive TV watching, Best was getting married and starting to raise a family. Best, who became moderator of the United Church of Canada in 1994, joined the church shortly after the birth of her first child. "I felt called that this child needed to be part of a community of faith that I hadn't been part of," she recalls.[38] Best spent the next 15 years raising her children, but still she experienced the pull toward community which eventually drew her to the United Church moderator's office in Toronto and to strong statements denouncing Canadian and international social inequities.

During her term as moderator, Best talked about early experiences which helped to shape her vision of community. One was her perusal of a church bulletin picture which depicted an obviously poor couple and their young child at home. "What brings that photo to mind for me now, is a deep concern about the widening gap between the haves and the have-nots, globally and here in Canada."[39]

Best's early perceptions of inequities within Canada's superficially prosperous and dynamic society were shared by United Church member and academic Stewart Chrysdale and others in the denomination. In a 1966 book commissioned by the church, Chrysdale wrote that "the number of dispossessed and deprived people in Canada is increasing as a result of rapid social change. If the church is to be effective in outreach, *it must understand how economic and social changes affect different groups of people.* Where inequities exist and injustices exist, the church should fight for redress."[40] Chrysdale's prescriptions were similar to the just-then-developing insights of Latin America's liberation theology. Both these kinds of Christianity were a world away from the piety I learned as a youth.

The rapid social and economic change in Canada at mid-century displayed many similarities to the explosive growth that was powering U.S. national life. Canada's differences from the U.S., however, were at least as striking as the similarities. Canada's economy was much smaller, less diverse, and more dependent on the export of staples such as lumber than that of the U.S. Canada, unlike Brazil and other Latin American countries, was never seen as underdeveloped or impoverished, but it shared basic economic weaknesses with third world countries, even as Canadians enjoyed a standard of living much higher than what was the norm in Latin America and other less developed regions. In a 1977 article, political scientist Daniel Drache described how, during the years just after World War II, "our liberal economists became increasingly puzzled by the country's continued lack of progress towards a fully advanced form of capitalism, under circumstances which should have encouraged this progress...Our ability to export manufactured goods actually declined between 1870 and the early 1950s."[41]

Though Canada's economy did not become fully developed during the immediate postwar years it—and the country's population—did grow bigger and more concentrated in Toronto, Montreal and the golden triangle between Montreal, Toronto and Windsor. At the same time it was becoming increasingly dominated by U.S. investment. The post war period was characterized by "increasing American ownership of our industry...Between 1948 and 1954 American ownership of mining and petroleum industries in Canada increased from 39 to 59 per cent."[42] According to Wallace Clement, the U.S. move into Canada was a direction deliberately taken as a reaction to World War II and the Korean War. "The Paley Report (Resources for Freedom) identified twenty-two key resources, with Canada designated as a major source for twelve of these."[43]

Unlike the U.S., Canada during the postwar boom generally did not marginalize large sectors of the population because they were members of a particular race or because they were immigrants from poor areas such as Puerto Rico. (Aboriginal people, who started the twentieth century poor and remained poor, are an important exception to this statement.) In addition, there has never been a headlong migration of people to any Canadian city the way people have jammed into New York; Sao Paulo, Brazil; and Mexico City, Mexico. The poverty of Canadians was caused by the economy's inability to generate anything near full employment and the government's unwillingness to try another economic strategy or redistribute resources in any important way.

The 401

In the beginning was the expressway, in Canada as well in the U.S. The road which hooked Ontarians into modernity was the Highway 401, the MacDonald Cartier

Freeway. The first section of the 510 mile road opened in 1947 and the last nearly twenty years later. The route extends from Windsor and Detroit in the west to the Quebec border in the east. In 1963, the 401 was called "the most important single development changing the economic and social patterns of Ontario" by Professor E. Pleva of the University of Western Ontario.[44]

Unlike the Long Island Expressway which had nowhere to go at its eastern tip except the Atlantic Ocean, the 401 connected Canada with the United States. This U.S.-connecting function was also performed by the Queen Elizabeth Way, the other major Ontario road to be completed after World War II. The 401 at first seemed to be more a highway for long distance commerce and travelers than a trap for tired commuters based in the Toronto area. The 401's original four lanes across Toronto were intended to handle traffic bypassing the city at a comfortable volume of about 35,000 vehicles a day. It didn't take long, however, for people to start using the 401 as a commuter road.

By early 1961, sections of the bypass were carrying up to 70,000 vehicles daily. Two years later, the traffic count had climbed to 85,000 a day, higher during peak periods. Checks showed that as many as 4,000 cars and trucks traveled in one direction within one hour—more vehicles than some sections of the provincial highway carried during a month or more.[45]

In 1962, plans were announced to widen the Toronto bypass to 12 lanes. And so was born that barely navigable stretch of highway at the top of Toronto where drivers spend their hours sweating, fuming, and riding their brakes.

That same year, 1962, Metro Toronto Council also approved over $73 million for construction of the Spadina Expressway. The Spadina was the final leg of a rectangle which would completely enclose the city with expressways in a New York style grid. Spadina critics even predicted that construction of the new expressway would inevitably create a need for a fifth, crosstown expressway from one side of the rectangle to the other.

Construction did start on the Spadina Expressway, but the road was short circuited and never proceeded to the heart of the downtown area as originally planned because of citizen opposition to it. Its crowning glory—from the perspective of big road lovers—was "a $13 million interchange at 401, a complex of bridges and roads that covered 150 acres of land,"[46] and incorporated 24 bridges and 25 miles of pavement.Former New Yorker and urban analyst Jane Jacobs wrote at the time that "up at the Highway 401 we could see what Marshall McLuhan calls the launching pad, a big, confident interchange poised for imminent attack on a wide swath of raw earth and for the subsequent invasion of the still unviolated ravine and pleasant communities to the south."[47]

Though the Spadina Expressway was stopped before it reached downtown, Toronto's domination by a motor vehicle oriented economy continued. As in the United States, an onslaught of new cars and drivers came with the highways. The

401 and the highways which intersected it became the province's key channels for commerce. "Between 1946 and 1952, motor vehicle registration shot up an amazing 75%. During those same years, the trucking industry in Ontario became a much more significant factor in the transportation field. By 1950, there were 200,000 commercial vehicles registered in the province, more than double the 1945 figure."[48] The number of passenger vehicles more than doubled between 1945 and 1955—from 555,000 to nearly 1,300,000.[49]

There was also a surge in the country's auto making capacity—mainly in the provinces of Ontario and Quebec. This growth occurred mainly because the Big Three auto makers in the U.S. starting building Canadian plants, usually near major highways such as the 401. As a prime example of this trend, the "Ford Motor Company of Canada Limited chose a location a few miles south of Highway 401 for its $65 million assembly plant at Talbotville Royal, near St. Thomas. The 1,331,318 square foot plant went into production in 1967."[50] Ford's Canadian President, Karl E. Scott, described the region bisected by highway 401 as being part of a "megalopolis stretching from Quebec City to Chicago, with similarities to the eastern seaboard of the continent."[51] The 1965 Auto Pact between Canada and the U.S., which allowed automotive products to cross borders without impediments, accelerated the growth of Canada's U.S. led auto industry, which had already grown by 40 per cent in just two years, from 1962 to 1964.

Population growth was another factor in the rapid multiplication of cars, roads, and manufacturing capacity. Toronto's population ballooned from one million in 1951 to two million in 1971. Toronto launched a two tier metropolitan government chaired by "Big Daddy" Fred Gardiner, who gave his name to the chronically overcrowded expressway which spans the south side of the city.[52] The authors of Building for People wrongly predicted that Toronto's population would surge to over four million by the millennium. In fact, population growth started flattening out in the 1970s as it did in New York City.

As in New York, Toronto's road building and population growth provoked a flurry of homebuilding and domesticity in the city's suburbs. In another book, Chrysdale noted that "distinctive of post-war urbanization has been the flight of hundreds of thousands of families to cheaper land, fresher air and new homes in suburbia. From 1951 to 1961 the population in fringe areas around [Canadian] cities grew by 96 percent, compared with an average increase of 19 percent in the cities themselves."[53]

Toronto's demographic growth had striking differences from New York's because Toronto never experienced a massive immigration of impoverished people from poorer areas of the country or from other countries (though there was a substantial influx of less affluent people from both inside and outside Canada.) There have always been rich and poor districts in Toronto, but sometimes these have not been split between inner city and suburbs, or according to race. Instead affluent and poor downtown neighbourhoods sometimes sit virtually on top of each other;

the best known example of this uneasy intimacy is in Cabbagetown, where upper middle class renovators live across the street from Regent Park, Canada's oldest and some would say least desirable public housing project. Some of Toronto's poorest residents also live at the outer edges of the city in high rise public housing projects. There have never been any "South Bronxes" in Toronto or other large Canadian cities. The poverty in Canadian cities can be spotted in details such as the kind of footwear children wear to school on snow days.

Housing Galore

In Canada, as in the U.S., there was a postwar boom in construction of housing for veterans, new immigrants, and for those who had remained underhoused during the depression and World War II. Social work professor Albert Rose, in a 1958 study of Regent Park, noted that home ownership had become the number one goal of Canadian families.

> Home ownership in recent years assumed the proportions of a national fetish. Along with this pride has come the notion in some communities that rental housing belongs in some other municipality and that tenant families constitute somewhat inferior citizens.[54]

Rose's account makes it clear that a great many Torontonians did not live in houses and were indeed severely underhoused. He includes descriptions, supplied by tenant selection officers for Toronto's housing authority, of some poor families' living situations.

> The house was, as far as he [the officer] could judge, fairly sound structurally. But the two attic rooms in which resided a family of two adults and five children (the Justice family, it will be called) were obviously inadequate on on physical grounds, not merely for this family but for any family. Seven people slept in one room under an inverted V-shaped ceiling. They shared the second floor bathroom with two other families...In all, nineteen persons lived in this house.[55]

Rose's figures also showed that families like the Justices were unlikely to find better accommodation they could afford. "The statistics of income distribution indicate that no more than one-third, perhaps less, of Canadian family heads can either rent or buy housing accommodation likely to be created during the next few years."[56]

The Canadian government took on some financing and ownership of housing. As in the U.S., the need to provide for returning veterans spurred action on the housing front. A major 1970s study of the country's low income housing by Michael Dennis and Susan Fish recounted how Wartime Housing Ltd., a Crown company created by C.D. Howe, constructed over 19,000 units from 1941 to 1945. At that time,

...psychologically Canadians crossed the hurdle of an almost universal abhorrence of the idea of state-owned housing. The flow of returning veterans, most of them clamoring for housing, started in 1945. By then government had realized from its wartime housing experience that direct action could put housing into place to serve a particular need, and the wartime housing agency was pressed into service to build houses for veterans. Between 1945 and 1949, more than 27,000 houses were thus constructed.[57]

The Central Mortgage and Housing Corporation was launched during the same period to administer the National Housing Act (NHA), and by 1949 became the landlord of over 40,000 families in 50 Canadian communities.[58] A 1949 amendment to Canada's NHA, which provided for federal-provincial low rental housing projects had produced only about 3,000 units by 1955. Ontario, with a worse-than-lacklustre performance in this sector, still became the national leader in low income housing programs. Many of these programs were managed by Progressive Conservative (PC) governments who took over policies and talking points from the Cooperative Commonwealth Federation (CCF), the United Church, trade unions and other progressive social housing advocates. In 1943, the PCs housing plank said that "an Ontario Housing Corporation will be created to plan a great housing program throughout the whole province...creating employment in the period of adjustment and, at the same time, bringing to an end the unsatisfactory housing conditions."[59] Between 1950 and 1964, Ontario provided 6,100 units of public housing—half Canada's total during that period, but less than one percent of the total housing units produced in the province.

The United Church at this time was exerting pressure and providing detailed suggestions about how to provide housing for people of moderate income. Participants in the church's 1968 General Council, for instance, affirmed that "adequate housing is a basic human right and is of the opinion that with proper policies it is economically and technologically possible for every Canadian to be adequately housed."[60] A report to the council named some of the forces driving up the price of housing —interest rates, the tax structure, and land costs—and urged provincial governments to implement mitigating measures. The council authorized the expenditure of $100,000 for a pilot housing project and urged the church to "consider the best way in which the resources of the Church, both in personnel and money, can be used to alleviate the housing crisis."

Slum Clearance

Toronto got started early on its low income housing program through its decision in the late 1940s to proceed with the Regent Park slum clearance project. Rose's study makes it clear that the low rise, low income housing project was a product, not of government initiative, but of pressure applied by the Citizens' Housing Association, which was formed in 1944, and, like the United Church, wanted to promote immediate action. In a seemingly prescient observation in his 1958 study, Rose remarked that,

> ...a hard lesson has been learned in almost every densely populated urban area in Europe, the United States and Canada during the past half-century: public housing, particularly housing to meet the needs of families of low income, does not 'just happen.' Only after much pressure and demand from a variety of groups in the community, including citizen's organizations, labour unions, boards of trade or chambers of commerce, church groups or veterans' organizations, is the required social legislation enacted and specific projects undertaken.[61]

Rose records how the association's appeals for slum clearance at first fell on an assembly of deaf ears. Still the association pressed its case for city council to proceed immediately with low rental housing in the Regent Park area. The plan would necessitate the demolition of 765 units, which would be replaced by 854 new units. The proposal had blemishes, including the large problem that it would almost certainly not house the area's current residents. Still the association wanted it because "it is a start in the direction which a public housing program should take."[62]

The association's encounters with the city council's board of control ultimately proved happier than that of East Tremont residents with New York's municipal government. When association members heard that the board was considering putting the Regent Park question to the electorate, they decided that they needed an audience with the mayor and the board to discuss the matter. They got their hearing on 20 Nov. 1946, when a delegation of about 250 crowded into the council chamber at 10 p.m. The delegation's first spokesperson, social work professor Stuart Jaffary, proclaimed that "housing is the most urgent question facing the City of Toronto today." The association knew that its points had been well received when Mayor Robert Saunders told the delegation that he was convinced that the question should be put to Toronto voters. "Thus a major victory was won," according to Rose's account.[63]

Regent Park was a not unattractive and well situated development close to the heart of Toronto's downtown. It proved an inimitable contribution to the urban scene, however, because slum clearance and development through demolition were soon subjected to critiques by community activists on the left (who rejected use of the wrecker's ball except in the most extreme cases) and business interests on the right (who wanted downtown real estate devoted to more profitable uses.) In the 1970s, the phalanx of activists led by aldermen Karl Jaffary (Stuart Jaffary's son) and John Sewell, among others, managed to create a social climate where a bit more than just lip service was paid to the goal of small scale development to benefit people of modest means. The half finished Spadina expressway and the peaceful coexistence of Cabaagetown's middle class renovators with Regent Park residents are two of the mid-century activists' enduring achievements.

Poverty Not the Exception

The fact that so many Torontonians were underhoused indicated that Canadians were poor even during the period of postwar expansion. A Senate committee study of poverty in the late 1960s in fact found that one-quarter of all Canadians were poor: one Canadian in four "was a member of a family unit whose income was below the poverty line."[64] The "average" low income family in 1967 received a total income of $2,442, with the head of the family earning approximately half of this, or $1,231.

In naming the causes of poverty, the Senate committee cited John Kenneth Galbraith's hypothesis in *The New Industrial State* that "there seem to be two distinct economies operating in North America. The first, according to Galbraith, is really the sphere of the giant corporations that dominate the nation's productive activity. The second economy is the one which employs the poor."[65] The truth of this observation about the unevenness of growth oriented capitalist development became abundantly clear during the 1980s and 1990s. Instead of drawing the conclusion suggested by its own observations, the committee criticized analysts who wanted to make a thorough exploration of the causes in poverty in Canada. The committee instead proposed a Guaranteed Annual Income as the solution to the problems it had discovered.

As in the United States, some of the poorest people in Canada at mid-century were the mentally ill and others who were not able to produce marketable goods and services. The great majority of mentally ill people in Canada were not homeless at that time. In fact there were few homeless people evident anywhere in the nations' cities. Toronto's earliest shelters, for single men only, were launched by the Salvation Army and the United Church. Then in the 1930s, the municipal government opened a shelter on Seaton St. for single male casualties of the depression. Toronto had no need of shelters for families and youth until the 1970s.[66]

At mid-century, Canadians diagnosed as emotionally or mentally unfit were usually confined in hospitals. Most of the country's mental hospitals were large institutions containing 1,000 to 2,000 patients. (The largest, with almost 6,000 patients, was in Quebec.) The federal government's Royal Commission on Health Care reported in 1964 that the number of mental patients in Canada considered as a proportion of the population was about the same as the number in the United States and the United Kingdom. "Most of these hospitalized patients (up to 85 per cent in some provinces) are chronic, and now receive residential care rather than active treatment...the number of old persons in mental hospitals has increased a great deal during the past 30 years. Since depression and war had stopped hospital construction, by 1945 most Canadian mental hospitals were severely overcrowded."[67]

The treatments at Canada's mental hospitals were the same as those prescribed to U.S. patients, with a few exceptions. The government of Alberta was alone in trying to curb emotional disorders by sterilizing many people diagnosed as mentally ill. The Royal Commission on Health Care noted that more than 2,000 people had been sterilized in 35 years.[68]

Starting around 1960, most of Canada's mental patients were gradually released into the community. During the fifteen year period up to 1976, two-thirds of Canada's psychiatric beds were closed. By the late 1990s, there were just 5,000 hospital beds remaining in Ontario.[69] Lack of community support made many ex-patients into homeless wanderers. The 1964 royal commission had already noted that follow-up and aftercare were grossly inadequate. "For the most part, after treatment psychiatrists discharge their patients from hospital with too little attention paid to their chances for future employment. In part, this neglect results from the traditional isolation of the mental hospital, and in part from the physician's too frequent aversion to concerning himself with the social problems of sick people."[70]

At mid-century, Canada's mentally ill people were frequently marginalized through denial of their basic civil rights as well as through their lack of employment and income. This was evident in measures such as the Alberta sterilizations. Many other groups outside the employable mainstream also found themselves short on rights in a society which placed economic growth at the top of its value hierarchy. Two groups that had to contend with pronounced disadvantages were African-Canadians and aboriginal people. The special problems of these two groups—related both to discrimination and economic marginalization—did not start or end in the 1950s; in fact their difficulties persist today even in instances where legislated human rights codes prohibit discrimination against them.

The Senate committee cited the special difficulties of both these groups. The African-Canadians referred to by the committee were the black people of Nova Scotia who took up residence in Canada many generations ago. The disadvantages Nova Scotia blacks have suffered are no less onerous because they are a very tiny minority instead of a very large minority, as black people are in the United States. Racial segregation by law was practiced in Nova Scotia too. A representative of the New Brunswick Association for the Advancement of Coloured People told the committee that "we black people understandably have expressed our plan, unvarnished views and deep concern, in numerous surveys and interviews, about the limited areas of employment, all seemingly to no avail."[71]

The committee acknowledged that Canada's aboriginal people are often the worst off people in the nation. Chief Walter Dieter explained that not all Indian people are poor, but those who are can be described as "the poorest of the poor." A solution to this problem recommended by the committee was to erase the unique opprobrium which came from being a poor Indian. "A poor man who is Indian or Eskimo should be regarded in the same light as a poor man who was a blacksmith, or one whose farm has given out, or whose outport has stagnated, or who is out of work because of economic conditions, or who is handicapped physically."[72] (The statement seems to say that being Indian is similar to being disabled.)

The committee report seemed to suggest that Indians should be treated as no different from other Canadians, and in fact this was the policy toward Indians adopted by the Trudeau government, which had commissioned the Senate committee report on poverty. In the history of aboriginal people in Canada there is no document more notorious than the Trudeau government's white paper, which sought to end special status for Indians. In its call for modernity as a salvation for oppressed minorities, the document was typical of mid-twentieth century North American thinking. The white paper, issued under the auspices of Indian Affairs Minister Jean Chretien, advocated a new policy "based on the principle of individual equality," a strategy which would lead to "full and equal participation by aboriginal people in mainstream Canadian society." The paper "spelled out the mechanisms that would dismantle special Indian status provisions…The government was convinced that the focus by native groups on their ethnicity was a negative response to their sense of exclusion, which could be better addressed through 'equality' and 'liberty.' "[73]

It turned out that Indian Affairs had badly misjudged what Indians wanted. It was true that aboriginal peoples' special status was the source of much of the discrimination against them. The government's mistake was seeking to end this discrimination by completely assimilating Indians to mainstream society, a policy that would lead to their eventual disappearance as a people.

Canada's aboriginal people were united in outright rejection of the white paper. Their response, *Citizens Plus*, refuted the idea that separation, isolation, or disorientation—i.e., special status for Indians—was the source of their poverty or other social problems. "Rather, the document charged, the paternalistic and improper manner in which government historically administered aboriginal rights had done most of the damage. Conscientious commitment by government to live up to its treaty obligations would have assisted in maintaining healthy, vibrant communities."[74] Instead, federal government failures to fulfill its obligations left aboriginal people without the resources they needed.

Concerted opposition from Indian nations prompted Ottawa to drop its white paper. Over a decade later, special rights for aboriginal people were recognized in Section 35 of the 1982 Canadian constitution, which stipulates that "the existing aboriginal and treaty rights of the aboriginal people of Canada are hereby recognized and affirmed." Abandonment of the white paper and eventual endorsement of aboriginal rights, however, did not mean that Ottawa was willing to take resolute action to protect aboriginal culture and institutions. During the era of the white paper, aboriginal people's poverty was interpreted simply as a result of society's inability to make the first nations full participants in growth oriented capitalism. It took a new analysis focused on rights instead of just on economic indicators to put aboriginal issues in a very different perspective.

A Critic Born in Brazil

Interest in social justice came early in life to Herbert de Souza, as it did to me. De Souza, better known as "Betinho," was born in 1935 in one of Brazil's rural provinces. A number of circumstances in Betinho's youth tended to promote a critical or gloomy view of the universe. His father ran a funeral home; he was a hemophiliac, and at the age of 15, he contracted tuberculosis. He read constantly during his three year quarantine for this illness.[75] Bethinho graduated from university in the early 1960s, an era of intense political turmoil in Brazil. Bethinho soon became politically active, and—like both Marion Best and me—he became involved in social issues through his identification with moral imperatives rooted in faith. In a 1996 CBC radio interview, he recalled that he had joined the student wing of Catholic Action, but was soon considered Christian activism too timid and was drawn to the radical ideas of Marxism and Maoism.[76] Betinho was too eclectic and pleasure-loving to remain a strict adherent of Maoism. He soon perceived that "people were not Maoists…my friends were crazy and I was crazy."

Betinho lived underground in Brazil after the 1964 military coup but eventually fled to Chile, where he lived until the military coup there nine years later. During the 1970s, he was a refugee in Canada, the country where I first met him while I was engaged in Latin America solidarity work. Our paths crossed again nearly twenty years in Rio de Janeiro, Brazil where Bethinho had returned to live permanently after the cessation of military rule. He was then a mainstay of Brazil's Institute for Social and Economic Analysis (IBASE) and a popular public personality as a leader of Brazil's Campaign Against Hunger and Misery. At that time Betinho was also emaciated and sick because he had contracted AIDS through a blood transfusion. He was getting closer and closer to death, which came in the year 1997. Even at that time, he liked a good joke. He appreciated the irony that he looked like an image of "Hunger" even as he led the campaign against hunger.[77]

The very first political article Bethinho wrote as a teenager was titled "Capitalism and Misery"; he remained a staunch opponent of misery all his life. For his summary on how political life should be organized, Betinho returned to his Christian roots for inspiration in the sense that he believed that the goal of politics should be human fulfillment and not just the acquisition of power or authority. "Politics has to be the way to be happy…Politics is not the art of unhappiness," he told the CBC in 1996. "Economists are the masters of unhappiness."

At mid-century, when Betinho was learning Marxism and officers were concocting their 1964 coup, most of the heated discussions among activists and politicians about how development should occur were focused on economic matters. This was because the material resources at stake in Brazil's development were unimaginably big and still largely unexploited. At the time, Brazil was a so-called "underdeveloped" nation striving to become developed; "underdeveloped" is a moniker it was still struggling to shake in the 1990s, when it had become the world's seventh most industrialized nation.[78]

As an "underdeveloped," "less developed," or "dependent nation," the course of Brazil's development was different in key ways from post-war development in the United States and Canada. For this reason, discussion of the development path taken by it and other third world nations occurs in Chapter Three, which focuses mainly on development issues in this hemisphere's less developed nations, especially Brazil and Mexico. The point made in this chapter is that there are similarities between the fiscal measures and development strategies employed in the wealthy and the less developed countries. The main differences—and they are big ones—are in the condition of these nations before development strategies are applied, in the way resources needed for the strategy are acquired and controlled, and in the distribution of the benefits gained through the strategy.

The first of these differences is the most critical in the decision about whether to call a country underdeveloped. A country like Brazil where so many people live below the poverty line[79] definitely needs some development or social change, and might well be termed underdeveloped. This is especially true in situations—and there are many such in Brazil—where poverty means lack of clean water, electricity, adequate nutrition and other basic necessities. A country where so many live in poverty may lack the capital and other resources to mount its own development projects, and in fact this has been one of the main assumptions of the U.S. Agency for International Development, the Canadian International Development Agency and other government aid agencies. Then there is the question about who designates the beneficiaries of development strategies: does a big increase in a country's energy generating capacity benefit its citizens, international business interests, or both?

Using these three standards to gauge development, there can be no doubt that Brazil is in a different development category from the U.S. and Canada because there is so much more what Betinho calls "misery" there than in North America. Yet the poverty measurements done in the world's wealthiest countries do not offer firm assurances that these countries are truly developed in the sense of offering their citizens a high standard of living. In the late 1990s, some 16.5 percent of U.S. residents lived below the poverty line, a score that seems to pull the country toward the "less developed" category. To the question about control of development resources, the answer in Brazil has very often been that U.S. companies or other outside agencies supply needed investment. Yet that has also been true in Canada, which no expert has ever termed underdeveloped.

These questions: how many are poor?; who controls resources?; and who benefits?; are political and not just technical questions. They suggest the strong possibility that development involves allocating resources rather than just making them grow bigger. In the 1950s, Bethinho, his friends who signed up with Catholic Action and later with Maoism, and most Brazilians were aware that development had a large political component. Brazilians at mid-century had fights about the politics of development which were much more intense and bitter than any which occurred in North America, where governments strove successfully for a national *modus vivendi*.

In Brazil, the struggle about development was between groups that backed populist, nationalist leaders such as President Getulio Vargas and his Minister of Labour Joao Goulart and those that instead favoured openness to foreign investment and strongly anti-Communist policies. The latter included backers of President Juscelino Kubitschek (1956-61) and the nation's key military leaders. The 1964 coup that brought down Goulart's government inaugurated two decades of military rule and sent progressive people like Betinho scurrying to safer havens.

The first general to take the presidency during the period of military rule was Humberto Castelo Branco, "a stocky, unhandsome man"[80] known for his military rectitude. His government replaced the country's numerous political parties with two on the U.S. model, dissolved or purged trade unions and arrested many trade unionists, abolished the National Union of Students, and disbanded the peasant leagues. Many well known public figures were *cassated* (deprived of civil rights). Later in the 1960s, detention, torture, and even murder of suspected subversives were widespread. Loyal alignment with the U.S. was the hallmark of the Castelo Branco government in the spheres of both politics and economic development.

> He turned Brazilian policy around from the pro-Cuban approach of Goulart to almost complete alignment with the United States in the global confrontation with communism. To clear relations with the United States, compensation was pushed through Congress for utility properties expropriated in Goulart days; they became the basis for the state electrical producer, Electrobras.[81]

Political upheavals in Brazil, Cuba, Chile, and elsewhere in Latin America sparked a fierce debate it the hemisphere about the three questions posed above and about the overall meaning of development. One of the participants in this controversy was Andre Gunder Frank, a practitioner of economics, and another mid-century social critic. Gunder Frank, who was brought by his father from Germany to the United States in the 1930s to escape Nazism, received a doctorate in economics, taught at Michigan State University, and then, to be where the action was, lived in various Latin American countries, including Brazil, where he was at the time of the 1964 coup. Like Bethino, he moved to Chile after the 1964 coup and then left Chile after the 1973 coup there. He was also at various times in Canada, where I met him in 1996.

Before leaving the U.S., he met some of the economic theorists who were responsible for U.S.-led development of the Alliance for Progress type, including Walt Whitman Rostow. "Walt Whitman Rostow 'confided to me' that since the age of 18 he made it his life mission to offer the world a better alternative to Karl Marx...Moreover, in case that were not enough, he then proposed to bomb Vietnam back into the stone age."[82]

Gunder Frank's writings, which enunciated some of the chief propositions of what came to be known as 'dependency theory,' asserted that economics was not a self-sufficient discipline and that the chief factors in economic development were really social.[83] He said what progressive Brazilians were learning through political struggle: that political conflict and social change were the instigators of economic development which would benefit the whole society and not just a tiny sector of it.

Since political change seemed difficult if not impossible to achieve through reform, the obvious answer therefore seemed to be the need to start change through political revolution. It became increasingly clear to me that all American, including my own, development studies and thinking therefore were not at all part of the solution to development problems. Instead they were themselves part of the problem, since they sought to obscure both the real problem and the real solution, which lay in politics.[84]

Gunder Frank's 1965 article about Brazil, "On the Mechanisms of Imperialism: The case of Brazil," is one of the founding documents of dependency theory; this theory is more fully discussed in Chapter Two, "Mid-century development theories." It should be noted here that the article shows awareness that there are similarities between the Robert Moses development style and U.S. led economic development in Brazil. In the article, a Brazilian politician—who is called "the Brazilian Barry Goldwater"—is roundly criticized for spending "his American-supplied dollars on parkways marked 'works of the government of Carlos Lacerda' and on projects such as forcing slum dwellers to move out to 'John Kennedy village' located twenty miles out of town, while burning down their houses in the center of town to make room for a new tourist hotel. That's development!"[85]

The idea that economics cannot be successfully pursued apart from broad political concerns such as housing and health care has been a widely held one by critics of capitalism since the 19th century and even earlier. Karl Marx's concern about social justice was what inspired him to discover dialectical materialism. In Brazil at mid-century, the principle that economic good sense must be combined with equity was applied by Betinho and his friends in Catholic Action, as well numerous other church based social critics who developed a complex of ideas which came to be known as liberation theology. Subscribers to liberation theology started with the idea of Christian charity and added economics to it, while Gunder Frank and other left wing economists proposed the injection of equity into investment decisions and fiscal matters. Gunder Frank has noted that "dependence theory and writing, including mine, also made a notable impact on and through the 'theology of liberation,' which was and still is spread through Catholic Church groups in Latin America."[86] The Peruvian theologian Gustavo Gutierrez acknowledged this influence. The notions of liberation theology, which were popular with this hemisphere's social critics under various guises and names, reached me and many Canadian people of faith, including those in the United Church. Liberation theology's mix of values, prescriptions, and strategies was and remains serviceable because it contains both economic good sense and high aspirations for equity.

Some Similar Characteristics

Despite the fact that the course of development in Brazil was much different from that in North America because Brazil was afflicted with underdevelopment and widespread poverty, there are some striking resemblances between the modernizing economic policies adopted in Brazil and in North American countries. In Brazil, as in the United States and Canada, there was a highway, but it was a trans-Amazonian highway, not an expressway moving commuters to their jobs or goods to the nation's most densely populated areas. There were dense traffic jams already in Sao Paulo, but these were not assuaged with crosstown expressways.

Highways in the Amazon are were intended to facilitate immigration and resource extraction. A highway from Belem at the mouth of the Amazon to Brasilia, the new inland capital city built during Kubitschek presidency, was completed in 1959. It stimulated a large immigration of *campesinos* from the impoverished northeast area of Brazil. Their small landholdings were soon taken over by large ranching and lumbering enterprises.[87]

The opening of the Amazon frontier area for colonization and resource exploitation did not create a great many holdings for an emerging group of family farmers and ranchers, as frontier settlement did in the United States. What it did do—in a way that suggests comparison with the U.S. and Canadian experiences—is increase the odds against the survival of Brazil's already pressured aboriginal nations.

Unofficial estimates in the 1960s were that they numbered 100,000…Their fate had been much better than those of the Indian populations in the U.S.A. and Argentina or even in the other countries of South America, but the prospects for their survival as an independent culture looked bad, as Amazonia and the Centre West were increasingly penetrated by the long-distance trunk roads.[88]

In addition to "the road," there was in post-war Brazil a burgeoning city-state, Sao Paulo, which was growing rapidly throughout the twentieth century and especially during the years after World War II. The forces that pushed population toward the big cities in Brazil's south were the same ones that prompted migrants to try their luck in the Amazon. High concentration of land ownership and increasing industrialization of the country's agriculture left little room for small holders or even for agricultural labourers in the country's rural areas.

Sao Paulo's postwar population explosion did not level off in the later part of the century as it did in New York. Population reached two million in 1950, then more than doubled to 5.9 million in 1970. The 1996 figure was 18.8 million and one projection for 2015 is 20.3 million.[89] The steady influx of newcomers has made Sao Paulo one of the world's most bustling and bewildering cities, with a street map as thick as a world almanac. The development of Sao Paulo as a world city state is more fully discussed in Chapter Three: "How did development fail?"

The incidence and impact of poverty in Brazil has been so serious that it cannot be rightfully compared with the economic deprivation suffered by people in the U.S. and Canada. An especially repellant feature of poverty in Brazil is that it co-exists in very tight proximity with excesses of fabulous wealth. One very important cause of extreme economic contrast in Brazil is the concentration of land ownership, which has also been the spur for migration within the country. At mid-century and still today economic development strategies cannot be discussed without reference to the need of millions for access to basic goods and services. The great contrasts in comfort available at different levels of Brazilian society have made its political struggles over development sharp and sometimes—as in the mid-1960s— violent.

The trajectory of Brazilian development in the postwar years is a striking demonstration that economic growth does not necessarily lead to poverty eradication. Economic indicators shot up during the military years, but poverty remained persistent and widespread.

When compared to Asian countries of medium and large sizes, Brazil's growth rates and creation of an industrial sector are seen to surpass any of these countries. Yet large-scale industrializing Asian countries, which often have had less growth than Brazil and have far lower per capita incomes, have achieved far better social results. Countries such as India and China, which are far larger than Brazil and have per capita incomes one-seventh of Brazil's relatively high rate, have better distribution of income (India), as well as better levels of health and education (China). Thus size alone cannot explain why Brazil has not achieved better social gains for its population.[90]

Problems associated with poverty were coupled with the denial of civil and political rights during the years of military rule. People suspected of being leftist or subversive were liable to be detained and tortured. Middle class Brazilians who were considered mentally ill were also likely to be deprived of civil rights. In fact, the categories of "leftist" and "mentally ill" were sometimes in danger of being confused or used interchangeably. This mixing of the notions of "sickness" and "subversion" also occurred frequently in the United States during the Cold War years.

A 1976 article by Gilberto Velho summarized a study he did of middle class Rio de Janeiro families from 1972 to 1974. He found that children in these families might be considered deviant or ill if they did not show a lot of interest in work, productivity, and achieving material success. He stressed that "observers of Brazilian society must be prepared to put into perspective these accusations and labeling situations. They must be aware of the complexity of contemporary Brazilian social processes, its changing patterns, and be able to identify the political interests that often lie hidden behind scientific language."[91]

Velho made it clear that definitions of mental illness, in Brazil as in other countries, are linked to the nation's dominant political ideology.

> I want to emphasize that for at least twenty years Brazil has been under the influence of a dominant ideology, more or less rightist and capitalistic, stressing the necessity of rapid growth of the Brazilian gross national product at any price. The more leftist approach, which was concerned with the necessity of dividing the results of the growth more equally, was completely put aside by the events of 1964...As a result, many families, especially in the mobile urban middle class, internalize this [economic] project and make it their own, stressing the possibility of individual success, big profits, buying goods, and a sophisticated way of life.[92]

Velho found that, in the families he studied, children who questioned the dominant economic project were subjected to strong negative pressures, including in some cases accusations of mental illness and hospitalization.

> So when a family member, especially a child, rejects the family's mobility project, it may create a serious crisis. If other mechanisms fail, the 'rebel' may be isolated through the accusation process. These middle class children not only reject their family's value system, they also adopt a different one. The new value system is not the invention of a 'sick mind,' but an alternative found in the child's sociocultural milieu.[93]

Velho stressed that problems that seemed individual could have sociological implications. He concluded that problems which seem to be pathologies or moral lapses can often be properly evaluated only in a broad social context.

Denial of civil rights and even of the right to exist was rife in the official treatment of Brazil's aboriginal nations. As in Canada and the United States, this disregard for first nations often took the form of widespread environmental destruction. A 1974 article on "Indigenous People and Sociocultural Change in the Amazon" described how penetration of the jungle and resource exploitation there were subjecting Indian nations to alien forms of social organization which treated them as a subordinate labour force. It pointed out that many of the indigenous groups occupying land along the route of the trans-Amazonian highways faced threats on two fronts: from mining companies and commercial agriculture.

The article provided case studies that showed how the operation of missionaries and government agents in the Amazon area during the 1960s served to pacify Indians and enlist them in the nation's modernization project. It described how missionaries were often the trail blazers for modern civilization who helped or pressured Indians to adjust to new ways of life. The article quoted researchers Ramos and Taylor's observations of missionary behaviour:

> Their position as the only effective source of manufactured goods and money gives the missionaries, up to a certain point, the power to control the behaviour of the Indians, which they exercise at their convenience.[94]

One of cases cited was the situation of the Guajajara, which was described by a researcher for the Summer Institute of Linguistics in 1967. "There are few who work for *civilizados*. The majority are involved in slash-and-burn agriculture or in husking babassu palm nuts. But due to the great influx of *civilizados* few of the people (Guajajara) still possess their own land. They perform any type of manual labour for the *civilizados*: porters, oarsmen, etc." The researcher indicated that virtually none of the women, but all of the men spoke Portuguese, since the latter came into contact with the *civilizados*.

How another group, the Gavioes, was incorporated into the modern economy is described through reference to the work of another researcher, Roberto de Matta. Harvesting Brazil nuts is an important activity for the Gavioes. "Formerly, Brazil nut trees were the collective property of the tribe. Now however, each Indian has his Brazil nut area (*ponto*) duly marked off and exploits his grove independently...The rationalization used by the leader is that the Brazil nut business has nothing to do with 'the affairs of the *caboclo* (of the Indian); it is the business of the *kupen* (Brazilian)." The article was not sanguine about the prospects for Brazil's first nations since the government, which had the job of protecting them, was also determined to help organize the extraction of the Amazon's resources.

The Haves and the Have Nots

The fact that development is a political issue and not just a matter of technical innovation or efficient organization was much more evident in Brazil at mid-century than in either the United States or Canada. It was no less political in those more developed countries, despite the fact that consensus building was more possible there. On this matter we'll give the last word to Betinho. "Either this is a planet for all of its inhabitants to live, eat, and have their rights respected, or let's admit outright that the earth is divided between the haves and the have-nots—then we'll see if war breaks out. If there's a war how will it be? An affluent white minority will be up against a mass of very poor and hungry people. Will the affluent minority live in bunkers? Will they migrate to the moon?"[95]

NOTES
1. Edward J. Smits, *Nassau. Suburbia U.S.A. The First Seventy-Five Years of Nassau County, New York* (Garden City, New York: Doubleday and Co., Inc., 1974), p. 202.
2. *Ibid.*, p. 204.
3. *The New York Times*, Nov. 5, 1996.
4. Charles Meyer, "The Politics of Inflation in the Twentieth Century," in Fred Hirsch and John H. Goldthorpe, eds. *The Political Economy of Inflation* (Oxford: Martin Robertson). Cited in Robert W. Cox, *Production, Power, and World Order* (New York: Columbia University Press, 1987).
5. Robert A. Caro, *The Power Broker. Robert Moses and the Fall of New York* (New York: Alfred A. Knopf, 1974), p. 895.
6. *An Illustrated History of Long Island*, p. 192.
7. *Ibid.*, 940.
8. *Illustrated History*, 194.
9. Caro, p. 949.
10. *Newsday*, 28 Sept. 1997, H19.

11. Caro, p. 875.
12. Jane Jacobs, "A City Getting Hooked on the Expressway Drug," *The Globe and Mail*, 1 Nov. 1969, quoted by David and Nadine Nowlan in *The Bad Trip: The Untold Story of the Spadina Expressway* (Toronto: New Press, 1970), p. 92.
13. Michael Forman, *The Making of a Slum* (New York: Delacorte Press, 1972), p. 181.
14. *Ibid.*, p. 181.
15. *Ibid.*, p. 185
16. Statistical Abstract of the United States, 1997, U.S. Dept. of Commerce, p. 42.
17. Riccardo Petrella, "World City States of the Future," *New Perspectives Quarterly*, Fall 1991, p. 59.
18. Stewart Chrysdale, *Churches Where the Action Is!*, United Church of Canada, 1966, p. 4.
19. *Newsday*, 28 Sept. 1997.
20. *Ibid.*, p. H25.
21. *Ibid.*, p. H23.
22. *Ibid.*,p. H13.
23. Forman, p. 214.
24. *Ibid.*, p. 182.
25. Caro, p.893.
26. Russell K. Schutt and Gerald R. Garrett, *Responding to the Homeless: Policy and Practice* (New York: Plenum Press, 1992),p. 5.
27. *The New York Times*, Nov. 5, 1996.
28. William Wallace Tooker, *The Indian Place Names on Long Island and Islands Adjacent* (Port Washington, N.Y.: Kennikat Press, n.d.), p. 160-1.
29. Letter to Virginia Smith from King's Park Psychiatric Centre, 8 July 1997.
30. D.G. McKerracher, *Trends in Psychiatric Care*, Royal Commission on Health Services, 1964.
31. *Ibid.*, p. 234.
32. Douglas H. Frayn, *The Clarke and its Founders: the Thirtieth Anniversary*. The Clarke Monograph Series No. 6., n.d.
33. Schutt and Garrett, p. 217.
34. *Newsday*, 28 Sept. 1997, H19.
35. *Illustrated History*, p. 17.
36. *Illustrated History*, p. 29.
37. Caro, p. 941.
38. Profile of Marion Best, Division of Communication, United Church of Canada, n.d.
39. *United Church Observer*, Vol. 59, No. 6, December 1995, p. 20.
40. Stewart Chrysdale, *Churches Where the Action Is!* (United Church of Canada, the Board of Evangelism and Social Service, 1966), p.3.
41. Daniel Drache, "Staple-ization: A Theory of Canadian Capitalist Development," in *Imperialism, Nationalism, and Canada*, ed. Craig Heron (Kitchener: Between the Lines, 1977), p. 17.
42. *Ibid.*, p. 22.
43. Wallace Clement, "Uneven Development: A Mature Branch Plant Society," in *A Passion for Identity: An Introduction to Canadian Studies*, eds. David Taras, Beverly Rasporich, and Eli Mandel.
44. Quoted by Ronald E. Richardson, George H. McNevin, Walter G. Rooke, *Building for People* (Toronto: The Ryerson Press, 1970), p. 1.
45. *Ibid.*, p. 22.
46. David and Nadine Nowlan, *The Bad Trip: The Untold Story of the Spadina Expressway* (Toronto: New Press, 1970), p. 2.
47. *The Globe and Mail*, 1 Nov. 1969, quoted in *The Bad Trip*.
48. Richardson, *Building*, p. 32.
49.
50. *Ibid.*, p. 12.
51. *Ibid.*, p. 13.
52. *The Junior Encyclopedia of Canada*, vol. 5 (Edmonton: Hurtig Publishers, 1990), p. 142.
53. Stewart Chrysdale, *The Changing Church in Canada* (The Board of Evangelism and Social Service, 1965), p. 9.
54. Albert Rose, *A Study in Slum Clearance* (Toronto: University of Toronto Press, 1958), p. 18.
55. *Ibid.*, p, 7.
56. *Ibid.*, p. 18.

57. A.D. Wilson, "Canadian Housing Legislation," Canadian Public Administration (Vol. 2, 1959), p. 219 quoted in Michael Dennis and Susan Fish, Programs In Search of a Policy. Low Income Housing in Canada (Toronto: Hakkert, 1972), p. 127.

58. Dennis, Programs, p. 129.

59. Quoted in Dennis, Programs, p. 147.

60. United Church of Canada, 23 General Council, Record of Proceedings, 27 August to 4 Sept. 1968, p. 190.

61. Rose, p. 46.

62. Citizens' Housing and Planning Association, A Statement on the Proposed Regent Park Public Housing Project (August 1946), p. 2, quoted in Rose, p. 57.

63. Rose, p. 60.

64. Poverty in Canada. Report of the Special Senate Committee on Poverty (Ottawa: Information Canada, 1971), p. 11.

65. Ibid., p. 53.

66. Daniel Anstett, The Experiences of Homeless Families in Metropolitan Toronto in 1997, Graduate Program in Social Work, York University, September 1997, p. 7.

67. McKerracher, Trends, p. 7.

68. Ibid., p. 6.

69. The Globe and Mail, 7 March 1998.

70. McKerracher, Trends, p. 16.

71. Poverty in Canada, p. 34.

72. Ibid., p. 35.

73. Tim Schouls, John Olthuis and Diane Engelstad, "The Basic Dilemma: Sovereignty or Assmiliation," in Nation to Nation, ed. Diane Engelstad and John Bird (Toronto: Anansi, 1992), p. 20.

74. Ibid., p. 21.

75. Interview with Bob Carty, "This Morning," CBC Radio, 8 Feb. 1998.

76. Ibid.

77. Ibid.

78. "Introduction," Social Change in Brazil 1945-85. The Incomplete Transition, eds. Edmar L. Bacha and Herbert S. Klein (Albuquerque: University of New Mexico Press), 1.

79. Luiz Ramos, Monica Perracini, E. Rosa Terza, Alex Kalachi, "Significance and Management of Disability Among Urban Elderly Residents in Brazil," Journal of Cross Cultural Gerontology, 8,4 (Oct. 1993): 313-23.

80. Robert Wesson and David Fleisher, Brazil in Transition, (New York: Praeger Special Studies, 1983), 26.

81. Ibid.

82. Andre Gunder Frank, "The Underdevelopment of Development," Scandanavian Journal of Development Alternatives, vol.10, no. 3 (September 1991), 17.

83. Ibid.

84. Ibid.

85. Andre Gunder Frank, "On the Mechanisms of Imperialism: The Case of Brazil," Readings in U.S. Imperialism, eds. K.T. Fann and Donald C. Hodges (Boston: Porter Sargent Publisher, 1971), 246.

86. Andre Gunder Frank, "The Underdevelopment of Development,"p.350.

87. Stephen G. Bunker, "The Eternal Conquest," Fighting for the Soul of Brazil (N.Y.: Monthly Review Press, 1995), 24.

88. Gordon Campbell, Brazil Struggles for Development (London: Charles Knight and Co. Ltd., 1972), 169.

89. B.R. Mitchell, International Historical Statistics (Detroit: Gale Research Co., 1983), p. 108; Encyclopedia of World Cities (Armonk, N.Y.: Sharpe Reference, 1999), p. 564.

90. "Introduction," Social Change in Brazil. The Incomplete Transition 1945-1985 (Albquerque: University of New Mexico Press, 1989), 6.

91. Gilberto Velho, "Accusations, Family Mobility, and Deviant Behaviour," Social Problems, vol. 23, no. 3 (Feb. 1976): 274.

92. Ibid., 272-73.

93. Ibid., 273.

94. "Indigenous People and Sociocultural Change in the Amazon," Man in the Amazon, ed. Charles Wagley (Gainsville: A University of Florida Book, 1974), 127.

95. An Interview with Herbert "Betinho" de Souza by Michael Shellenberger, Soul of Brazil, 63.

2

◆ ◆ ◆

WHY TALK THEORY?

During the 1950s and 1960s, many Long Islanders did not espouse any development theory more complex than "that and ten cents will get you a cup of coffee." A lot of us were proud of eschewing ideas more complex than those expressed in the ten commandments and the bill of rights. To this day I am scornful of people who promote values that lack a strong material foundation. What I did not realize during those Cold War days was that my appreciation of the "material world" might make me a good Marxist. I did not understand that the theory phobia, which was widespread in the U.S., was a way of avoiding Marxism and other ideologies which were seen, not just as overly complicated, but as downright subversive. In his recently revised book on development theory, Canadian political scientist Colin Leys pointed out that the avoidance of complex theorizing by postwar U.S. intellectuals was actually a form of self-defence. "But, whereas the early theorists of rising capitalism thought it essential to locate it in a broad conception of history, most Western theorists of development in the post-war years (and most of them were Westerners) avoided doing do because it meant, unavoidably, taking seriously the work of Marx."[1]

In fact, no adequate description and explanation of post-World War II economic development can occur without an understanding of the theories which guided it. Most political and social movements have some theoretical foundation. This truth applied even in the post-World War II United States, where belief in growth was the intellectual fuel that powered the economy. The growth ethic and the equation of economic development with growth are products of of the industrial revolution and the rise of capitalism. Before industrial production burst onto the world scene during the late eighteenth century, the study of economics as we understand it today was unknown. Industrialization brought a new self-awareness to the provision of goods and services: diligent thought was applied to how production could be improved and expanded. Study of the industrial revolution in the Academy started in the late 19th century. From this seeking of constant improvement came the goal of economic development, a teleological concept that suggests that there are economic goals which all human beings seek. During the postcolonial, modernizing years after World War II, economic development came to be seen as the goal of the underdeveloped countries of the third world.

During the 1980s and 1990s, the goal of economic development came to be rejected by postmodernists who proclaimed that they were interested in understanding what is in all its complexity rather than in prescribing what should be. The idea that any theory of human behaviour could be a guide to action became increasingly unpopular. Still the goal of development —freedom from poverty and oppression—and the need for strategies to get there retains a modicum of credibility even into the twenty-first century.

Post-World War II development theory was suffused with intellectual imperialism which at the time went largely unacknowledged. Most of the ideas intended to guide poor countries to prosperity were hatched in the U.S. by economists such as Rostow and Milton Friedman. Some other, more equity oriented capitalist economists came from developed powers such as the U.K. (John Maynard Keynes) or Canada (John Kenneth Galbraith).

W.W. Rostow was a very political thinker who gave his 1960 book *The Stages of Growth* the subtitle, *A Non-Communist Manifesto*. In this volume, Rostow talked about Four Graduating Classes Into Stages of Economic Growth. Using straight-faced pedagogy, Rostow demonstrated the timing of these graduating classes by plotting them on a graph. Great Britain is the only member of the first class (1783-1802), while the second (1830-50) includes the United States, France, and Germany. In the fourth class (1933 to the present) are ten less developed countries—Brazil and Mexico among them— that are said to have entered the takeoff stage. No indication is given of when or whether the 100 or so other third world countries in the world may be expected to attain the takeoff stage.[2]

Rostow boiled down development to the mastering of some universally applicable techniques. "For in the end the lesson of all this is that the tricks of growth are not all that difficult; they may seem so, at moments of frustration and confusion in transitional societies; and they seemed so when our own societies got stuck between maturity and high mass consumption, as they did between the wars" [the 1930s depression]. It would not be surprising if poor countries short of capital rejected and even resented this depiction of how development is achieved.

To date, Marxism has been the chief refutation of growth oriented capitalist development theory. Up until the 1980s, Marxist philosophy was espoused by many Communist and workers' parties in both industrialized and poor countries. Marxism was not a theory which applied specifically to the third world; in fact Marx, who was based much of the time at a desk in London's British Museum, focused his work on the course of economic development in the most developed capitalist countries and particularly in England. His work does not have much to say about the world's colonies with the exception of Ireland. In his writings on Ireland and the Irish question, Marx sometimes seems to say that resolution of the Irish question must precede social revolution in England. Such remarks, however, do not constitute a theory of imperialism.

Marx in fact expected revolutions to occur in the industrialized countries where the capitalist productive forces were most highly developed. The fact that the world's first Communist revolution happened in a less developed country—Russia—presented Marxist thinkers with a problem which became the subject for a large number of twentieth century books, articles, and polemics.

The century's leading Communist theorist about the role of capitalism in underdeveloped countries was V.I. Lenin, who was also a leader of the Russian revolution and later of the Soviet government. His book, *Imperialism, the Highest Stage of Capitalism*, written in 1916 in Switzerland, was in the mid-twentieth century still the seminal work which had to be reckoned with by all Communist and socialist writers on imperialism and third world development. In this work, Lenin argued that the age of imperialism is marked by an end to competition, the growing dominance of monopolies, and the need to export capital in order to boost profit levels. *Imperialism* included both detailed information about the export of capital and passionate polemics about the injustices perpetrated by early 20th century capitalists.

Even at the century's end, some of Lenin's discourse remains convincing. "We see a new type of monopoly coming into existence. First, there are monopolist capitalist combines in all advanced capitalist countries; secondly, a few rich countries, in which the accumulation of capital reaches gigantic proportions, occupy a monopolist position. An enormous 'superfluity of capital' has accumulated in the advanced countries." Beside this superfluity stands the wretchedness of the world's poor. The contrast makes Lenin positively livid.

"If capitalism did these things [raised living standards] it would not be capitalism; for uneven development and wretched conditions of the masses are the fundamental and inevitable conditions and premises of this mode of production. As long as capitalism remains what it is, surplus capital will never be utilized for the purpose of raising the standard of living of the masses in a given country."[3] (Extreme unevenness is in fact one of the failures of growth oriented development discussed in Chapter Three.)

Western political thinkers have very often dismissed Lenin's assertions about imperialist development or not considered them at all. Mid-century U.S. analyst Henry Mayo concludes that "if Lenin's *Imperialism* is judged as a theory to explain why overseas trade and investment took place, it is hard to see what it contributed...Imperialism has passed from being a rational theory into becoming a term of abuse for all overseas activities."[4] This rejection of Lenin's work was overly facile. Mayo and others have found it hard to separate Lenin's failings as a person and political leader from his achievements as a revolutionary intellectual.

Leftist third world thinkers and their supporters discovered in Lenin's writings a treasure trove of ideas that helped them to understand their lack of economic advancement in terms very different from the ones presented by W.W. Rostow and other postwar U.S. economists. For many, it was like discovering that the dog's biting of their knee wasn't their fault; it was the dog's fault or the dog owner's fault! U.S. based radical economist James O'Connor concluded that Lenin's portrayal of imperialism's five basic features—the concentration of production and capital, the fusion of bank capital with industrial capital, the export of capital, the formation of international capitalist monopolies, and the division of the whole earth by the great powers—was largely accurate even in the light of 50 or so more years of history.[5]

Latin American political writer Eduardo Galeano was another who discovered important analytical resources in Lenin's work. (Galeano also found inspiration in Andre Gunder Frank's work.) In a 1970 article, Galeano cited Lenin's argument that the domination of finance capital accentuates inequalities and contradictions in the world economy. "Time has passed and proven him [Lenin] right. The inequalities have become sharper. Historical research has shown that the distance that separated the standard of living in the wealthy countries from that of the poor countries toward the middle of the nineteenth century was much smaller than the distance that separates them today. The gap has widened." Galeano quoted a 1969 speech by U.S. President Richard Nixon at the Organization of American States to the effect that, if hemispheric growth rates persisted, "at the end of the century the per capita income in the United States will be fifteen times higher than the income per person of our friends, our neighbors, the members of our family in the rest of the Hemisphere."[6]

Though Lenin was right about the extreme economic disparities caused by worldwide laissez-faire capitalism, his ideas could by no means be adopted holus bolus by third world governments and movements seeking prosperity for all. This was so for several reasons. First of all, Lenin as a theorist had all the vices as well as the good qualities of the committed activist. You can hear his axe grinding throughout your reading of *Imperialism*. (This is true also of Rostow's *Stages*, but Rostow was at least not an underground revolutionary at the time he wrote his books.) Then there is the fact that, when Lenin wrote, imperialism meant political domination and not just economic control of underdeveloped countries. Forty years later, in the mid-1950s, development theory was designed specifically to chart an economic course for decolonized countries and at the same time to ignore the imperial history that preceded the drive to graduation and "takeoff."

One of the most limiting aspects of Lenin's work is its concentration on the situation of the capital exporting countries. It has little to say about what capital importing countries can do to respond constructively to their colonized situations. Lenin said imperialism "greatly affects and accelerates" the development of capitalism in the host countries without giving a full explanation of "accelerates." Galeano many years later contradicted him on this point.

The imperialism that Lenin knew—the greed of industrial centers in the search for world markets for their excess production and the capture of all the possible sources of raw materials; the extraction of iron, coal, and oil; the railways cementing their control of the areas under exploitation; the usurious loans made by the financial monopolies; the military expeditions and the wars of conquest— certainly did not accelerate anything except 'the development of underdevelopment,' as Andre Gunder Frank expresses it so well. Contrary to Midas, imperialism has turned everything it touched into scrap.[7]

At the start of the 21st century, Marxism-Leninism is reputed to be a stale, dogmatic, and slogan ridden discourse with little to offer people who need strategies to achieve social justice here and today. A careful review of Marx's and even some of Lenin's analyses about the flaws of capitalist development suggests that this conclusion may be overly hasty. Karl Marx and V.I. Lenin got a lot wrong, that's true, but so did John Maynard Keynes and W.W. Rostow.

By the waning years of the twentieth century, progressive (what used to be called leftist) critics of both capitalism and Communism had compiled a list of both systems' shortcomings. First of all, both systems were overly preoccupied with capital accumulation and the strictly money related aspects of human development. "The economic theory of growth thus largely coincides with the theory of capitalist formation," according to U.S. economist Aldolph Lowe.[8] After over 30 years in the field, Andre Gunder Frank concluded that "all these back and forths in economic development theory and praxis make it appear that the real economic development problem or insufficiency is not human and other capital, social structure, or values and ideology, but foreign exchange!"[9]

Many postmodern critics of both capitalism and Communism address themselves to questions other than "where can capital be found?" There are a number of reasons for this shift in emphasis. First, some theorists have concluded that adequate capital for third world development will never be found, and therefore attention must be turned to problems which have solutions. Then there is the very accurate criticism that the acquisition of capital in any venue does not mean that development will occur there. Growth may occur, i.e., through the opening of a sports stadium, but this cannot be called "development." Neither capitalism nor Communism, in other words, provides answers to the questions posed in Chapter One: "who controls development?" and "who benefits?"

These critiques of classical development theory are much needed reminders that economic development is not strictly business—that it includes political and social issues such as racism and women's rights. Many non-national investors who wanted to do business in South Africa, for instance, could not see that true economic development would not occur there until apartheid was dismantled. In Brazil, the exclusion of most black people from economic opportunity is an ongoing economic development problem, despite the fact that it has no direct connection to the process of capital accumulation.

What needs to be noted is that Marxism did ask the important questions about control of resources and distribution of benefits. What it lacked was fine discrimination among different social situations that is so evident in much late twentieth century writing. Dependency theory and its religious sibling, liberation theology, also introduced questions about human fulfillment into the standard economic development recipes. They have lost popularity in recent years, not because they lack the ability to describe unique situations, but because they are for now history's losers, pushed aside by triumphal right wing rhetoric. At least one lasting insight contributed by liberation theology is the truth that underdevelopment is not a problem confined to countries with low GDP or per capita incomes.

Popular educator Paulo Freire was one of the theorists who observed that many New Yorkers and people in poor countries were in fact very similarly situated. In the *Pedagogy of Hope*, he recalls his first visit to New York in 1967.

> It was an exceedingly important visit for me, especially because of what I was able to observe in places where blacks and Puerto Ricans were discriminated against. I visited these places by invitation of educators working with [Monsignor Robert] Fox. There was a great deal of similarity between what they were doing in New York and what I was doing in Brazil....I saw and heard things in New York that were 'translations'—not just linguistic ones, of course, but emotional ones as well—of much of what I had heard in Brazil, and was hearing more recently in Chile. The`why' of the behaviour was the same.[10]

What was revealed to Freire and what I already knew in my underdeveloped Long Island home—that an adequate development theory must encompass problems of insufficiency in the developed countries as well as in obviously poor ones—is one of the main contentions of this book.

Development Theory in the United States

U.S. economic preeminence after World War II made its development theory a little more "equal" than others. In fact U.S. led development theory was indiscriminately applied in nonsocialist third world countries as well as within its own borders. The way that Rostow and others advocates of capitalist growth developed their theory was to look at the way the industrial revolution had occurred and then assert that industrialization would occur in a roughly similar fashion in countries around the world.

In the 1960 *Stages of Growth*, the 1963 *Economics of Takeoff into Sustained Growth* (a book of conference proceedings edited by Rostow), and the 1975 *How It All Began: Origins of the Modern Economy*, Rostow used the experience of Britain and the United States, the two original takeoff graduates, as examples or prototypes of how growth should occur. Rostow pinpointed the first takeoff as occurring in Britain between 1785 and 1802 with the explosive growth of the cotton textile industry; during this period "modern growth began."[11] Rostow makes passing reference to the fact that this takeoff was partially based on the intense exploitation of slave labour in the U.S. South, which exported cotton to Britain. The launching of the textile industry stimulated activity in other sectors of the economy. "In the 1780s, the building of canals, turnpikes, and houses and the enclosure and improvement of land were, in scale, the main avenues of investment. Brick production, a good index of investment at this time, almost doubled between 1785 and 1792."[12] In *How It All Began*, a later, more reflective work than *The Stages of Growth*, Rostow pointed out that the rise of the British textile industry and its exports led to the demise of muslin manufacture in India. At first English products could not match the quality of Indian muslin, but English textiles started a large scale movement into India early in the nineteenth century. Rostow quoted an Indian historian who noted that, by 1800, "India was now well started on the road to transformation from being the industrial workshop of the world to one of its richest raw material-producing regions...India entered on a period of de-industrialization."[13] In the United States, the textile industry was also a prime instigator of industrialization at a slightly later date. "New England was able to move into a regional takeoff in the 1820s, centered on the mass production, with American-built machinery, of cotton textiles. There were 795 cotton factories in the United States by 1831, with 1.2 million spindles. Industrialization was well on its way."[14]

Rostow's work as a whole has indicated that underdeveloped countries can and indeed must seek to imitate the industrial takeoff experienced by Britain and the United States. Using their history as a model, he constructed a prototype for takeoff. Takeoff, Rostow asserted, usually starts because of the application of a particular sharp stimulus. "What is essential here is not the form of the stimulus but the fact that the prior development of the society and its economy result in a positive, sustained, and self-reinforcing response to it."[15] Rostow pointed to three conditions that facilitate such a positive response: (1) a rise in the rate of productive investment from, say, 5% or less to over 10% of national income, (2) the development of one or more manufacturing sectors with a high rate of growth, (3) the emergence of a political, social, and institutional framework which supports expansion. All these conditions imply that a national economy has a lot of money, i.e., what Rostow calls the "capability to mobilize capital from domestic sources."[16]

Another identifying mark of takeoff is the multiplicity of its effects, including backward, lateral, and forward effects. An example of a backward effect is a requirement "for new inputs of raw materials and machinery which require, in turn, an extension of modern contriving attitudes and methods." A lateral effect might be the transformation of the whole region where takeoff occurred. "For example, the cotton textile revolution transformed Manchester and Boston and the automobile industry transformed Detroit. Wherever they went, the railroads induced the transformation of old urban centres or the creation of new ones." Forward effects are those which move an economy to the next stage of industrial takeoff or development.[17]

Rostow made it clear that constant innovation is necessary to sustain a capitalist economy, as leading sectors—such as steel in the early twentieth century—slow down or become obsolete. "It follows also that the average performance of an economy can be held constant only by the introduction of new production functions which will compensate for the deceleration built into the older ones."[18] This conclusion about the nature of capitalist economies is one also drawn by Marx and Lenin. In fact this need for constant growth is the characteristic of capitalism that Lenin identifies as the spur for imperialism.

In the immediate post-World War II era, Rostow, like many U.S. economists and politicians, seemed very optimistic that the countries of the less developed world would soon take off and get their "development wings." This confidence in the future inspired his idea of development as a "trick" and of four development graduating classes which had mastered the trick. In *Stages*, Rostow also used the analogy of hardening to depict third world development.

> The central fact about the future of world power is the acceleration of the preconditions or the beginnings of take-off in the southern half of the world: South-East Asia, the Middle East, Africa, and Latin America. In addition, key areas in Eastern Europe (notably Yugoslavia and Poland), and, of course, China, are hardening up, as their take-offs occur; and while they remain vulnerable to military conquest and occupation…they have lost or are losing their old spongy character…In short, looking ahead some sixty years it can be said with reasonable confidence that the world will contain many new nations which have achieved maturity…they will have the capacity to apply to their resources the full capabilities of (then) modern science and technology.

This passage appeared in *Stages'* first edition; Rostow quoted it in the 1990 third edition, but by that time termed it a piece of "high risk speculation."

Nagging Doubts

Even during growth's heady heyday in the 1950s, there was limited, and sometimes covert, admission among mainstream economists that growth theory was not globally applicable and not even all that successful in developed countries. In those days, the 1930s depression was still a remembered reality for many.

One of the conference papers in *The Economics off Take-off into Sustained Growth* was given by University of Glasgow economist A.K. Cairncross, who displayed more sobriety and skepticism than Rostow did about the prospects for global growth. In his paper on "Capital Formation in the Take-Off," Cairncross asserted that,

...the apparatus of thought and analysis which economists have devised for studying capital accumulation in advanced countries is not necessarily applicable [in less developed countries]. Many of the models that seek to relate capital formation to economic progress do so in order to show how difficult it is to move steadily along a continuous path of growth. But while it may be interesting to be reminded that there is a certain connection between the amount of alcohol consumed and the unsteadiness of our subsequent movements, this reminder does not help us to learn to walk. We cannot assume that capital plays the same part at the outset of industrialization as it does once industry is well established.

Cairncross made a direct admission of the fact that capital accumulation was a big problem for less developed countries: "Development poses different problems for rich and poor and nowhere so strikingly as in the matter of finance. The problem of generating adequate savings hardly troubled European countries as industrialization proceeded."[19]

Then there was the fact that cheap or free slave labour, one of the assets available during the early days of the industrial revolution, would not be adequate for the job of economic development in the more capital intensive times of the twentieth century. Rostow's contention in *The Economics of Take-off* that "ample supplies of cheap labour provide a basis for effective competition with more advanced economies, once the other conditions for an industrial surge have been established" was an outdated contention even in the early 1960s when he made it.[20]

Then there was the issue of agriculture's role in economic development; this question was skirted by mainstream economists. Post-war capitalist economists asserted that agriculture should somehow generate the capital needed for industrial development, but without any apparent conviction that savings and investment would actually occur. Rostow asserted that "a rise in domestic income (which in most poor societies implies a rise in agricultural productivity and retained income) is an essential market foundation for the spread of industrialization, unless leading sectors are to be built around the requirements for military expansion."[21] This suggestion that "guns or butter" is only growth path open to underdeveloped societies does not promote optimism about their prospects.

Cairncross' paper talks about why reliance on agriculture to fund development is so problematic. "Data on investment in agriculture, by far the most important activity in pre-industrial countries, is inevitably defective. In such countries, the problem of measuring capital formation is aggravated by the more limited role of the market and the consequent difficulty of imputing value to the assets that are created."

Most mainstream economists said little about the inequities which have plagued third world agriculture; in other words, the theory that agriculture could fund industrialization was disproved first of all by landholding systems in most less developed countries (even before considering the often low prices of agricultural commodities). This issue is discussed in Chapter Three. There were a few other hints that the world was not, and indeed as currently structured could not, unfold into a prosperous future for the third world. One was the fact that many countries (including a number in Latin America) had not yet taken off despite the fact that they had been politically independent for many years and had the infrastructure needed for development.

Rostow hints that Latin America's failure to take off was the fault of its Indian cultures and also of its colonizers. (The latter were Spanish Catholic, not English Protestants.) "As the Latin Americans turned to the long, slow task of building viable modern nation states out of their ancient cultures, and the colonial heritage, they began also the long slow task of economic modernization."[22]

Then there was the hard to acknowledge fact that even railroad building—a transforming event in Canadian life—did not turn the "trick" of takeoff in many countries. Rostow notes that "it was the railroad and all its works that was to lift many nations in the northern half of the world into takeoff between 1830 and 1914."[23] Cairncross is, however, skeptical on this point. "The railroad was, in its day, as modern as the sputnik, but there are many countries that have had a good railway system for nearly a century and are still struggling to 'take-off.' "

Among mainstream thinkers, there was even some acknowledgment of the truth proclaimed by dependency theorists, Marxists, Communists of all stripes, and liberation theologians: that development meant more than just getting your economy to grow bigger all the time. Rostow himself admitted that "a part of the challenge posed by these hard cases [poor countries which don't take off] is that economists cannot usefully come to grips with them unless we are willing to make cultural, social, and political factors—as well as history—a living part of our analyses."[24] To this, Cairncross said "Amen": "Social change is interwoven with economic change and may dominate both the process of capital accumulation and the process of innovation that lies at the root of economic progress. In any society growth can never be a purely quantitative affair."[25] Still these insights were momentary for mainstream economists. The assumption remained that the U.S. and other most advanced industrial powers had the correct theories to promote development.

Development Theory in Canada

There is no one "made in Canada" development theory; as noted in Chapter One, Canada has not yet learned even how to develop itself properly, partly because it contains so many sparsely populated spaces and so many diverse peoples. In Rostow's stages, Canada is ranked as a fully graduated "class three" developed country which took off between 1870 and 1901. Other class three graduates are: Sweden, Japan, Russia, Italy, and Australia. In his chart, Rostow does not rank the countries which have graduated according to their relative strength, but he does in his writing. He notes that, around the turn of the 20th century, there is "a sharp relative improvement in the position of Britain and the United States at the expense of France, Spain, and Portugal. Thereafter, the pattern persists, with Russia joining Spain and Portugal in relative decline; Belgium, Holland, and central Europe holding their own; and the world outside beginning to gain a little on Europe."[26] It is not hard to guess where Canada might fit in this rather impressionistic scheme.

In *Imperialism*, Lenin describes a category of dependent country which sounds a bit like Canada. The only countries named by Lenin as examples of this condition are Argentina and Portugal, but his implication is that they are numerous. "There is also a variety of forms of dependence; countries which, formally, are politically independent, but which are, in fact, enmeshed in the net of financial and diplomatic dependence."[27] Canada is certainly an example of a country which used a railroad bankrolled outside its borders to achieve a modest degree of take-off. Britain provided bond money for the railroad and so freed a considerable amount of Canadian capital to move into the West Indies, where it operated in co-operation with British institutions there.[28] This dual role as both recipient and a supplier of capital is typical of Canada's global stance both at the time and in later years.

Canada's use of development theory has been consistent with its agent/recipient international identity. Mid-century Canadian political leaders such as Lester B. Pearson and Pierre Trudeau adopted U.S. bred development theories holus bolus, but at the same time they utilized approaches, including some associated with dependency theory, with more distributive and democratic goals. Since the 1950s, Canada has used its home grown theoretical savvy mainly as one guide for the dispensation of development assistance through the Canadian International Development Agency (CIDA), the federal government's aid-giving agency. Canada's development ideas have usually not been drafted to the service of imperialist political or military goals, as they have in the United States. Canada does not dispense military aid, and its aid-giving activities have not had the close association with counterinsurgency which has tainted so much U.S. development aid.

At mid-century, there were basically two, in some ways clashing, theories that guided CIDA's activities. One was the assertion that aid-stimulated growth is the economic dynamic needed to achieve prosperity both in less developed countries and at home in Canada. In the early days of Canadian aid-giving, during the 1950s and early 1960s, aid was seen as a temporary filler that would plug the gap between third world domestic savings and domestic investment. It was assumed that domestic savings would rise. By the late 1960s, many Canadian aid givers already realized that growth oriented development theory was proving a flop. CIDA's 1969 *Annual Report* acknowledges that "the gap between the rich and poor countries continues to widen."[29] Despite the problems with growth—its failure to occur or to promote widespread prosperity in countries such as Brazil where it did occur—CIDA and many other aid agencies continued to promote it as a development ideal. As late as 1991, the World Bank, the world's premiere multilateral aid agency said that its strategy was to encourage "broadly based economic growth."

One reason for the continuing popularity of growth oriented development theory in Canada and elsewhere is that aid has very often served as an agent of growth in the donor as well as the recipient country. This is so because, up to the 1980s, 80 percent of Canadian bilateral aid was tied to procurement in Canada; what this meant was that CIDA provided a goverment with money to buy certain products, but then most of the products would have to be purchased in Canada.[30]

The idea that aid promotes growth in both the donor and recipient countries might be termed the "railroad building" theory of development. Just as Britain supplied the bond money to build Canada's railroads, other wealthy and relatively older countries have supplied railway building capital to less developed nations. Lenin is just one of many commentators who have noted that this provision of infrastructure is a way that donors generate orders for their railway equipment and other infrastructural items.

His *Imperialism* cites a report from the Austro-Hungarian Consul at Sao Paulo, Brazil, which stated that "the construction of the Brazilian railways is being carried out chiefly by French, Belgian, British, and German capital. In the financial operations connected with the construction of these railways the countries involved also stipulate for orders for the necessary railway material."[31]

In the 1950s and 1960s, Canada supplied railway equipment and other kinds of infrastructure for industrial development—hydro-electric and telecommunications capacity—to numerous less developed countries; these deals benefitted the Canada based companies which supplied equipment and personnel for the projects. Some of the most massive and costly infrastructural items ever provided by Canada were during the 1950s and early 1960s: "the Warsak Hydro-Electric and Irrigation project in Pakistan ($35 million disbursed between 1952 and 1959), the Kundah Hydro-Electric Power Development in India ($44 million between 1955 and 1965), steam locomotives to India ($21 million between 1952 and 1955), and the Canada-India Atomic Research Reactor at Trombay ($11 million between 1958 and 1965).[32] The Warsak dam—a huge concrete structure almost 750 feet long and 220 feet high—was built on the Pakistan-Afghanistan border in an effort to stabilize a volatile front in the Cold War. On a 1975 list of equipment suppliers for tied aid were a number of Canada's largest corporations, including a number with head offices in the U.S. or Europe. Some of the names are: Alcan, Canadian General Electric, de Havilland, Hawker-Siddeley Canada, Northern Telecom, and Westinghouse.[33]

During the 1980s, CIDA was still in the infrastructure-providing business. In its largest bilateral development project ever, CIDA and Canada's export promotion agency, the Export Development Corporation, were providing $217 million and $403 million respectively to construct a 540 megawatt hydroelectric power station in northwest India. Some 200 Canadian companies were participating in the project, which was intended to bring power to one-third of India's population. During its 1985-86 fiscal year, a quarter—$88 million of $346.5 million—of CIDA's bilateral disbursements in Asia were for energy and transportation projects.[34]

One of the chief results of the "buy my railroad" approach to aid is that the economic development of the recipient countries comes to resemble that of the donor; the faults in the developed economy are duplicated or transferred to the world's less industrialized economies. This statement does not mean that the economy of the poor country becomes a mirror image of the bigger economy. (This failure of advanced capitalism to duplicate itself throughout the world has already been noted by Cairncross and even to some extent by Rostow.) Instead what often happens is that the less developed country acquires the railway, the electric power, and the roads, but still fails to take-off. Some theorists—some dependency theorists—would say that the infrastructure-acquiring economy becomes a complement or subordinate rather than a twin sibling of the developed donor economy. In the case of CIDA's giving, Canada has shifted to the third world some of its own weaknesses as a developed, yet not fully industrialized country. Its promotion of gigantic hydroelectric projects is a case in point. Their acceptability as aid has become increasingly questionable since they have come under heavy fire from citizens's rights groups and environmental activists both here in Canada (over projects like James Bay) and in a number of third world countries, especially India. (Just one example was the widespread opposition in India and overseas to the $3 billion Sardar Sarovar dam project which would flood forests, farms, and over 200 villages. The World Bank canceled part of its loan for Sardar Sarovar early in 1993.[35])

By the early 1970s, growth-oriented, "buy my railroad" development theory was facing competition from another line of thought and practice, which came to be known as "basic needs" aid. Advocates of the basic needs approach preferred to focus on providing the essentials for less affluent people rather than on expansion of an economy's leading sectors. Most people in development circles know the story about how the basic needs approach got started; it was announced by World Bank president Robert McNamara in 1973. There is no one account of how McNamara (formerly a U.S. Secretary of Defense) developed this kind of concern for the world's most disadvantaged people. Instead, there seem to be a number of accounts.

It may first of all be said that basic needs theory, unlike growth oriented third world development theory, does not bear a sharply etched "made in USA" label; it may therefore be called a Canadian idea in at least a limited sense, since CIDA enthusiastically adopted it in 1975 in its publication *Strategy for International Development Cooperation 1975–1980*. It was first of all the product of a global reality check—non-oil producing third world countries were becoming economic basket cases—and of statistical research. A study of 43 countries cited by development analyst Diana Hunt found that "economic growth was not only associated with increasing inequality but with a worsening of absolute poverty, particularly in the early stages of economic development."[36] In the *Strategy*, which pledged that Canada would adopt the basic needs approach, CIDA links the basic needs approach, not just to global crisis, but also to new demands from the third world. In the early 1970s, there was, according to CIDA, "a revolution of expectations on the part of the poor, who seek a more balanced distribution of resources and opportunities through a more equitable international economic and social order."[37] Colin Leys asserts that basic needs was "influenced by the (unacknowledged) impact of dependency thinking" and in turn links dependency theory back to Marx and Hegel—to a critique of capitalism made in a broad historical framework.[38]

The *Strategy*, which presented a 21 point plan for change, had the potential to change CIDA's way of working, perhaps radically. Its commitments to redirect aid to the world's poorest were rather specific. Some of these were: to focus on the most critical development problems (food production and distribution, rural development, education and training, public health and demography, shelter and energy), to direct the "bulk of its resources and expertise" to the world's poorest countries, and to concentrate bilateral aid on a limited number of countries.[39]

None of the *Strategy*'s goals was was ever met, partly because the era of budgetary constraints set in soon after its publication and never ended, even to this day. The departure from the agency in 1977 of CIDA's much criticized second president and *Strategy* originator Paul Gerin-Lajoie also helped to put the kibosh on basic needs as an official Canadian theory. Another factor was the perceived need to keep juggling goals and programs in over 100 countries (134 in 1992-93).

Still the idea of meeting basic needs, presented under a few different guises, retained credibility as a goal for aid and development even into the 1990s. It often appears under the heading of rural development: multi-faceted projects that help to improve agriculture, education, health care, and/or other aspects of life in rural areas. One such project on CIDA's books during the mid-1980s was in Nepal's Karnali-Bheri region. It included small hill irrigation, livestock improvement, reforestation, and soil conservation. Another, in Pakistan's Barani (dryland) areas, was intended to increase agricultural production on terrain that includes 30 percent of the country's cultivated area, but produces only 10 percent of its crops.[40]

"Aid to the poorest" is another aid label which indicates that a program or project is intended to meet basic needs. It appeared in the *Strategy* and again over ten years later in a CIDA goal-setting document, *Sharing Our Future*. *Sharing's* statement of principles and priorities says that "the primary purpose of Canadian official development assistance is the help the poorest countries and people of the world." Rural development and basic needs projects at the time appeared and still sometimes seem able to function as not insignificant correctives to growth oriented development trends.

Non-governmental organizations such as Canadian churches and volunteer groups are often the organizations best suited to delivering basic needs aid, just as big corporations and infrastructure aid go together like a horse and carriage. Canada is home to hundreds of organizations which do overseas development work. From about 20 in 1963, the number jumped to over 120 in 1972 and to about 220 in 1988.[41] By the late 1980s, Canadian government contributions to NGOs were the third highest in the world; only West Germany and Japan gave more.[42] With this enhanced prominence came an increase in NGOs' ambitions; many Canadian NGOs started wanting to do more than just participate in and guide overseas basic needs projects. They wanted to help equip the poor with the tools they needed to become political actors on the world scene. Canadian aid analyst Brian K. Murphy calls this advocacy phase of NGO activity "Stage Three," a stage characterized by "preoccupation with communications and the democratization of information flow; collaborative research, analysis, and dissemination; and action networking."[43] The evolution of NGOs has brought to their participants the realization that, to help people meet their basic needs, the NGOs must place themselves at odds with the large corporations which construct aid-funded dams and other kinds of infrastructure in the third world. This conjuncture presents us with a puzzle: could a CIDA funded dam ever be opposed by a CIDA funded NGO? (The paradoxical situation of NGOs is further discussed in Chapter Four and Chapter Five.)

Development oriented to meeting basic needs sounds like what the development doctor ordered for the world's poor people but it has not worked out extremely well in practice. This is because basic needs theory most often makes its way in the world under the banner of what Marxists call "reformism." It usually skirts the critically important questions posed by at least some dependency theorists: "who controls resources for development?" and "who benefits?" Development analyst Diana Hunt poses the basic needs dilemma in her book *Economic Theories of Development: An Analysis of Competing Paradigms*. Hunt identifies two streams in basic needs theory, one reformist and one non-reformist; the non-reformist option involves what she calls a "paradigm switch." The reformist, "improved public services" approach has "generally sought to minimize the extent to which a focus on meeting basic needs requires radical policy change while, as just noted, emphasizing the potentially positive effects on economic performance of improvements in a country's stock of human capital."[44] According to Hunt, a more thorough basic needs approach could not occur in most countries without a redistributive land reform. "Political commitment is a *sine qua non* for the implementation of a comprehensive basic needs oriented development strategy, and the lack of such commitment is the dominant impediment to its implementation. It is significant that in Taiwan and South Korea, two countries often cited for their success in meeting basic needs, land reform was initiated in the late 1940s by the American military government in response to mounting social unrest."[45] Hunt's assessment of the need for land reform leads to the conclusion that, in most third world countries, radical political change or even revolution is necessary before effective basic needs strategies can be enacted. This may be the reason why in his 1991 publication, Andre Gunder Frank dismissed basic needs as "hot air pie in the sky."[46]

The final question remains: can basic needs truly be called a Canadian development theory? Certainly it is not in the sense that its originators were not theorists based in Canada, but instead practitioners at an international development institution. Basic needs theory is more like dependency theory, which is the product of a group like minded political thinkers, than like Marxism. What can be said is that basic needs is not a distinctively American idea and that Canada's aid agency has promoted and practiced it under various guises during the past quarter century.

Dependency theory

Dependency theory is to date the only "made in the third world" development theory. It was developed to analyze a specific area of the third world—Latin America—but it has also been used as a basis for action in some African countries and also elsewhere in the third world. Dependency theory's brief life span was less than two decades, from the early 1960s to the late 1970s. One of the first statements by a dependency theorist to be published in the developed world was Andre Gunder Frank's essay "The Development of Underdevelopment," which appeared in the September 1966 issue of *Monthly Review*, a New York based, leftist periodical. (Dependency theory did have to be read and acknowledged somewhere in the developed world if it was to become a forceful presence in world politics.) I did not read it at the time, but its ideas filtered through to me from Mexico, where it was written, via a multitude of leftist meetings and publications. By this I do not mean that there was a worldwide "dependency theory" conspiracy, but that the essay was one element in an anti-imperialist ferment that was occurring in Vietnam, Cuba, and numerous other third world countries.

Dependency theory could not survive the 1980s triple whammy of mounting third world debt, falling commodity prices, and structural adjustment. In fact, Gunder Frank had decided that the theory was already dead as a political force nearly a decade earlier, in 1972, when "at the UNCTAD III meetings in Santiago, I heard 'development of underdevelopment' sloganized by establishment Third World delegates from afar."[47]

Dependency theory is really not just one theory, but a loose conglomeration of ideas about national economic development in countries where the government, business, and the economy as a whole rely heavily on capital and technology acquired outside their borders for new projects, and even, in some cases, for their everyday workings. Its practitioners, who were based mostly in Latin America, very often worked in that region's universities and international agencies, including UN agencies. "Basic needs" bears a World Bank imprint; "dependency theory" is associated with the UN and especially with the Economic Commission on Latin America (ECLA) and the United Nations Commission on Trade and Development (UNCTAD).

Dependency theorists had a wide variety of prescriptions for how to cure dependency, including some that contradicted each other.

> 'Bourgeois' dependency theorists in Latin America, such as Oasvaldo Sunkel or Celso Furtado, could perhaps be considered (however unfairly, in terms of their actual party-political sympathies) 'organic intellectuals' of their own national capitalist class, chafing at its subordination to the interests of foreign companies and the influence of the US state in domestic politics. Radical or 'left' dependency theorists such as T. Dos Santos and Rui Mauro Marini, on the other hand, aligned themselves openly with the Latin American labour movements, or with radical parties such as the MIR in Chile, and paid a high price by losing their jobs, being forced into exile or even being murdered during the era of the military dictatorships.[48]

Another dependency thinker with moderate tendencies was Fernando Henrique Cardoso, who eventually became Brazil's president during the second half of the 1990s.

Though dependency theory did not have a strong alignment with either of the world's two main competing ideologies, capitalism and communism, there can be no doubt that some of its leftist proponents were inspired by the work of Marx and Lenin, and by new left and "insurrectionist" writings such as those by Regis Debray. Another Communist stream of thought, Maoism, was especially attractive to many people in Latin America and other parts of the less developed world because it explained how a revolution could occur in an agricultural society instead of in an industrialized setting; Marx had predicted the latter scenario. Betinho acknowledged that he had at least a brief encounter with Maoism. Gunder Frank says that, after the Sino-Soviet split, he accepted the Chinese line.[49]

One characteristic shared by dependency thinkers was that they did ask the political questions—"who controls development?" and "who benefits?" —that growth oriented theorists were so reluctant to pose. This inclusion of social, political, and even personal matters under the banner of economic development made dependency theory similar to other progressive contemporary Latin American social currents and especially to liberation theology. Brazilian liberation theologians Leonardo and Clodovis Boff have explained why their religious expression sometimes sounds so much like an economic theory. "Placing themselves firmly on the side of the poor, liberation theologians ask Marx: 'What can you tell us about the situation of poverty and ways of overcoming it?'...To put it in more specific terms, liberation theology freely borrows from Marxism certain 'methodological pointers' that have proved fruitful in understanding the world of the oppressed."[50]

There is a dark or potentially pessimistic side to leftist dependency theory. This is so because its asking of the questions "who controls?" and "who benefits?" elicits information not all to the liking of the world's less affluent people: the ones termed "the wretched of the earth" by political analyst Franz Fanon. It is in response to this negative reading of the poor's situation that liberation theology (like other people-promoting philosophies) raises the flags of human agency, positive thinking, and social revolution.

In answer to the two big questions, it should be noted that Britain and the U.S. took a commanding lead in the industrial revolution and stayed there. Even the admission to the world's top industrial ranks of a few newcomers such as Japan—a process which started in the late 1960s—did not displace the old frontrunners. Small third world countries started at the back of the pack and stayed there. The obdurate reality of unchanging inequality threw the notion of takeoff into the realm of unsubstantiated speculation. Eduardo Galeano, who found inspiration for his writings in dependency theory, was one Latin American analyst who noted this seemingly permanent inequality as a fact of global economic life. "The oppressed nations will have to grow much more rapidly just to maintain their relative backwardness. The present low rates of development feed the dynamic of inequality: the oppressor nations are becoming increasingly rich in absolute terms, but they are richer still in relative terms. The overall strength of the imperialist system rests on the necessary inequality of its component parts, and that inequality is achieving every greater proportions."[51]

This continuing and ever widening disparity was also demonstrated mathematically by Fidel Castro in a 1968 speech at the University of Havana. Casto pointed out that the countries "that initiated the era of the Industrial Revolution, succeeded in increasing their gross product per inhabitant, per year, by only one per cent in the first 60 to 100 year of their development." In contrast "any underdeveloped country that increases its population by 2.2 per cent, will triple its entire population in 50 years and will need to invest no less than 12 percent of the gross product to compensate for that population increase...If, because of that enormous population growth, such a country wants to increase its gross product per inhabitant by one percent annually, it must invest no less than 16 per cent of its gross product."[52]

Not only are the original leaders in the industrial revolution still way ahead, they are actually frustrating efforts to catch up with them. This is the argument advanced by Gunder Frank and other leftist dependency theorists. In his 1966 essay "The Development of Underdevelopment," Gunder Frank advanced a number of hypotheses about underdevelopment. The first hypothesis is that "in contrast to the development of the world metropolis which is no one's satellite, the development of the national and other subordinate metropoles is limited by their satellite status." The second is "that the satellites experience their greatest economic development and especially their most classically capitalist industrial development if and when their ties to their metropolis are weakest."[53] This bleak view, i.e., that the strongest economies were blocking the weaker ones, was not shared by more moderate, reform minded dependency theorists, who declared that third world nations could make progress even without shaking their subordinate status.

Some dependency theory writings assert that the inequality between the most advanced economies and the underdeveloped world is reproduced within underdeveloped countries. Investment in key sectors such as petroleum and auto making tends to create isolated enclaves of prosperity, while the poor outside the enclave grow more impoverished than ever. Gunder Frank, for instance, said that the explosive growth of cities such as Sao Paulo was creating such enclaves. "The development of industry in Sao Paulo has not brought greater riches to the other regions of Brazil. Instead, it converted them into internal colonial satellites, decapitalized them further, and consolidated or even deepened their underdevelopment."[54] This extreme unevenness of postwar development in Latin America is taken up in more detail in Chapter Three.

The widespread perception and also the evidence that ties with the wealthiest countries were making development more difficult instead of helping it to occur led some dependency thinkers to promote the concept of self-reliance, which was most often seen as a series of measures which would enable less developed economies meet their own basic needs, without depending solely or even largely on loans, technical support, or investment from abroad. This idea that "we can meet our own basic needs" was often coupled with the goal of raising the nation's overall standard of living. Basic needs aid dispensed through NGOs was tied in at least some respects to this notion of self-reliance.

An autonomy-promoting measure tried by some Latin American governments during the 1960s was import substitution, which meant that products such as automobiles were manufactured inside the country instead of imported. Import substitution tended to promote self-reliance in a way that did not alter or threaten the existing relationships between third world countries and the largest producers of expensive consumer goods; these companies needed and indeed wanted to invest overseas. Import substitution also did nothing to enlarge the domestic market for consumer goods; it simply made those goods available at home for consumers of means.

Dependency theorists' claims that more authentic and fuller self-reliance could be achieved were made credible by the citing of evidence that less developed countries had potential or in some cases already actualized sources of capital that would enable them to decide on investments. This claim that "we have enough ourselves" was often coupled with the assertion that the resources of less developed countries were being plundered by the most industrialized powers, which then returned a fraction of what was taken and called it "aid." The contention that the world's poor were being robbed by the rich was at the root of the revolutionary struggles that wracked the third world at mid-century. Most politicians and intel-

lectuals based in the strongest nations alleged that third world guerrilla movements were fueled mainly by paranoia. The third world revolutionaries rejoined that
first world leaders always presented a version of the world's workings that was totally self-serving. The presence of communist powers on the world stage made
touchy situations even tenser; the help extended by some communist governments
to leftist revolutionaries provoked strong bouts of paranoia among first world policy makers.

Apart from the question of who was taking resources from whom, dependency theorists did make a convincing case that foreign companies and other kinds
of investors in less developed economies often utilized domestic capital for their
projects. This contrasted with their widely circulated image as bearers of money
and technology to non-industrialized areas of the world. In his 1964 essay on the
mechanisms of imperialism in Brazil, Andre Gunder Frank pointed out that "in the
public utility sector especially, the ownership and earnings of so-called American
capital are based, not on original investment of capital, but on concessions, exorbitant use rates, and other privileges. The capital is provided by Brazil. The Sao
Paulo Light Company...in 1907 took over a concession already granted to two
Brazilian individuals until 1950 and then got it extended to 1990...Following the
usual procedure, the various light companies financed expansion of service to new
areas by assessments on, and more recently by loans from the communities to be
served, while equipment was purchased out of earnings from exorbitant utility
rates. Even so, as any user can testify, service always lags far behind demand."[55]

Other writers also pointed out that, in Latin America particularly, U.S. companies mobilize local capital for their operations. Eduardo Galeano cited several
sources for this assertion, including some based in the United States.

> According to the OAS, an unimpeachable source in this respect, barely
> twenty cents of every dollar that U.S. industrial affiliates use for their
> operations and expansion come from the U.S. The remaining eighty cents
> come from Latin American sources, through credits, loans, and the
> retention of profits...This channeling of national resources into foreign
> enterprises is due in large part to the proliferation of U.S. bank branches
> spread throughout Latin America in order to pour national savings into
> foreign hands. There were 78 branches of U.S. banks in the area in 1964; in
> 1967, the number had risen to 133.[56]

Other contemporary leftist writers, including James O'Connor, Paul Baran, and
Paul Sweezy, confirmed this interpretation of the facts about global flows. The
idea that Latin American and other less developed countries already possessed at
least some of the resources needed for their development was very often coupled
with the idea that the agricultural sector could or should provide a large portion of
the resources needed for development in the third world. The line was that, if agriculture was not already contributing its bit to national development, it had to be

restructured so that its productivity and its capacity to provide capital for industrial development would increase. (Remember that Rostow suggested that that the only alternative to agriculture was military production.) Thinkers on both the left and right seemed to agree that agriculture was somehow the key which would open the door to prosperity for the third world. The question was: how is this to be done?

On both the left and right, the theory—which almost never worked out in practice—was that farmers, who form a large portion of the population in most third world countries could move beyond the level of subsistence agriculture by improving their agricultural methods and developing a greater capacity to sell their goods, either at home or for export. As they became more prosperous, they would have savings to contribute to the national economy either as savers or consumers. Moderate thinkers who proposed a basic needs perspective seemed to believe most that this scenario might become actual. Leftists instead called with increasing conviction for land reform, and that cry has never ceased in countries such as Brazil. Economists on the right in the meantime were pushing for the green revolution and agribusiness as solutions. Rightists' stress on productivity and increased exports led them to overlook completely the basic needs of small farmers and their claims for justice.

By the late 1980s, the fall in price for many third world agricultural commodities led many exporting countries into a downward spiral; the more they exported, the more the price of their commodity dropped and the less they had available to pay off their debts. The idea of industrial investment funded by agriculture seemed to have fallen out of the world's development syllabus. Yet there were a few theorists left who still asserted that self-reliant development was possible; one of them was Samir Amin who had occasionally collaborated on publications with Gunder Frank. As late as the 1980s, Amin was promoting what he called a "national and popular auto-centred strategy." Some of the chief elements of this strategy are: A declaration of agricultural priority, industrialization geared to the maintenance of agricultural productivity, and national and popular forms of social organization.[57] By that time, Gunder Frank had concluded that delinking was not a development option for the third world.[58]

Another ingredient of some dependency theory was the formulation of development goals which deviated from those set by growth oriented development. These different goals—including distributive justice, equal rights and respect for peoples, and protection of the environment—were the social and not just economic benefits called for by leftist dependency thinkers including Frank, practitioners of liberation theology, and community activists in centres throughout North and South America. The problem was then and still is that these goals cannot not be adequately met until national wealth is used to acquire the goods and services people need. The setting of alternative development goals involves distinguishing necessary goods and services from superfluous or even harmful ones. This effort to

restrain consumerism and promote simpler ways of life was started by leftists and
subsequently has been continued and intensified by postmodernists. The choices
required to change personal patterns are often stark, particularly for people whose
lives have always included TV: yes to porridge, no to 20 kinds of sugary cereals;
yes to bicycles, no to poison-puffing, gas-slurping, road-hogging hulks!

The effort to set development goals focused on people's health rather than on
business sector buoyancy is what led some dependency thinkers to the perception
that underdevelopment is a chronic condition, not just in the third world, but in
many areas areas of the most developed countries. In the United States, the civil
rights movement, the growing militancy of Latino and first nations' people, and
massive protests against the Vietnam War all fueled the widespread conviction that
post-World War II development had careened way off course. This was the epiph-
any Paulo Freire experienced on his first visit to New York. I had such thoughts too
as I fed the already overstuffed and out of shape ducks in the park at Roslyn
Heights, New York. (I could have assured Holden Caulfield—the anti-hero of J.D.
Salinger's *The Catcher in the Rye*—that these ducks weren't going anywhere in the
winter; they could barely waddle.)

There is still another question to pose in this very brief review of development theory. Were there national governments which actually used dependency
theory as the basis for their policies?

The answer to this is a qualified yes. Dependency theory and associated
streams of thought certainly influenced a number of third world governments that
hewed a line of economic nationalism during the 1950s, 1960s, and 1970s. In
these cases, Marxism, Communism, and social democracy, which were the sources
for many ideas advanced by dependency theorists, were equally as or more important than dependency theory itself. Tanzania during the presidency of Julius
Nyrere is one outstanding example of socialism geared toward national
self-reliance (which some would say is another name for dependency theory). A
government that had direct links with dependency theory and the people who in-
vented it was Salvador Allende's in Chile. This happened partly because many progressive political thinkers went to Chile after the 1964 coup, only to become
political refugees again in 1973, when Allende's government was toppled. World
imperialism's retaliation against measures such as Allende's nationalization of
Chile's copper industry convinced many leftist activists and thinkers that economic nationalism based on dependency theory could never succeed; the forces
aligned against it were just too great. Nearly all the events of the next two decades—such as the failure of the Nicaraguan revolution—seem to confirm that hypothesis.

Yet the question needs to be asked again: where can a theory or belief system
be found which was made in the less developed world, and has the best interests of
marginalized peoples at heart? Theories can move people to constructive action,
but the third world currently has no theory to call its own; instead it experiences

only the imperative to keep scrambling in the race not to lose more ground. Marxism as developed by the bearded philosopher in the British Museum is not adequate to the development needs of third world peoples. It never was wholly suitable, if only because it was a theory made in Europe for Europeans. Third world peoples needs to make up the ideas that they will use to liberate themselves. To date, dependency theory and liberation theology are the two approaches to this hemisphere's development dilemmas which are meant to be tailored to specific communities' characteristics. These two disciplines do not reject the ideas proposed by the thinkers of Europe, but instead say that these ideas must be assimilated and used by the world's poor in ways that are conceived by the poor themselves. Today, when the poor are repeatedly told that they can hop on the caboose of globalization, if they are lucky, is a good time to re-examine dependency theory to see what of value it might still impart.

NOTES

1. Colin Leys, *The Rise and Fall of Development Theory* (Bloomington: Indiana University Press, 1996), p. 6.
2. W.W. Rostow, *The Stages of Economic Growth: A non-Communist Manifesto*, 3d edition (Cambridge University Press, 1990), p. xviii.
3. V.I. Lenin, *Imperialism, The Highest Stage of Capitalism*, in *The Essential Works of Lenin*, edited and with an introduction by Henry M. Christman (New York: Bantam Books, 1966), p. 216.
4. Henry B.Mayo, *Introduction to Marxist Theory* (New York: Oxford University Press, 1960), p. 113,115.
5. James O'Connor, "The Meaning of Economic Imperialism," in *Readings in U.S. Imperialism*, K.T. Fann and Donald C. Hodges eds. (Boston: Porter Sargent, 1971), p. 36.
6. Eduardo Galeano, "Latin America and the Theory of Imperialism," in *Readings in U.S. Imperialism*, p. 206,207.
7. Galeano, p. 212.
8. Adolph Lowe, *On Economic Knowledge. Toward a Science of Political Economics* (New York and Evanston: Harper and Row, 1965), p. 287.
9. Gunder Frank, *The Underdevelopment of Development*, p. 53.
10. Paulo Freire, *Pedagogy of Hope* (New York: Continuum), English translation, 1994, p. 54.
11. Rostow, *How It All Began: The Origins of the Modern Economy* (New York: McGraw Hill, 1975), p. 191.
12. *Ibid.*, p. 197.
13. R. Mukerjee, *The Economic History of India*, 1600-1800 (Allhabad: Kitab Mahal, 1967), pp. 193-4, quoted in Rostow, *How It All Began*.
14. Rostow, *How It All Began*, p. 203.
15. W.W. Rostow, *The Stages of Economic Growth: A Non-Communist Manifesto*, 3d edition (Cambridge University Press, 1990), p. 37.
16. Rostow, *Stages*, p. 39.
17. W.W. Rostow, "Leading Sectors and the Takeoff," in *The Economics of Take-Off into Sustained Growth*, edited by W.W. Rostow (London: Macmillian and Co. Ltd., 1963), pp. 3-6.
18. W.W. Rostow, "Leading Sectors and the Takeoff," in *Economics of Takeoff*, p. 3.
19. Cairncross, "Capital Formation in the Takeoff," in *Economics of Takeoff*, p. 242.
20. W.W. Rostow, "Leading Sectors and the Takeoff," in *Economics of Takeoff*, p. 12.
21. *Ibid.*, p. 17, footnote 1.
22. Rostow, *How It All Began*, p. 217.
23. Rostow, *How It All Began*, p. 221.
24. Rostow, *Stages*, xxiii.
25. Cairncross, "Capital Formation in the Takeoff," p. 240.
26. Rostow, *How It All Began*, p. 219-220.
27. Lenin, *Imperialism*, p. 234.

28. Development Education Centre and Latin American Working Group, "Canadian Power, the Canadian State, and Imperialism,"in *Imperialism, Nationalism, and Canada*, p. 49.

29. Canadian International Development Agency, *Annual Review* 1969, p. 5.

30. Canadian International Development Agency, *Sharing Our Future*, Ministry of Supply and Services Canada, 1987, p. 53.

31. Consul's reported cited in Lenin, *Imperialism*, p. 219.

32. *Ottawa Citizen*, 2 Jan. 1975 cited in Robert Carty and Virginia Smith, *Perpetuating Poverty: The Political Economy of Canadian Foreign Aid* (Toronto: Between the Lines, 1981), p. 46.

33. Government of Canada, Treasury Board and Financial Post, *Survey of Industrials*, various years, cited in Carty and Smith, Perpetuating Poverty, p. 103.

34. CIDA, *Annual Report* 1985-86, p. 42.

35. *The Globe and Mail*, 31 March 1993.

36. Diana Hunt, *Economic Theories of Development: An Analysis of Competing Paradigms* (Hertfordshire: Harvester Wheatsheaf, 1989), p. 261.

37. CIDA, *Strategy for International Development Cooperation 1975-1980 (Ottawa: 1975)*, p.1.

38. Leyes, *Rise and Fall*, pp. 12,13.

39. CIDA, *Strategy*, pp. 24-27.

40. CIDA, *Annual Report 1985-86*, p. 41.

41. CIDA, *Partners in Tomorrow* (Minister of Supply & Services Canada, 1984), p. 7.

42. OECD, *Development Cooperation: 1990 Report*, p. 248, cited in Jean-Philippe Therien, "Canadian Aid: A Comparative Analysis," in *Canadian Development Assistance Policies: An Appraisal*, ed. Cranford Pratt (Montreal and Kingston: McGill-Queen's University Press, 1994), p. 231.

43. Brian K. Murphy, "Canadian NGOs and the Politics of Participation," in *Conflicts of Interest. Canada and the Third World*, Jamie Swift and Brian Tomlinson eds. (Toronto: Between the Lines, 1991), p. 178.

44. Hunt, p. 270.

45. *Ibid.*, p. 285.

46. Gunder Frank, "The Underdevelopment of Development," *Scandanavian Journal of Development Alternatives*, vol. 10, no. 3 (September 1991), p. 45.

47. Gunder Frank, "The Underdevelopment of Development," p. 43.

48. Leyes, p. 12.

49. Gunder Frank, p. 21.

50. Clodovis Boff and Leonardo Boff, *Introducing Liberation Theology* (Maryknoll, N.Y.: Orbis Books, 1984), p.30 quoted in Christian Smith, *The Emergence Of LIberation Theology* (Chicago: University of Chicago Press, 1991), p. 30.

51. Galeano, "Latin America and the Theory of Imperialism," *Readings in U.S. Imperialism*, p. 207.

52. Fidel Castro, "On Underdevelopment," *Readings in U.S. Imperialism*, pp.189 , 190.

53. Andre Gunder Frank, "The Development of Underdevelopment," in *Imperialism and Underdevelopment. A Reader* (New York: Monthly Review Press, 1970), Robert I. Rhodes ed., pp. 9-10.

54. *Ibid.*, p. 9.

55. Gunder Frank, "The Mechanisms of Imperialism," p. 92.

56. Richard M. Nixon, speech to the OAS, 14 April 1969 and International Banking Survey, *Journal of Commerce*, New York, 25 February 1968, cited in Eduardo Galeano, "Latin America and the Theory of Imperialism,"p. 214.

57. Samir Amin, "Is an Endogenous Development Strategy Possible in Africa?" in *World Economy in Transition*, eds. Krishna Ahooja-Patel, Anne Gordon Drabek, and Marc Nerfin (Oxford: Pergamon Press, 1986), pp. 159-73.

58. Gunder Frank, "The Underdevelopment of Development," p. 58.

3

◆ ◆ ◆

DEBACLE AT IPANEMA BEACH: HOW DID DEVELOPMENT FAIL?

On 18 March 1963, jazz saxophonist Stan Getz had a much fabled New York City date with Brazilian musicians Joao and Astrud Gilberto; their mission was to record Antonio Carlos Jobim's "The Girl from Ipanema," a song that became so greatly loved that, on its thirtieth anniversary, the international press ran articles on the fate of the "girl," a flesh and blood Brazilian woman who by then was middle aged. I have always known that the girl from Ipanema is not as complexly interesting a figure as Shakespeare's dark lady or Dante's Beatrice, but still I like her better, because she is an icon of our modern times, a briefly glimpsed image of earthly fulfillment. The song also has a little noticed dark side. To this day, I feel a bit tearful when I hear the song, partly because it makes me nostalgic for the youth I feel I never really had. The song makes me cry not just for myself but also for all the mid-century political goals never reached and for all development that failed.

To me, "The Girl from Ipanema" is song about colonial relationships as well as a dirge about lost love. Its lyrics are redolent of all the promises and bitter disappointments in the relationships between the third and first worlds since 1960. In the song, we first of all see the radiant life of youth paraded before us, but then there's the catch: "He smiles, but she doesn't see." So the two remain forever locked in this sad tableau, the young girl separated from her bashful worshiper; the song offers no way out of their dilemma.

As a tale about politics and economic development, "The Girl from Ipanema" proceeds in this fashion. The developed world (the worshiper) doesn't have the moral resources to strike up a relationship with the girl (the third world). He is paralyzed when he has to deal with this stranger, because he has never learned how to build good relationships in his own home (i.e., his own domestic economy.) So he tries a small smile, but backs off in frustration when this strategy is a flop. On the part of the girl, there is also an uncertainty about how to proceed.

A more detailed reading of "The Girl from Ipanema's" sub-text produces these results: after World War II, the U.S. and other nations, including Canada, tried to win the adherence of less developed nations to their own growth based model of economic development. (When she passes, he smiles.) When this model failed to eradicate poverty or to protect human rights and the environment (i.e.,

She just doesn't see.), various mitigating measures were instituted. Equity oriented measures, such as basic needs oriented rural development projects in the third world and job creation schemes, such as Opportunities for Youth in Canada and the Office for Economic Opportunity in the United States, also failed to correct the flaws in the growth oriented development model or to achieve social justice in either the first or third worlds. (He continues to smile, but she still doesn't see.)

The late 1980s and 1990s then became the era when world leaders openly abandoned the effort to generate prosperity for all the world's people. The growth oriented model—this time including a stiff dose of deficit reduction—was again embraced with even greater fervor than before, despite its past failures. Policy makers were able to justify this seemingly contradictory behaviour because they blamed global economic failures on the *correctives* to growth-oriented capitalism rather than on unbridled capitalism itself.

It became fashionable to ridicule activist governments as "nanny states," and to dismiss all their efforts as ill natured meddling. Business guru Peter Drucker, for instance, in his 1993 book *Post-Capitalist Society* dismisses the U.S. model of the nanny state in sweeping terms. "By and large it has been almost as great a fiasco there as in Hitler's Germany or Stalin's Soviet Union."[1] Drucker does not mention the evident deficiencies of capitalist development strategies. If growth oriented capitalism doesn't work, then, what the heck, we'll go on doing it anyway. (She still goes on walking to the sea every single day, and he continues to smile ineffectually.)

This chapter depicts and tries to explain the causes of the chief failures in growth oriented development efforts in two Latin American countries. As noted in Chapter One, it is important to treat development's deficiencies in Latin America and other areas of the third world separately from the failures noted in the most developed countries, because poverty and other social ills are extremely dire in third world countries in a way that they are not in North America and Europe. In explaining these differences, a very important issue to economic theorists is whether the direness is caused by too much intervention or too little intervention from the industrialized world. This was a question addressed by Lenin, Rostow, and Gunder Frank alike.

I chose Latin America as the region for my study because many of its countries have for many years been inserted into the sphere of world business and closely tied to industrialized economies such as those in the U.S. and Britain. Within Latin America, Brazil and Mexico have been selected for examination because they are important actors in the hemispheric and the global economies, and home to deeply rooted social movements that are affecting their nations' development outcomes. Both—and especially Mexico—have been targets of expensive trade and development initiatives launched from North America.

Uneven Development

One firm generalization that can be ventured about the drawbacks of post-World War II growth oriented development in Latin America is that it has been extremely uneven, with lots of money, technology and land adhering to one pole of society and only scant resources to the opposite pole. The pole with little money, technology, or land has very often had a high birth rate and population density.

In Latin America and other areas of the third world, the distinction between the two poles has often been labeled the difference between the "traditional" (or marginal) sector and "modern" sector, with the traditional sector seen as that part of the economy which so has failed to "take off" into modernity, but which will eventually take wing. One mid-century characterization of Mexico's traditional sector by a U.S. based political scientist, for instance, concluded that,

> ...although 'marginal Mexico' is growing in absolute size, its *rate* of growth is nevertheless much lower than the rate of growth of the total population. Accordingly, the marginal Mexicans represent a steadily decreasing *proportion* of the total population. More importantly, perhaps, it seems unwise to extrapolate the gap in standard of living between the two sectors into the indefinite future. By its nature, development does not occur evenly throughout the society in its early stages, but rather focuses in the most favourable zones, in the Mexican case the national capital, the largest cities, and the areas close to the United States border.[2]

If poverty is seen as an stage of capitalism, then the suffering is causes can be seen as a necessary consequence of marginal populations' lack of education and life skills: ignorance which will later be corrected by modernity. A recent article in the *The Economist* on Brazil attributes the appalling infant mortality statistics in northeast Brazil to the incapacity of rural mothers. "The true problem is the mothers. Their ignorance of even the most basic facts of child care, of feeding and hygiene is terrifying," said a doctor in an interview.[3]

Latin America poses a special problem for stages of growth theorists like Rostow because the path to imputed takeoff has been so long, tortuous, and, in many cases, anguished. Unlike many Asian and African countries, most Latin American nations achieved independence in the 19th century, but by the mid-twentieth century, they were still struggling to achieve a measure of prosperity for the majority of their citizens. In *How It All Began*, Rostow seemed to attribute Latin America's slow progress to its Spanish Catholic origins.

Dependency theorists, liberations theologians, and other Latin Americans concerned about justice tend to see the gaping chasm between the traditional, usually poor, and the modern sectors in Latin America (which were labeled as such in so many words only after World War II) not as a stage of capitalism but as an ongoing result of it. Land holding is an area of the economy in most Latin American countries which is deeply marked by lopsided allocation of resources, uneven development, and a long standing split between a small number of proprietors who control a large share of land resources and a large number of rural workers (*campesinos*) who own little or nothing, and yet produce a lot of the food that they consume. In his 1971 classic study of Latin America's agriculture, Ernst Feder noted that this division had grave consequences because "in agrarian societies such as those of Latin America, land is traditionally the main source of wealth."[4]

Knowledge of the causes and consequences of Latin America's landholding systems is critically important to development of an economic development theory for the region because land is such an important resource in itself and because its use also affects the direction taken by other sectors of the economy. A key question asked by dependency theorists and other analysts of third world development is whether agriculture can produce capital to fund other kinds of economic activities. Another issue has been whether Latin America's lopsided landholding system are pre-capitalist (feudal), capitalist, or both. In a 1966 work on Mexican agriculture, Gunder Frank took the position that "since the Conquest Mexican agricultural (under)development was commercially driven and affected by transatlantic economic cycles."[5] What seems to have happened is that Latin America's huge *haciendas* and *fincas,* which predate the industrial revolution, eventually became capitalist production units without losing any of their enormity or concentration in the hands of a few.

A number of mid-century studies sparked by the Alliance for Progress or social developments related to it showed clearly just how exorbitantly land distribution was skewed throughout the region. In *The Rape of the Peasantry,* Feder wrote that,

> ...it is now amply demonstrated that in all countries the distribution of farmland is more unequal, and that a larger proportion of farm people live and work on an excessively small land base, than had been known prior to the Alliance for Progress...Less well known is the fact that the inequality in the distribution of land resources seems to be increasing. The most complete information is available from ten Latin American nations with a total rural population of nearly 70 million in 1960, which represents about 70 per cent of the entire rural population of the hemisphere, excluding Cuba.

> In these ten nations...the large multi-family farms alone—2 per cent of all farms—controlled about 46 percent of all farmland. In the other nations of Latin America which are not included here, these inequalities are similar, although the situation in Bolivia and Mexico is somewhat more complex.[6]

Problems arose from the quality as well as from the distribution of land. "Even casual observation suffices to show that small holdings are usually of inferior quality, as the best land is occupied by the estate owners. Most small holdings are located on eroded hillsides and other poor soils, often of difficult access."[7] Feder's depiction of the life at mid-century of most of the rural poor has the tone of a Pieter

Bruegel painting gone to hell. "Poor conditions with respect to diet throughout Latin America are equaled by conditions of housing, clothing, sanitation, and education. The bulk of the farm population live in huts which are windowless earthen or straw shacks with dirt floors. Adults and children crowd into one or two rooms. There is no direct water supply and drinking water is frequently from canals or brooks that double as sewers...There are no indoor or outdoor toilet facilities."[8]

Racism is a longstanding cause of the many deprivations (including landlessness) endured by Latin America's rural poor. "In some sense the poor in Latin America are the objects of racial discrimination as blatant as that in South Africa," wrote William Thiesenhusen in a 1990 article. "Inadequate incomes, illiteracy, landlessness or near landlessness, and dark skin are closely correlated in all the countries of the area. In general, the closer the relationship to European stock, the more apt a population cohort is to have a high income level, land, and education; the closer the relationship to indigenous or African stock, the more apt the group is to lack land, to have a low income level and little schooling, and to suffer discrimination."[9]

Studies by other authorities confirmed that the overall situation depicted by Feder, Thiesenhusen and others also existed in individual countries. A 1973 study by the Inter-American Committee for Agricultural Development (CIDA), which was set up to give advice to the Alliance for Progess, concluded that, in Brazil, "it is not unrealistic to assume that, after taking multiple ownership into account, latifundistas control not 53 percent, but somewhere between 60 and 70 percent of the land resources."[10]

The pattern was different in Mexico, where an ambitious—yet not thorough—program of land reform was instituted by the government of Lazaro Cardenas during the 1930s. This reform changed and mitigated, but did not eradicate, longstanding inequities in land distribution. In the 1940s and 1950s, the government continued to transfer resources from the urban to rural activities, but in a way that promoted a high technology, commercial system of agriculture that existed side-by-side with a neglected subsistence sector. In other words, "resources did not follow the agrarian-reform beneficiaries."[11] It was noted by some observers that regions with a lot of *ejido* (communal, *campesino*) land received a only a small portion of public investment in irrigation during that period. "Investment in roads during the 1940s and 1950s similarly favoured the north and north-Pacific. These areas also accounted for two-thirds of private investment in agriculture from 1940 to 1960, with benefits largely accruing to commercial growers. Meanwhile, the *ejidatario* or landless laborer, the *minifundista* and the *comunero* remained immune from these developments."[12] Even by the 1990s, fewer than half of the *ejidos* used any kind of modern technology, and 58 percent used oxen for ploughing.[13]

At mid-century, it was clear to millions of Latin Americans and also to the U.S. that the problem of land distribution had to be solved one way or another.

The perception of a veteran U.S. missionary in Latin America, Roy May, was widely shared: "The unjust distribution of land and the rapacious assaults by the powerful on the lands of the poor are fundamental causes of poverty and misery in Latin America...Indeed, in one way or another, nearly all social injustice can traced to land—who owns it and how it is used."[14] The cries for justice and the perceived threats to U.S. interests in the region were becoming too intense to be dismissed. If land reform in Guatemala, initiated but not finished by the government of Jacobo Arbenz in the 1950s, was a warning bell to Washington, then the 1959 Cuban revolution, which instituted a thorough land reform, was a deafening siren.

U.S. governments since the nation's earliest days have believed themselves to be champions of a certain kind of egalitarian reform, including land reform. In the nineteenth century, the U.S. had a great deal of fertile land in its mid-West and West that was occupied by first nations, but not yet by farmers of European origin. The 1862 Homestead Act, which gave settlers of modest means full title to 160 acres of land after five years of residence and evidence of improvements, has long been seen as a measure which made the U.S. a nation of petit bourgeois owners, rather than of lords and serfs. The Homestead Act was, however, less a boon to the general population than it seems at first glance. The Act was passed during the Civil War because enough votes to approve it could be garnered only after the southern states seceded. Slave states had opposed a free land policy because it was a threat to the slave system, which was essential to the functioning of cotton plantations.

The benefits provided by the Homestead Act have to be stacked up against the failure to institute any post-Civil War land reform. According to Peter Dorner, an academic and former senior staff economist on President Lyndon Johnson's Council of Economic Advisers, "The failure to follow through with a land reform after the Civil War has cast a century-long shadow over race relations and the economic opportunities of Afro-Americans. The slaves were free, but they did not have the independent economic opportunities that could have been theirs had a land reform been carried out."[15]

Another severe limitation of the "free land" method of land reform was that it was a occurrence which could not be repeated or even imitated, even in a country like Brazil, which has ample land resources, but not of the same type as the U.S. Some Latin American land-reforming governments have taken an approach that is somewhat comparable by focusing on the redistribution of large estate lands which are not being utilized.

The U.S. did become the sponsor of some fairly sweeping non-Latin American land reforms in the 1940s and 1950s: in South Korea, Taiwan, and Japan. The reforms have often been cited as causes of these countries' economic success after World War II.

A critically important difference between the Asian reforms and the earlier one in Mexico was that the former were approved and controlled by the United

States. Latin American reforms with unforeseeable outcomes—such as those in Mexico, Guatemala, and Cuba—were much less welcome. U.S. sanctioned and funded land reform became widespread in Latin America during the 1960s. Land reform legislation was enacted in 19 countries after the 1961 declaration by the Inter-American Economic and Social Council that set up the Alliance for Progress.[16] In some cases, the drive for reform came as much or more from progressive governments as from the Alliance for Progress. In Chile, for instance, the reform sponsored by the governments of Eduardo Frei and Salvador Allende was reversed after the 1973 coup that toppled the Allende government.

Reform approved by the Alliance for Progress was coupled with injections of foreign aid from the U.S. and other developed nations; this capital was intended to modernize agriculture and make it more commercial. U.S. economic assistance to Latin America during the 1960s totaled over US$10 billion. "However, the level of official flows began to slow down in the 1960s as the effects of the Cuban revolution were seen to have been contained."[17] In the early 1970s, the basic needs approach to agricultural development discussed in Chapter Two replaced the 'reform plus capital infusion' approach of the 1960s. This shift sent out a number of mixed signals: that the U.S. (which had accumulated big bills for the Vietnam War) was running out of money to spend in Latin America; that land reform was either an irretrievable failure or else had accomplished its goals and was no longer needed; or perhaps that agricultural productivity and social justice in the countryside could be achieved without redistribution of land. Whatever the motives behind it, basic needs was seized on in the 1970s as the more practical alternative to the "throw-money-at-poverty" approach of the 1960s.

The Alliance for Progress era of land reform did not alter the land holding regimes in Mexico and Brazil in any important way. Brazil got through the 1960s, 1970s, and 1980s without any significant reform because the nation had right wing military governments throughout the period. In Mexico, the government of Gustavo Diaz Ordaz distributed about 25 million hectares of land (more than the Cardenas government had), during the 1960s but only about 10 percent of it was arable. At the same time, government policy continued to favour commercial, export agriculture, while production of basic food crops received little official bolstering.[18]

By the 1970s, it became apparent that the push to change Latin America's agriculture and land-holding systems during the 1960s had brought modernity and growth to that sector, but had not delivered economic development which would benefit the nation as a whole and satisfy the basic needs of the majority. In his 1995 assessment of recent land reform in Latin America, William Thiesenhusen concluded that "agrarian reforms in the region have not done very well in ameliorating rural poverty, improving equity, or creating employment largely because of the multiplicity of their expected accomplishments and because they are vulnerable as policy instruments."[19]

In Washington and most other capitals in the hemisphere, except Havana, there was little breast-beating about this failure, partly because it had become apparent that the revolutionary onslaught of the 1960s was subsiding. Owners of large helpings of land and/or capital felt a shared relief that radical alterations might not be necessary. A 1951 article by John Kenneth Galbraith succinctly stated their position: "The world is composed of many different kinds of people, but those who own land are not so different—whether they live in China, Persia, Mississippi, or Quebec—that they will meet and happily vote themselves out of its possession."[20]

Mid-century Latin American land reforms were hobbled by mixed, unclear goals as well as by the miserliness of politicians and landowners. Justice and not productivity was the primary goal of the 1930s Mexican land reform. The idea seemed to be that all people deserved some land, whether or not they used it very efficiently. Many analysts in fact argue that small holdings can be more productive than very large ones. Does this mean that the goals of justice and productivity can both be achieved by using the same method: breaking up large land holdings into smaller units? There is also a debate about whether land should be used primarily for food crops or for potentially more profitable export items such as broccoli, fruit, or flowers.

There is still the question about whether agricultural production can be used to generate capital needed for a nation' industrial development. This was a question seldom asked directly by most 1960s land reformers in Latin America. The reform minded military government of Juan Velasco Alvarado in Peru (1968-75) did try to use land reform as an instrument of capital formation. Yet "price controls to keep prices low in the cities discouraged production for the national market."[21] The issue of how to deal with the impact of cheap food policies on *campesinos* with small holdings was for the most part neglected.

The impact of failed reform and the subsequently increased unevenness in the distribution of national resources was evident in the lives of poor *campesinos* during the 1970s, and is still present today. In his 1995 book on land reform, Thiesenhusen depicted a starkly bleak landscape for the lives of very large numbers of Latin American rural people as they approached the millennium. "Like the homeless in U.S. cities, the rural landless in Latin America are people whom society chooses to ignore…Tragically, the chances today seem slim that the rural poor will be positively affected by public policy anytime soon…Meanwhile, rural poverty is particularly stubborn in Latin America, accounting for three-fifths of the so-called 'hungry poor' of the region."[22]

Current Rural Conditions

At the turn of the millennium, chronic desperation and poverty are still the lot of most rural Brazilians, and these conditions are tending to grow worse. Conditions are especially bad in the country's impoverished northeast. According to figures published by Brazil's Landless Workers' Movement, *Sem Terra*, the child mortality rate in the northeast is 287 per 1,000, compared with 116 per 1,000 in the country as a whole. The average life expectancy in the northeast is just 47; the average for the country as a whole is 60. In the nation as a whole, about 26 percent of the adult population cannot read or write their own names; in rural areas that percentage is 42 percent.[23]

Sem Terra attributes these appalling conditions to the nation's extremely uneven distribution of resources. Just one percent of landowners own 44 percent of the land, according to Sem Terra. The country's 20 largest ranches control 15 million hectares. In stark contrast, 53 percent of all properties—or a total of 3,099,632 properties—are just one to 10 hectares.[24] The four million families in the country's rural areas who are landless share croppers or tenant farmers are the very large group that *Sem Terra* aims to organize.

Sam Terra, which started organizing in the mid-1970s in response to increased land concentration, was constituted as a national organization in 1984. In a 1995 interview in *Sem Terra*'s Sao Paulo office, MST representative Neuri Rossetto told me that, before 1975, *campesinos*' struggles tended to be local rather than national in scope; still many *campesinos* were assassinated during the late 1960s and early 1970s. MST's current ambitious agenda of goals includes: modification of the country's structure of landholding, a special development program for semi-arid regions, and a rural development system which grants better conditions of life, education, and culture for all.

In Mexico, revolution, land reform and the modernizing measures of recent governments still have not brought prosperity to rural areas. Thiesenhusen noted in his 1995 book that, still, "although sparse rainfall characterizes much of the country, only 17 percent of *ejido* land is irrigated. Of the 50 percent of Mexicans who live below the poverty line, 70 percent reside in rural areas…Most of the 10 million whom the Mexican government deems 'critically nutritionally deficient' live in rural areas."[25] In the same book, Thiesenhusen asserted that Mexican agriculture was at a turning point in the mid-1990s.[26] During the past decade, a critical point was indeed reached on a number of fronts. In 1991, Mexico's globalizing president, Carlos Salinas de Gortari, announced that he would amend the country's much revered constitution to roll back the land reform measure, Article 27, which specified that *ejido* land could be passed along within the community, but not sold or rented. Salinas' action was geared to preparing Mexico for the North American Free Trade Agreement (NAFTA). The reversal of Article 27 was one of the measures that prompted indigenous people in southern Mexico, under the leadership of the Zapatista Army of National Liberation, to rise up and fire shots heard 'round the world' on 1 January 1994.

A number of Mexican citizens' groups, and not just the Zapatistas, have recently focused their publicity and public actions on the plight of Mexico's rural poor under the regime of globalization. The platform for the 1995 Citizens' Referendum for Freedom, an initiative to promote a justice oriented national economic strategy, noted that, historically, the countryside has been abandoned and "with modernization, has been devastated." The platform calls for a repeal of Article 27's repeal as the only way to "respect rights and promote productivity."[27] A Charter of Rights adopted at a July 1995 meeting in Mexico City proclaimed that all citizens have the right "to live and work in the country, with dignified ways of satisfying our basic needs for food, health care, housing, education, culture, and recreation."[28]

The failure to effect thorough agrarian reform in Latin America has had numerous serious consequences during the now more than half century since World War II. One is the chaotic expansion of the region's capital cities and other key urban centres. This precipitous growth has created not just megacities but monster cities where a large percentage of new arrivals go without sufficient food, basic services, and housing. Mexico City and Sao Paulo are two of the area's largest cities, which experienced the most torrential demographic growth after World War II. Population growth in many other cities, e.g., Lima, while not so huge as in the largest cities, has been no less rapid and unplanned.

Riccardo Petrella, the European Community's head of Forecasting and Assessment of Science and Technology and an originator of the notion of postmodern "city states," points to great cities such as Sao Paulo as the most important economic and political units of the future. In a 1991 article, he predicts:

> Rather than an order of nation-states weighing in on a new global balance of power, an archipelago of technologically highly developed city-regions —or mass consumer technopoles—is evolving. These city-regions are linked together by transnational business firms that by-pass the traditional nation-state framework in their ceaseless pursuit of new customers, as well as by thousands of local and transnational Non-Governmental Organizations active in promotion of customer protection and citizens rights.

The goal of the largest corporations—which will be the key movers and shakers rather than national governments—will be to "capture the allegiance of those with the means to be consumers; that is about seven hundred to eight hundred million people worldwide." The other billions of people on the earth will become part of what Petrella calls a "global underclass."[29] The centres participating in this new "Hanseatic" (i.e, resembling 14th and 15th century Europe) economy will be London, New York, Tokyo, Toronto, Chicago, San Francisco, Los Angeles, Houston, and Miami; Mexico City and Sao Paulo; Seoul, Taipei, Hong Kong, Singapore, and Bangkok; Paris, Zurich, Vienna, Milan, Madrid, and more of less the whole of Holland. Petrella bemoans this seemingly inexorable onslaught as unjust and "also unsustainable in a well-armed world that is ecologically interdependent and exposed to unstoppable waves of mass migration." His brief article offers few ideas about how to counter the movement toward a Hanseatic order.

The Cities' History

Rapid, early urbanization marked Latin America's development from its earliest days. In his book on *Industrialization and Urbanization in Latin America*, Robert Gwynne notes that,

> ...the Latin American urban system was created in less than a century. Indeed what were to become some of the principal urban foci of Spanish Latin America were founded between 1520 and 1541— Mexico City, Puebla, Guadalajara, Oaxaca, Guatemala, Bogota, Cali, Quito, Trujillo, Lima, Cuzco, Arequipa, Asuncion, Buenos Aires, and Santiago de Chile...Between 1540 and 1580, the basis of the Brazilian city system was laid with the founding of Recife, Salvador, Sao Paulo, and Rio de Janeiro in the Portuguese territories.[30]

Gwynne notes that the more gradual growth of cities in the U.S. and Canada was linked to the westward movement of the frontier. In North America, according to Gwynne, the town evolved to serve rural needs, while in Latin America the town became the focal point for occupying and administering the New World.[31]

Different patterns of urbanization in North and South America have persisted into the twentieth century. In Latin America, a continuing strong trend to urbanization after World War II was fueled not so much by the prospect of an industrial job in the city as by the certainty that economic prospects in the countryside would not improve anytime soon. By 1940, 19.6 percent of Latin America's population lived in urban centres with over 20,000 inhabitants, but that figure had climbed to 61 percent in 1979, according to the Population Reference Bureau. Within this overall figure there were significant regional variations. "In temperate South America, urban population constituted as much as 80 percent of the total, although the tropical and Central American regions recorded levels of 60 per cent and 58 per cent respectively."[32]

Latin America's rate of urbanization at the end of the 1970s was much higher than in other areas of the less developed world and had reached levels approaching those in the developed world. A decade later, the United Nations Department of Economic and Social Affairs reported further big jumps in the population of Latin America's largest cities. The department pegged Mexico City's population at 20.19 million, Sao Paulo's at 17.40, and Rio de Janeiro's at 10.71 million. Mexico City was the largest city in Latin America, while Sao Paulo and Rio stood at second and fourth in the region. (Some of the department's figures may have been inflated, but estimating population is these cities accurately is very hard to do.)

Cartrek: Life in the Monster City

Population assessments say little about what life is like for most people in Mexico City, Sao Paulo, and Rio de Janeiro. I went to all three in 1995 to find out for myself how human and economic development had fared in the Latin American metropolis (which, according to dependency theory, is still a hinterland to a developed world metropolis such as New York). Even a veteran big city dweller like myself found that life in these cities mounts sometimes unbearable sensory overloads on innocent pedestrians. I found myself overstimulated by the abundance of life at every street corner; yet I also sometimes found myself in tears at the failures of development and the fathomless depths of human suffering in these cities.

Sao Paulo and Mexico City are particularly hard to reduce to a manageable sketch, Bruegelian or otherwise. Is one of these cities tougher than the other for working, buying, and getting around? The two are hard to compare. Sao Paulo is a harsher environment than Mexico City in some respects because it is unrelievedly sprawling and lacks a historic downtown core comparable to Mexico City's Zocalo. There is a spacious square occupied by the Roman Catholic cathedral, a stately but very new building finished in 1954. Sao Paulo's neighbourhoods also appear more like armed camps than Mexico City's, though residents of both cities express strong fears about the safety of their persons and property. Most middle class and rich Paulistanos barricade themselves into their homes. In the affluent neighbourhood near the Ana Rose subway station, for example, small but elegantly appointed homes are protected by seven or eight feet high iron fences made of thin bars spaced about two inches apart. The bars are topped by very sharp metal arrowheads; a thief would have to be exceptionally nimble to avoid impalement on them.

In many other important respects, the two cities are very similar in character if not in appearance. Mexico City's most memorable aspect is its sometimes surrealistic chaos, while Sao Paulo makes a strong impression by being very, very big. Both cities seem to provide overpowering evidence that God made too few roads, and far too many people and gasoline powered vehicles. There is no Long Island Expressway to provide at least for an orderly gridlock. In Sao Paulo, the traffic jam starts the moment the visitor leaves the airport, and it continues throughout the day and late night, for those who care to stay up late and gawk at it. Statistics bear out this casual observation. Between 1960 and 1974, the number of cars in Sao Paulo rocketed from 120,000 to almost a million, while public transport stagnated.[33] The poor state of Brazil's public utilities was cited as a proof of underdevelopment in Gunder Frank's article "On The Mechanisms of Imperialism: The Case of Brazil," which was cited in Chapter One. (This neglect was a development in some ways comparable to what happened in New York during the same period).

Below ground, in Sao Paulo's and Mexico City's subways, the scenes of traffic are comparable but with a different twist. Mexico City's efficient, well kept, nine-line subway system, which was built in the late 1960s, by the turn of the century was just barely viable as a transport system. This failure is evident at key transfer stations, particularly at rush hour. Six o'clock brings an oversized, tightly packed, but generally courteous crowd to the transfer station Hidalgo, for example, for the purpose of cramming itself into too small cars and thence proceeding home. If only God had a shoe horn! Getting swept along by the multitudes is a scary experience even for a veteran of Bloor St. line and 7th Ave. line subway scrimmages like myself. I enter the car with my feet barely touching the ground and my arms locked to my sides. Bringing my hand to my nose for the purpose of scratching it requires an intense bare knuckled fight with the riders closest to me. *Los rituales del caos,* a book by Mexican journalist Carlos Monsivais on the grotesque in Mexican society, presents many such scenes in words and photographs. One photo reveals a public swimming pool so full of bodies that there isn't more than a drop or two of water in sight.

Sao Paulo's metro is much less packed than Mexico City's. It's possible to use busy downtown stops at rush hours without a lot of crowd-caused discomfort. At the turn of the century, Sao Paulo's metro was much more limited than Mexico City's, three lines compared to nine. It was still fairly modern and glossy looking partly because it was built about a decade after Mexico City's. A likely cause of its continuing adequate capacity in the 1990s is that it is so big that it looks like it was built to be used by herds of very large elephants. Sao Paulo's metro is to subways what the Amazon is to other rivers. The city's gigantic bus station near the Tiete metro station is a similarly immense facility with buses leaving from 59 different gates for all corners of the country. Like the metro, it works well despite, and indeed partly because of, its ungainliness and staggering size.

Despite the fact that both cities are equipped with subways that can move millions of people, as well as with large fleets of buses and taxis, the job of getting to and from work every day continues to be so difficult for many commuters that it dictates where and how they live. The poorest people in Mexico City and Sao Paulo very often live on the cities' fringes; they are the most recent arrivals from the country. To get to their work as street venders or domestic servants in the cities' centres, they may have to travel one, two, or even more hours morning and night, packed like pickles in a jar with their fellow citizens. In "The Logic of Disorder," an article about life in Sao Paulo, Lucio Kowarick, points out that lots of poor Paulistanos try to find a way to live close to their jobs in the core. There are,

> …615,000 inhabitants of slum dwellings which are concentrated in decaying parts of the more central districts of Sao Paulo: Bom Retiro, Bras, Bela Vista. As a result of the housing shortage as well as the 'slum clearance' operations in other areas, these slum tenements tend to spread, following especially the run-down areas adjacent to the railway lines: Perus, Pirituba, etc. Faced with the choice of worse housing or worse location, people in these areas live at a rate of 3.6 persons to a room—of which a quarter have no outside windows—but 67 per cent spend less than a half an hour getting to work. Like the shanty towns and the jerry-built houses on the periphery, these tenements house the working class, who live in enormous numbers in the old mansion houses, in sheds or in cellars.[34]

At the mid-point of the twentieth century, public transportation in Brazil's largest cities was so inadequate and the frustration of riders so extreme that riots, known as "*quebra-quebras,*" erupted in the mid-1970s. The first incident, when a train was set afire, was in July 1974. In 1975, transport riots became more frequent and intense. Within a single month, there were five *quebra-quebras* in Rio and one in Sao Paulo. "All of them were triggered by breakdowns and delays or were the direct result of accidents."[35] The decision to build a new subway line in Sao Paulo followed closely on the heels of these disturbances. Still Brazilian commentators tended to blame the rioters for their unruliness rather than to upbraid officials for the system's notorious failures. The right wing daily *O Estado de Sao Paulo* reported in June 1977 that the new subway line was "especially adapted to meet the particular characteristics of the passengers who will use it...The carriages have been reinforced against the inevitable vandalism that will occur, since these passengers have a lower standard of living and less education than those who travel on the other lines."[36]

Lolling in the Park

The nonstop roar of vehicular traffic in Latin America's two largest cities becomes downright insignificant when compared with the uproar created by the millions of people who rush to and fro on the cities' streets, pack the sidewalks with their vending stands, and stand bunched ahead of you on all kinds of lines. Nowhere is this overabundance of humanity more evident than in the parks which are meant to serve as oases of tranquillity and also as the cities' oxygen-producing lungs.

Like just about everything else in the city, Sao Paulo's Ibirapuera Park is enormous. Just outside the park is Bandeiras, a huge monument commemorating the city's pioneers. Inside there is greenery and a host of attractions, including a planetarium, a lake, monuments, a Japanese pavilion and museums. Ibirapuera Park is also packed with Paulistanos seeking a break. On a sunny Sunday afternoon, the park has a carnival atmosphere, with walkers, bicyclists, and roller bladers careening past each other to find some fun. Peace and quiet, it's not.

Mexico City's parks are also stretched way beyond their limits. Chapultepec Park, the city's largest park, covers more than four square kilometers and includes lakes, a zoo, and a number of museums including the Anthropolgy Museum, which houses a priceless collection of national treasures. On Sunday afternoons, the park is overrun with families seeking relaxation, an ice cream or a tortilla, and a space to enjoy life. Crowded as it is, Chapultepec is a unique resource; there are nowhere close to enough other public green spaces in Mexico City for people who want to swing, see-saw, or fly a kite. Triné Lopez of the Environmental Studies Group (GEA), an environmental protection group based at the Autonomous University of Mexico (UNAM), told me in an interview that Mexico City falls way below the World Health Organization standard of 10 square metres for each resident; in Mexico, it's more like four.[37] The situation in Sao Paulo is comparable;

Lucio Kowarick pegged the amount of green land at 4.5 square meters per inhabitant.[38] This average says nothing of the millions of Mexico City and Sao Paulo residents who don't have even four meters of green; instead they live in dusty, stony urban landscapes cut off from any vestige of natural beauty (not to mention tree generated oxygen).

A park lover since my earliest years, I put in hours wandering and bench-sitting in Ibirapuera and Chapultepec. What I missed seeing were paddling formations of plump ducks comparable to the Long Island ducks who quacked and gobbled up the overly substantial bread snacks I offered. I saw skinny dogs, dozens of motley birds, and the occasional rodent, but no sleek, pampered ducks. This lack of ducks only deepened my sense of melancholy about being cut off from one of the few pleasures of my childhood and also about how poorly development turned out in these megacities.

Like their parks, Sao Paulo's and Mexico City's markets—profusely stocked with food, odds and ends of housewares, and handicrafts—are also greatly oversupplied with people bent on staying alive. Entrepreneurial drive is very much in evidence at Sao Paulo's Praca da Republica, where many hundreds of painters, jewelry makers, keychain salespersons, and food venders ambitiously set up their stands day after day. On the rua 7 de Abril side of the Plaza, stands are so closely packed together that the shopper has difficulty threading her way among them.

It is hard to believe that all these venders make enough to pay for a comfortable spot in the world; indeed some of the venders sleep in the park bandshell and other nearby nooks. One of the bandshell squatters is Eduardo, a jewelry maker from Rio, who told me that he earns only enough for food from his work at the Plaza. He might go back to Rio, he says, but for now he can make a bare subsistence working from the bandshell.

Surely the grandma of all Latin America's markets is Mexico's City's La Merced, which became a congregation point for more and more venders as the country's unemployment rate soared in the 1990s. On a frantically busy Saturday in 1995, I saw a lot of typical farmers' market activity proceeding in the crowded market building, while outside a new group of unsheltered and otherwise unaccommodated sellers spread its wares helter-skelter style. Still there was some order to the proceedings; garbage was piled at agreed upon spots. As the sun went down and the market wound up, a group of adults and children could be seen clawing through one La Merced's biggest garbage piles, seeking tomatoes, lettuce, and other edibles. They worked the pile systematically and at high speed. At the same time, a long line of other shoppers was unsuccessfully trying to pack itself into the La Merced subway; just then I had neither the patience nor the physical endurance needed to worm my way through the crowd, past the turnstile, and down to the steaming platform, so instead I hopped into a taxi, which immediately got stuck in a traffic jam.

Favelas and Colonias

The geographic boundaries of Latin America's urban centres are constantly being stretched through settlements set up by new arrivals in the big cities. These new communities are called *pueblos jovenes* in Peru, *favelas* in Brazil, and *colonias* in Mexico. During the past 30 years, some of Latin America's new towns on the big cities' peripheries have become relatively well established and even affluent compared with the settlements of the very latest arrivals. This rootedness, however, does not relieve older town residents of the burden of being poor, surplus beings in the economies of their cities.

Santa Marta, perched at a very steep angle on the hills above Rio de Janeiro, is an older favela with community leaders who help to imbue a strong sense of social solidarity. People from around Pernambuco in the north of Brazil started coming to Santa Marta in the early 1940s. Though the government tried to stop the migration, the community expanded greatly during the 1960s and 1970s. There was no running water, electricity or plumbing in Santa Marta at that time. Still people organized with the help of the church, community activists told me.[39] In the years just before 1980, there was some precarious operation of electricity. Its full installation after that "changed life in the *favela* a lot. Before, there was a danger that the government would move the people. People after that were able to invest in houses."

There is a wide range of housing in the 1990s community of about 8,000 people—ranging from makeshift shacks to very solid, well furnished houses. TVs and other electricity powered household items are common. One modern necessity most residents continue to lack is phones. Santa Marta's community organization, ECO, has opened a computer school where young people can learn Windows and a variety of programs. ECO also runs a summer school for children and publishes a regular newsletter. The fact that Santa Marta's people have been successful in building a community which ECO calls "serious, honest, and working class" does not mean that the community has landed a spot in mainstream Brazilian society. The students in the computer school have no way of knowing if they will find work. Santa Marta is also plagued by with drug related problems and police violence. "There is a struggle between the police and the drug dealers," according to a community leader. An October 1995 police invasion of Santa Marta left a 19 year old boy dead. His mother has complained to the media and to the human rights commission about arbitrary police violence and their summary infliction of the death penalty. Despite it successes, Santa Marta is still a hillside town totally separate from Rio's affluent neighbourhoods and from Ipanema and Copacabana beaches to the south.

Corpus Christi, a neighbourhood perched on a hillside at the southern edge of Mexico City, is, like Santa Marta, blessed with community spirit but poor economic prospects, at least for now. Corpus Christi got started in the middle 1970s with settlers from Hidalgo, Michoacan, Tampico, Veracruz, and other states. Corpus Christi has running water, electricity, some phones, schools and stores. Life there is in some ways better than downtown since the air is a bit cleaner and the traffic a lot thinner than they are below at the city's centre. Some women told me that they never go downtown unless they must. Life in Corpus Christi is far from idyllic, however. People lucky to have jobs must make a long trip by minibus or other means every day. Residents estimated that the unemployment rate in their community rocketed to 60 percent after the 1994 peso crisis.

One focus of community life in Corpus Christi is the women's health centre, which is funded by churches, but not by the government. The health centre idea got started after the 1985 Mexico City earthquake as a project to provide aid with health to "damnificados"—people whose homes were destroyed—for one year. Subsequently, the project's location was shifted to the colonias on the city's periphery, according to project staffer Norma Baleazar Silva.[40] The Corpus Christi health centre used mainstream medicine for seven years, then switched to greater use of naturopathy in 1995. On the afternoon of my visit, women had gathered at the centre with the woman naturopathic doctor who works there for a discussion about how to keep the spine a well part of the body. Some of the Corpus Christi residents who participate in the centre also act as health promoters in the wider community.

Life at the Edge

The experience of people in Santa Marta and Corpus Christi is by no means typical of the life lived by other new arrivals in the cities of Brazil, Mexico, and other Latin American countries.

Many periphery dwellers are doing a lot worse than the people in Santa Marta and Corpus Christi. Many of the dwellings in Sao Paulo's *favelas* and Mexico's *colonias* are so minimal and so lacking in any kind of amenity that it seems an exaggeration to call them homes at all, except that they are, for millions of souls. The statistics depicting the poverty of those who live in the downtown slums or on large cities' peripheries in both Mexico and Brazil are shocking no matter how often they are repeated. While people in the Mexico City's *colonias* and comparable communities consume about 60 litres of water a day, the average for more affluent communities is an estimated 640 litres, Trine Lopez of Mexico City's Groupo de Estudios Ambientales told me in a November 1995 interview.[41] She also said that 40 percent of the city's people don't have access to running water in their homes.

Other elements of basic infrastructure are very often missing as well. Mid-century statistics for the Sao Paulo metropolitan area, for instance, indicate that "out of 8 000 km of roads used by traffic, only 40 percent are paved; 870 000 inhabitants live in houses with no electric light; only about 30 per cent of homes are connected to the drainage system, and 53 percent to the water supply system." Kowarick describes the situation in the city's periphery as even worse: "only 20 per cent of the houses are connected to the drainage system, and 46 per cent to the water supply. To have some idea of the high rate of environmental pollution, it is sufficient to say that at least three-quarters of the dwellings in the 'peripheries' empty their drains into simple blind sewers."[42]

For people in situations of such dire deprivation, personal development and upward mobility may seem impossible dreams. In an article on "Networks and Social Marginality," Larissa Lomnitz reports on the educational and job profiles of residents in Cerrada del Condor, a Mexico City shanty town. Among heads of families and their wives, "nearly 30 per cent are illiterate, and slightly over 2 per cent have schooling beyond the sixth grade."[43] Among those in the labour market, the most frequent occupation among men is that of *peon*, i.e., a manual laborer who may work at various trades according to demand. Among women the most frequent paid occupation is that of domestic servant.[44]

The bottom of the economic ladder in Latin America's biggest cities is very low; the top is as high as the highest in New York or Los Angeles. Wealthy people in Sao Paulo and Mexico City are fully plugged into the Internet; they sport designer clothes, camcorders, laptops and all the other gadgets of globalization; to their backs and feet are strapped gismos made by Nike, Apple, and Gianni Versace.

The differences between the booming economic life of the most well off and the poor shanty town life in Latin America's cities are so pronounced that many modern and postmodern commentators—for instance M. Santos in his 1979 book *The Shared Space: the Two Circuits of the Urban Economy in Underdeveloped Countries*—see them two very different economies. The division is often characterized as that between the capital intensive and the labour intensive sectors of the economy. Gwynne notes that "a wide variety of terms has been used to categorize the division—the firm versus the bazaar economy, the upper against the lower circuit, the large-scale versus the small-scale sector, the formal versus the informal sector."[45] The two economies correspond roughly to the paradigms of development and, in contrast, underdevelopment or dependent development outlined in Chapter Two.

At mid-century, many writers based in the developed world viewed the marginal life of the shanty town with horror; they saw nothing in it but squalor which badly needed transformation, or—as Rostow would put it—"takeoff." Daniel Lerner wrote in 1967: "The point that must be stressed in referring to this suffering mass of humanity displaced from the rural areas to the filthy peripheries of the great cities is that few of them experience the 'transition' from agricultural to urban-industrial labour called for by the mechanism of development and the model of modernization." Political science professor Martin Needler also found that Mexico's urban poor were unpromising raw material for modern life. "Political attitudes among the urban poor are oriented especially to immediate gratification, rather than to questions of ideology or program." He also reported: "Statistics indicate that for Mexico, as for other countries [e.g., the U.S.], lower-class organization is accompanied by social disorganization, the weakening of family ties, the absence of a male head of household or a succession of temporary occupants of this role, higher rates of juvenile delinquency, and so on."[46]

Other commentators—usually with a more postmodern, inductive, and less judgmental cast of mind—have found some things to admire and even celebrate in Latin America's marginal settlements. Their residents have been applauded for the work they do to keep mainstream society going, for their ability to cooperate with each other in difficult circumstances, for their ability to build their own houses, and for the smart ways they make do with the odds and ends discarded by more affluent sectors. Larissa Lomnitz, for example, noted in "Networks and Social Marginality" that "the rise of an urban middle class in Latin America is greatly indebted to cheap labor and services provided by marginals: domestic servants, gardeners, delivery boys, drivers, and a host of menial helpers of every description."[47] She also pointed out the "obvious contrast between the successful adaptation of the marginals to a situation of scarcity of resources, generating mechanisms of social solidarity and methods of intense utilization of waste, and the crisis of Western industrial societies attributed precisely to a lack of social solidarity and wasteful utilization of dwindling resources."[48]

The sometimes formidable political savvy of shanty town community organizations and leaders has been noted by some analysts, including Anthony and Elizabeth Leeds, authors of the essay "Brazil and the Myth of Urban Reality: Urban Experience, Work, and Values in the 'Squatments' of Rio de Janeiro and Lima," which was published in the same volume with Martin Needler's paper. The Leeds take quite a different approach; they emphasize that "a great many *favela* residents are not only interested in, but value actual participation in political matters of all sorts. Along with the professional politicians ad administrators of the Brazilian polity, the favela residents are the most subtle and conniving politicians we have ever met anywhere, far and away more politically-minded in all senses than the American populations a whole, and quite incomparable to any equivalent categories of people in it."[49]

My personal experiences in Latin America's marginal neighbourhoods have led me to conclude that, while there is much pluck and enterprise to extol in marginal neighbourhoods, it would be a mistake to idealize a way of life that is on based on offering services to the better off classes and on recycling goods discarded by those same classes. There are only slight rewards in a life spent traveling in the wake of the economic sectors which have the capital to take off into real prosperity. Still the very real achievements of the informal economy have to be acknowledged.

Taking a quite different tack, Robert Gwynne rejects the premise that Latin American cities have dual economies with sharply separated sectors. The way that he depicts the relationship between the two economic sectors tends to blur the distinction between them. While this blurring may be politically unsatisfying, it does allow for or seek some positive interaction between sectors. Gwynne points out that,

> ...any dichotomy is arbitrary but its greatest flaw is that it shifts analysis away from the interface. The urban dual economy model has generally been used as a framework within which to analyse the lower circuit or small-scale economy. Analysts have generally assumed that firms within the small-scale economy *stay* there. Capital accumulation, it is assumed, is too small for firms to make the transition from small to large-scale.

Perhaps for this reason, research has tended to focus on activities such as street vending or garbage picking. Gwynne instead focuses on home grown urban enterprises with some capital, such as the furniture-making (*biblioteca*) industry in Caracas, Venezuela. Such enterprises, he suggests, might be businesses which promote a measure of economic growth and at the same time meet urban residents' needs for regular employment.

One Thumb Up

Despite the fact that even a short downtown trip can be quite a challenge for the denizens of these cities, many of their residents are stubbornly bullish about prospects for themselves and their cities as a whole. In Mexico, there are a host of groups such as GEA and Greenpeace with proposals for how to make the city work better. Greenpeace, for example, launched a proposal to get at least cars off the street by deploying a fleet of large buses with fixed stops.[50] "I don't think Mexico City is so damaged that it can't come back," Mariclaire Acosta, president of Mexico's independent Commission for the Defense and Promotion of Human Rights, told me in a 1995 Mexico City interview.[51] One change that would help the city a lot is a large measure of self-rule, according to Acosta. In the early 1990s, over 300,000 voted for more autonomy in a citizen-organized plebiscite on self rule, despite the fact that the government "did its best to sabotage the plebiscite," according to Acosta.

In Brazil, the diverse projects of a large number of non-governmental organizations themselves have created a ground swell to make the monster cities liveable. Three of these are FASE (*Federacao de Orgoas para assistencia social e educacional*), IBASE (Brazilian Institute for Social and Economic Analysis), and CEAP (*Centro de Articulacao de Populacoes Marginalizadas*). FASE, the oldest Brazilian NGO, launched in 1961, currently has a few different urban projects on the go, FASE staff person Fatima Mello told me.[52] One FASE team working in Sao Paulo is working simultaneously on a three fronts: pressuring the government for adequate housing and sanitation, organizing people to build their own houses, and training women in the community to be leaders. This kind of effort obviously does make some positive changes for homeless people. (The role of NGOs in economic development is more fully discussed in Chapter Five.)

In addition to organized action for social change, the noisy good cheer found on most streets of Latin America's two largest cities must be noted as a sign that some kind of good development is happening. Paulistanos, for instance, are by no means a downcast lot; lots of people I talked to on the street said that they enjoyed living in Sao Paulo because the city's hustle and bustle are intriguing. (Enjoyment of life was not mentioned by any homeless person, however.) The "thumbs-up" gesture that concludes so many Sao Paulo conversations expresses the popular will to prevail.

The Homeless

In Latin American cities, the growing population of homeless people is even lower on the economic ladder than the shanty town dwellers. The recent surge in the number of homeless people in Mexico City, Sao Paulo, Rio de Janeiro and other Latin American cities is fueled, not by a release of mentally ill people from hospitals into the streets, but by the very rigorous application of growth oriented development theories during the 1990s.

Homelessness in Brazil is qualitatively—if not quantitatively—worse than homelessness in Canada, the United States, and Mexico. In the downtown of Brazil's two largest cities, the presence of the homeless is pervasive and inescapable. (Inescapability is also a quality of homelessness in some U.S. neighbourhoods, such as San Francisco's Haight-Ashbury. Still the life of a homeless person is very different in San Francisco from what it would be in Rio. In San Francisco, food and services for the homeless are much more readily available.) The streets of Sao Paulo and Rio de Janeiro are literally littered with the bodies of homeless people. So common are small encampments of the homeless that they go unnoticed on those cities' downtown streets. It is also common in either city for homeless individuals to doze off as they are stretched across the sidewalk or spreadeagled at a street corner; pedestrians walk gingerly around the bodies, usually without examining or even glancing at them. One afternoon on Rio's busy Rua Voluntarios de Patria, I watched with some hope as ambulance attendants hopped out of their vehicle to tend to a homeless man sprawled on the sidewalk. Hope was, however, fleeting; after picking the man up by his shirt and looking him over, they decided he had no need of an ambulance, set him down on the sidewalk again, and off they drove.

A lot but by no means all of the homeless are single men, for instance, the jewelry maker, Eduardo, who had been sleeping in the bandshell at the Plaza of the Republic for about two months when I met him in November 1995. There are also a lot of two parent and one parent families who huddle together on the sidewalk or in corners here and there. A homeless mother told me that her new daughter was just two days old. As we talked, she doggedly swept the sidewalk and the mat she kept under her baby's basket.

By no means all the people living on the streets of Brazil are chronic street people who are homeless at least partly because they lack basic coping skills. Two of the members of a small encampment of homeless people who lived, for a few days anyway, outside the Banespa bank on the Avenido Rio Branco told me that they were from Sao Paulo and were not recent arrivals in the city. They formerly had fixed dwellings, but had then lived on the street for about a year and a half. The group included a mother and a child about 18 months old as well as the two men who conversed with me. The child showed a toddler's usual playfulness as he frolicked on the sidewalk. This spirit of fun was totally absent in the adults, who appeared despondent and bereft of any resources which they could use to improve their situations.

In answer to my queries, some staffers at Brazilian NGOS said that their impression is that globalization has increased homelessness in Brazil's major cities. Hard data is lacking; homelessness is hard to quantify in any country where it occurs. Still, empirical evidence of homelessness is overwhelmingly present in Sao Paulo and Rio.

In addition to the homeless children accompanied by their parents, there are the by now world famous street children of Rio and Sao Paulo, who have only a slight attachment or no attachment at all to a parental home. Many of these Brazilian street children are murdered by death squads that include off duty police and hired killers. Very often fearful storeowners are the ones who instigate and pay for the hits, according to Nancy Scheper-Hughes, an anthropologist at the University of California, Berkeley, and author of a book on violence in everyday Brazilian life.[53] According to the federal police, close to 5,000 Brazilian children were murdered from 1988 to 1990, most of them boys from 15 to 19 years of age.[54] One of the most highly publicized of these killings was the Candelaria massacre: the murder of seven children and an adult in the doorway of a church on the night of 23 August 1993. Rio's Centre de Articulao de Populacoes Marginalizadas (CEAP) and others allege that such killings have been organized by the police working in the service of businessmen. Black children who have committed minor illegalities are very often the victims.[55]

In an interview in CEAP's office on the Rua da Lapa, CEAP's president Ele Semog told me that poverty and the neglect of children are caused by Brazil's structural problems, such as the concentration of wealth. Indifference to all kinds of violence against children can be construed to be "a cultural attitude of Brazilians; four children a day die from the violence of poverty." Semog reflected on how the transition "from poverty to misery to exclusion is a quick passage." Some people talk about "a generation with out hope," but it is not helpful to say that "people don't have hope...Our job is to help people form attitudes. Our job is to construct political consciousness."[56] With the support of UNICEF CEAP distributes posters as well as written materials. One recent CEAP poster strikingly depicted Miss Brazil 2,000 as a barefoot pre-adolescent girl with a tattered blanket around her shoulders and a long breadstick—her scepter—in her hand.

International publicity about Brazil's street kids very often leaves out the most important information about why so many children have been pushed to the edges of society: poor, marginalized parents have children who are also poor. "Until Brazilians reverse the chaotic economic and social conditions that cause desperately poor parents to 'lose' their children to the streets, childhood for the vast majority in Brazil will be a period of adversity to be survived and gotten over as quickly as possible, rather than a time of nurturance to be extended and savored."[57]

In Mexico City too, where family homelessness has not been highly visible, there are tens of thousands of children who have had to take to the streets, either to work, to live, or both. An estimated 10,000 children work in Mexico City's streets; 30,000 more children are said to be panhandlers.[58] The *Toronto Star's* Linda Diebel has written about some of Mexico's street kids and about the staff of Casa Alianza, who try to provide some support and help for the children. One of the children Diebel met was the smart talking, 12 year old Marcus, who coughed all the time and didn't know where his parents were. He did have a big dog named Negra; he assured Diebel that "I'm not alone...I have Negra."[59]

During my Mexico City sojourn, I met with staff people at the Mexican Foundation for Social Reintegration, another Mexico City agency that works with street children, particularly with children who have come in conflict with the law. The foundation has a six to twelve month program to support children with employment, schooling, and reorientation to the child's family. What is needed even more than this remedial work is action "to prevent children from going into the street in the first place." After they are in the street they undergo a process of "streetification" which makes it difficult for them to return to a homebound life, foundation director Carmen Perez Rocha told me.[60] The most pressing requirements are for work, education, and recreation for the whole family, said Perez Rocha.

The foundation has a joint project with the YMCA to help deal with the problems of Mexican children who end up in San Diego and other U.S. cities. One staff member observed dryly to me that "children in Mexico City are washing windows to make money, not selling crack. The social disintegration is more advanced in the United States than here."

Human Rights Concerns

Neglect of human rights as a component of development is another serious deficiency in post-World War II capitalist economics in Latin America. Though human rights discourse has been part of national and international politics since the 18th century, the meaning of rights remained highly circumscribed for almost two centuries thereafter. In nations where citizens rights' were specified and written down, "human rights" very often referred to the entitlement of individuals to say what they like, carry guns, and be free from arbitrary arrest.

The meaning and practice of human rights were greatly altered the 19th and 20th struggles over slavery, the emancipation of women, colonialism, and also by the genocidal murder of six million Jews during World War II. Enactment of the United Nations Universal Declaration of Human Rights in the late 1940s was a big step in the recognition that economic and social rights are as important as civil rights to human well being. A number of other agreements, such as the 1990 convention on the rights of the child, have also strengthened international consciousness of the need to meet the basic rights of all human beings and also to recognize their worth. Demands for rights by a very broad array of marginalized groups have picked up force especially since the 1960s, when the women's movement, the black power movement, and new third world liberation forces burst on the world scene all at once. Even the steamroller of world recession in the 1990s has not flattened the enthusiasm of a new generation human rights advocates, who now champion a newly discovered crop of rights that need defending, including the rights of homosexuals, the rights of the disabled, and animal rights.

In the United States, human rights became an important foreign aid and general foreign policy concern during the Jimmy Carter's post-Vietnam War administration, but the 1979 hostage taking in Iran dampened both concern for human rights in other countries and also public respect for Carter as a foreign policy maker. In Canada, human rights acquired a niche in the country's foreign policy during the 1980s. The Canadian International Development Agency's 1975 *Strategy for International Development Cooperation* makes only an indirect references to human rights: that one goal of aid is "to enhance the quality of life and improve the capacity of all sectors of their populations to participate in national development efforts."[61] A decade later Canadian aid policy makers considered human rights such an important aspect of development that they made a commitment to reduce or deny aid to gross human rights violators[62] and to launch an International Centre for Human Rights and Democratic Development. Despite these initiatives, racism, arbitrary arrest, abuse of women, and other human rights violations remained rampant in many aid receiving less developed countries, and also in the United States and Canada.

Some of the rights which have become important in international discussions about economic and social development are: women's rights, rights of racial minorities, individual civil rights, the right to sexual preference, children's rights, labour rights, the rights of refugees, and the right to have basic human needs fulfilled. The rights dealt with briefly in this chapter—in the Brazilian and Mexican contexts—are the right to freedom from racial discrimination and individual civil rights.

The Black and Indigenous People's Burden: Racism

That race and racism are explosive issues in Brazilian society there can be no doubt. Over 50 percent of the country's population is black, according to Antonio Carlos Arruda da Silva, president of Sao Paulo's Council for the Participation and Involvement of the Negro Community.[63] Some estimates of the black and mixed race population go as high as 70 to 80 percent. Brazil has the second largest black population in the world.

Discrimination and ill treatment of blacks, which is pervasive in Brazilian society, has to be traced back to Brazil's particular slave history. Brazil was the last country in the world to abolish slavery; this did not occur until 1888. Slaves had no rights at all under Brazilian law until 1860, when the "sexagenarian law" was passed, giving freedom to slaves over the age of 60 (when there was not much further need to feed and maintain them for work anyway). Under the slavery regime, black families were routinely separated—a violation that made it hard for them to establish any identity at all, either at the time or in future centuries. It would be impossible to have a Brazilian version of Alex Haley's *Roots*, Arruda Da Silva told me in a Sao Paulo interview.

Racism in Brazil is hard to pinpoint and isolate because there are no laws which create disadvantages for black people, as there were until recently in South Africa and in many states of the United States. "We know that the slavery of today does not use metal chains, but uses another kinds of oppression," said Arruda da Silva in a recent paper.[64] Ele Semog of CEAP even told me that "here racism is a greater problem than in South Africa."[65] Arruda listed four major kinds of discrimination against blacks: in the country as a whole, blacks get 30 percent of the salary of whites. Only four percent of university students are black. Police violence—up to and including murder—against young blacks is also a big problem in Brazil's cities. Recently, however, "the black movement and the human rights movement are making it more difficult to kill people in police stations."[66] There is also a great lack of public visibility for Brazilian black people. "All the people on Brazilian TV are white," Arruda da Silva told me. "If you see black people on TV, it's because they are singers, athletes, or criminals." A flip through the dials will confirm Arruda's statement.

Since the mid-1980s, there has been some very limited redress of racism. Racism was made a crime in Brazil's new constitution. The Council which Arruda da Silva heads was founded in 1984. He calls the Council "a mixture of government and civil society. This is a new instrument to discuss public policy for blacks."[67] To some extent, Brazilian blacks look to people of African origin in other countries as well as to their own society for ways to end racism. Arruda da Silva has a large photo of Malcolm X talking to Martin Luther King in a place of honour in his office, and a much smaller shot of himself together with the U.S. civil rights leader and politician Jesse Jackson. As a visiting scholar at the L.B.J. School of Public Policy in Texas, he wrote a paper on "Working together: possible strategies for Afro-Brazilians and Afro-Americans."

The harsh reality is that the racism of Brazilian society is by no means unique or even unusual. Racism—particularly against black and indigenous people—remains a large obstacle to equitable development in just about every country in the world, the G8 world and the less developed world alike. It has never received proper attention as a development issue from aid agencies or governments; CIDA, for instance, does not treat anti-racism as a special concern on a par with women or the environment. This neglect of issues related to racism happens because racism's occurrence is often unprovable and because people who are not its targets are usually reluctant to acknowledge its reality or to take action on it. Until racism gets proper recognition as an economic development issue, people of colour in Brazil and elsewhere will continue to have a hard struggle against economic misery and social isolation.

Civil Rights

The right to freedom from arbitrary arrest, torture, and execution is the most basic of all civil rights. The fact that respect for the right to physical survival is needed as foundation for all economic development has never been straightforwardly acknowledged by most experts in the development field or by politicians in any country. In fact, Brazil and Chile were greatly touted in the 1970s in the Western world as "economic miracles" despite the fact that both countries had military governments that stifled dissent through arbitrary arrest, torture, and execution.

For many years, Mexico enjoyed a sometimes undeserved reputation as home to governments which were seen as somewhat undemocratic (because dominated by the PRI) but still basically respectful of human rights. The signing of the North American Free Trade Agreement in the 1990s focused new attention on the serious, pervasive human rights abuses long committed by many Mexican authorities for the sake, they thought and sometimes said, of modern development. A November 1995 Amnesty International (AI) delegation to the country reported that serious human rights violations were widespread. AI Secretary-General Derek Evans said at a press conference that "only a firm political decision by the Mexican Government to eliminate impunity will make it possible to eradicate the practice of torture and other human rights violations. In a press release, AI criticized a 1993 measure that gives the Public Ministry "almost discretionary powers of arrest without a court order" and the power to "hold people in detention for up to four days without bringing them before a judge." During this period, "people are often held incommunicado and frequently tortured, often to force them to sign confessions. Despite evidence of such torture, these confessions are frequently the only evidence used to convict people and their claims of torture are almost never investigated."

Murder also became a frequently used weapon in the PRI's battle to retain political supremacy. The massacre by state police of 17 *campesinos* on their way to a political rally in the state of Guerrero, southwest of Mexico City, in June 1995 became an international scandal. It was frequently suggested in the Mexican press that Guerrero governor Ruben Figueroa was implicated in the killings, but special prosecutor Alejandro Vidales conducted an investigation which exonerated him. Despite the national and international publicity to the Guerrero case, official violence against *campesinos* continued unabated. On 18 February 1996, nine coffee planters and small ranchers were assassinated by judicial police in three separate incidents near Atoyac de Alvarez—in the same area as the 1995 massacre. Four days later, another four *campensinos*, also said to be lawbreakers, were killed in the southern Sierra Madre.[68] The subsequent discovery of an uncensored, unabridged videotape of the June 1995 incident raised a public furor. The tape showed that the *campesinos* carried no weapons, that the order to open fire came almost immediately after the *campesinos* were detained, and that police tampered with the crime scene.[69]

It is difficult to investigate lawbreaking by public authorities in an intimidating and hostile atmosphere which promotes the lawbreaking in the first place. Mexico's official human rights commission, which reviewed the case, has "moral weight but little real power."[70] The independent Commission for the Defense and Promotion of Human Rights, founded in 1990, has a lot of risky, hard work cut out for itself. "There's a real rise in human rights violations," human rights commission President Mariclaire Acosta told me in a 1995 Mexico City interview. "Last year there was a rise in the assassinations, arrests, and torture of members of the opposition." At the same time, "there is an increase in opposition and there is also a breakdown in the political system. The president gives the impression of being cornered against a wall. He scolds people who say that his policies are not the best."[71]

The pre-NAFTA rush of self-praising, high priced "infomercials" distributed by the government of Carlos Salinas de Gortari was successful in deflecting attention from the long-term and increasing human rights violations committed by PRI governments. The chickens of misused official power did, however, come home to roost in form of bad international publicity about the Zapatista rebellion, the Guerrero massacre, and other abuses. Eventually it led to electoral defeat for the PRI. Still bad publicity and losses at the polls, as unpleasant as they are, have not saved the lives of socially isolated *campesinos* whose political doings as seen as threats to the dominant power structures.

Coming up for Air

A final failure of growth oriented post World War II development in Latin America must be mentioned here: the failure to halt environmental degradation and to protect people, especially in big cities, from pollution and disasters caused by the carelessness of employers and governments. The supposition might be made that the job of coping with the pollution created by modern development is evenly distributed among all social sectors in Sao Paulo, Mexico City, and the world's other monster cities. Once a traffic jam starts, everyone gets stuck in it, right? The supposition is, however, largely wrong; a disproportionate amount of the world's pollution-generated gasping and rash scratching is done by the poor. The economically strongest residents of monster cities have getaway places in Cuernavaca (Mexico), Ubatuba (Brazil), or other relatively cleaner and more peaceful spots.

Then there is the fact that the dirtiest facilities are usually located in any city's least affluent districts. A February 1996 gas explosion at the Fain Chemical Plant in Mexico City resulted in the hospitalization of five people, including three children, and the evacuation of thousands from their homes. Residents of Iztapalapa and Tlahuac told the *Toronto Star* that they had been fighting for years to get the plant shut down after a number of explosions and repeated contamination of their water supply.[72] "This isn't the first time this has happened. It's the third. But nobody comes to ask us if anyone is hurt," area resident Antonio Rodriguez said.

The severe health hazards faced by many Mexican industrial workers and by communities near industrial plants have become internationally well known (but seldom corrected) during the post-NAFTA era. These life-threatening working situations are found both in Mexico City and in the industrial centres of *el norte* near the U.S. border, where maquilas—plants owned by multinational corporations and given important tax breaks by the Mexican government—have proliferated especially since 1982. Some of the most important industrial centres in the north are Tijuana, Monterrey, and Matemoros, which is directly across the border from Brownsville, Texas.

Health and safety inspection is almost non-existent at the plants in Matemoros, according to a study team from the University of Lowell, Mass. "In Matemoros, where there are more than 100 plants, there is not a single ministry of labour inspector in the city. The nearest one is 200 miles away." This lack is a symptom that even minimal standards are neglected. Few systematic surveys have been done of health and safety in the maquilas. One such effort was the University of Lowell study of 267 workers—over 80 percent female—in the Reynosa-Matamoros region, which uncovered many complaints about workers' health. Almost half of those in the survey reported that on every shift, they were exposed to gas or vapours, chemicals, and dust. The study team found that "nausea or vomiting, stomach pain, urinary problems and breathing problems were significantly related to the frequency of exposure to airborne contaminants." Its conclusion was that the findings were an "indication of the likelihood that there will be substantial chronic health effects in the future." In fact the future predicted by the Lowell group has already arrived in Matemoros. Twenty children afflicted with some kind of retardation have been born to women who worked at a Matamoros battery plant, where they wore no protective masks while they breathed battery acid fumes containing PCBs.[73]

Pollution of the poor is a practice not confined to Mexico or other Latin American nations; in Toronto, for instance, two well known polluters—Canada Metal and Toronto Refiners and Smelters—are located near less affluent residential neighbourhoods. For years during the 1970s, community groups pressured the companies, Toronto city council, and the provincial government for action to cut lead emissions from the plants and clean up the neighbourhoods. The Toronto lead pollution story had a fairly happy ending; lead emissions were better controlled, but continued monitoring has been needed to prevent high levels of toxicity that could can cause brain damage in children.

The Mexico and Toronto situations are comparable, but also different in ways that are so important that, in the end, they seem to fall into different categories of experience. Torontonians had the advantages working with a not-too-uncooperative governments that did take action to control and monitor the polluters. Moreover, Canada Metal and Toronto Refiners and Smelters were less dangerous polluters than Fain Chemical and the maquilas of Matamoros.

These and many other similar cases illustrate this axiom of world pollution: pollution is unevenly distributed within the G8 world and then even more unevenly distributed between the developed world as a whole and the third world as a whole. In the third world, pollution is again unevenly apportioned between the affluent and the poor.

A few exceptions to this rule must be noted. First of all, there are some industry-caused environmental hazards (other than pollution) that affect most human beings to some degree. One of these is the thinning of the ozone layer; the burning sun wreaks its havoc on the just and the unjust of the earth alike. (Still, people in the G8 world have better sunblock.) Then there is the fact that many people in the world's poorest countries do not get directly hit by a lot of pollution because there is not much industrial development in their countries. (Instead they suffer environmental blights such as desertification.) In contrast with these largely nonindustrial countries—many of them in Africa—Mexico and other nations which are able to attract polluting industries are seen as lucky.

In the 1990s, everyone, including captains of industry, agrees that environmental deterioration must be stopped, but the inattention of most world leaders to the earth's most pressing environmental problems since 1945 has taken a heavy toll, especially in less developed nations, including those in Latin America. The good news to report on this is that there's a new political stripe in world politics these days, and it's colour is green. Nowhere knows yet where the greening of politics will take us, mainly because champions of the environment do not control the affairs of any country and do not even usually have the ears of the people who do. Their marginalization could end in the 21st century, as we struggle against the slow landward creep of shorelines. Certainly we don't want Ipanema Beach and the Brazilians who still go to the sea each day to vanish under the wave of global warming.

NOTES

1. Peter F. Drucker, *Post-Capitalist Society* (New York: Harper Business, 1994), p. 131.
2. Martin C. Needler, "Political aspects of urbanization in Mexico," in *City and Country in the Third World, Issues in the Modernization of Latin America*, ed. Arthur J. Field (Cambridge, Mass. and London: Schenkman Publishing Company, 1970), p. 290.
3. *The Economist*, 25 April - 5 May 1995.
4. Ernest Feder, *The Rape of the Peasantry* (Garden City, New York: Doubleday and Co. 1971).
5. Gunder Frank, "The Underdevelopment of Development," *Scandanavian Journal of Development Alternatives*, vol. 10, no. 3 (September 1991), p. 31.
6. Feder, *The Rape of the Peasantry*, p. 53.
7. *Ibid.*, p. 54.
8. *Ibid.*, p. 27.
9. William Thiesenhusen, "Human Rights, Affirmative Action, and Land Reform in Latin America," in *The Political Economy of Ethnic Discrimination and Affirmative Action*, ed. Michael L. Wyzan (New York: Praeger, 1990), pp. 25-48.
10. *Agrarian Structure in Latin America*, A Resume of the CIDA Land Tenure Studies of Argentina, Brazil, Chile, Colombia, Ecuador, Guatemala, and Peru, edited by Solon Barraclough, 1973.
11. William C. Thiesenhusen, *Broken Promises: Agrarian Reform and the Latin American Campesino* (Boulder: Westview Press, 1995), p. 37.
12. *Ibid.*
13. *Ibid.*, p. 29.
14. Roy H. May, *The Poor of the Land* (Maryknoll, New York: Orbis Books, 1991), p. xi.
15. Peter Dorner, *Latin American Land Reforms in Theory and Practice. A Retrospective Analysis* (Madison: the University of Wisconsin Press, 1992), p. 3.
16. *Ibid.*, p. 33.
17. Robert N. Gwynne, *Industrialization and Urbanization in Latin America* (London and Sydney: Croom Helm, 1985), p. 9.
18. Dorner, p. 40.
19. Thiesenhusen, p. xi.
20. John K. Galbraith, "Conditions for Change in Underdeveloped Countries," *Journal of Farm Economics*, 33: 689-96, cited in Dorner, p. 4.
21. Dorner, p. 37.
22. Thiesenhusen, p. 1.
23. Material published by *Sem Terra*, 1995, p. 6.
24. *Ibid.*, p. 8.
25. Thiesenhusen, p. 29.
26. *Ibid.*
27. "Vamos al referendum. Para salir de la crisis," 1995.
28. Encuentro Nacional de Organizaciones Ciudadanas, *Carta de los Derechos Humanos*, July 1995, p. 17.
29. Riccardo Petrella, "World City-States of the Future," *New Perspectives Quarterly*, Fall 1991, p. 39.
30. Robert N. Gwynne, *Industrialization and Urbanization in Latin America* (London and Sydney: Croom Helm), p. 136.
31. *Ibid.*, p. 137.
32. *Ibid.*, p. 135.
33. Jose Alvaro Moises and Verena Stolke, "Urban Transport and Popular Violence in Brazil," in *Latin America*, eds. Eduardo Archetti, Paul Cammack and Bryan Roberts (Houndmills, 1987), p. 232.
34. Lucio Kowarick, "The Logic of Disorder," in *Latin America*, eds. Eduardo P. Archetti, Paul Cammack, and Bryan Roberts (Houndmills, 1987), p. 225.
35. Alvaro Moises and Stolcke, "Urban Transport and Popular Violence in Brazil," p. 237.
36. Ibid, p. 240.
37. Interview in Mexico City, 14 November 1995.
38. Kowarick, p. 222.
39. Interview with the author, 7 November 1995 in Santa Marta, Botafogo, Rio de Janeiro.
40. Interview with the author, 16 November, 1995.
41. Interview with the author, 14 November 1995.
42. Kowarick, p. 222.

43. Larissa Lomnitz, "Networks and Social Marginality," in *Latin America*, eds. Archetti, Cammack, and Roberts, p. 270.

44. Lomnitz, p. 271.

45. Gwynne, p. 158.

46. Martin C. Needler, "Political aspects of urbanization in Mexico," in *City and Country in the Third World. Issues in the Modernization of Latin America*, p. 292, 293.

47. Lomnitz, "Networks and Social Marginality," p. 267.

48. *Ibid.*, p. 272.

49. Anthony and Elizabeth Leeds, "Brazil and the Myth of Urban Reality: Urban Experience, Work, and Values in the 'Squatments' of Rio de Janeiro and Lima," in *City and Country in the Third World*, ed. Arthur J. Field.

50. Interview with Trine Lopez, GEA, 14 Nov. 1995.

51. Interview in Mexico City, 16 November 1995.

52. Interview in Rio de Janeiro, 6 November 1995.

53. Nancy Scheper-Hughes and Daniel Hoffman, "Kids Out of Place," *Fighting for the Soul of Brazil*, eds. K. Danaher and M. Shellenberger (New York: Monthly Review Press), p. 147.

54. *Ibid.*, p. 146.

55. *Pixote*, Revista Sobre Meninos E Meninas, Ano 1, no. 2, 1993, p. 4.

56. Interview in Rio de Janeiro, 8 November 1995.

57. Nancy Scheper-Hughes and Daniel Hoffman, p. 150.

58. *Toronto Star*, 17 December 1995.

59. *Ibid.*

60. Interview with Carmen Perez Rocha in Mexico City, 16 November 1995.

61. Canadian International Development Agency, Strategy for International Development Cooperation (Ottawa, 1975), p. 23.

62. Canadian International Development Agency, *Sharing Our Future*, Ministry of Supply and Services Canada, 1987, p. 31.

63. Interview with the author in Sao Paulo, 6 November 1995.

64. "Working Together: Possible Strategies for Afro-Brazilians and Afro-Americans," presented in Washington, October 1994, p. 4.

65. Interview in Rio de Janeiro, 8 November 1995.

66. Interview in Sao Paulo, 6 November 1995.

67. Interview, 6 November 1995.

68. David Crow and Javier Media, Fonteras Comunes, Analysis #61, *The Heartbeat of Mexico*, 28 February 1996.

69. Javier Medina and David Crow, Fronteras Comunes, *Heartbeat of Mexico*, Analysis #62, 7 March 1996.

70. Analysis #61, *The Heartbeat of Mexico*.

71. Interview with Mariclaire Acosta in Mexico City, 16 November 1996.

72. *Toronto Star*, 21 Feb, 1996.

73. Rafael Moure-Eraso, Meg Wilcox, Laura Punnett, Leslie Copeland, Charles Levenstien, "Back to the Future: Sweatshop Conditions on the Mexico-U.S. Border," University of Lowell-Work Environment Program, 11 April 1991, cited in *Crossing the Line*, ed. Jim Sinclair (Vancouver: New Star Books, 1992) p. 58.

4
◆ ◆ ◆

THE TOLL OF GLOBALIZATION

Cut to Toronto, Canada, 17 December 1995. On this frosty northern day, it was hard to believe that there was ever a girl from Ipanema who had been spotted sunning herself on a tropical beach. Marion Best, who by then had raised her family, was Moderator of the United Church and commuted between the church's Toronto office and her home in Naramata, British Columbia. Best was a groundbreaking moderator in a few different ways because she was a woman, a non-ordained lay person, and formerly the chairperson of a committee which dealt with the very controversial issue of gay and lesbian ordination. (The church decided that it would ordain them.) When she became moderator, Best was also given the Ojibwa name "Beh Beh Minwahjimoot." ("Who Goes Forth With the Good News.") In Dec. 1995, however, Best took on the task of reporting some decidedly bad news: that political change and the overhaul of social priorities were badly hurting many Canadians. She and other United Church executives penned a letter that was read to all congregations on 17 December that year. The letter deplored the dismantling of Canada's post-World War II social security system and noted that "the people we've hired through our taxes to tend the safety net are being laid off as federal and provincial governments cut their budgets. In many provinces, the cuts are happening with little thought to how people will cope. Some political leaders use a dangerous rhetoric—dividing our communities into those of 'us' who have enough income to be taxed and 'them'—people who are sick, disabled, unemployed, in need of education, medical care, or enough income to survive." This controversial thought was voiced in the pulpit because the times seemed to require a new kind of plain speaking.

The fall of 1995 was when I talked with Betinho at the IBASE office on Rio de Janeiro's Rua Vicente Souza. After a stint in Chile, where Betinho fled after Brazil's 1964 coup, and then in Canada—which offered him residency after Chile's 1973 coup—he had returned to Brazil for good in 1979. In 1995, Bethinho was a very tall and much too thin man nearing the age of 60. Despite his ill health, he was still *in media res* on many projects, including the National Campaign for Agrarian Reform and Citizens' Action Against Misery and for Life. (The latter is described in Chapter Five.) "We are trying to change Brazil so that everyone can eat, work, have a job, have land, and be a citizen," he told me.[1] His final words were to the effect that Rio needed food banks comparable to those in Toronto. This thought left me scratching my head; why would one of Brazil's most progressive thinkers champion food banks? Most left-of-centre Torontonians want to see food banks replaced by more adequate food suppliers as soon as possible. You just couldn't predict what the heterodox Bethinho was going to tell you.

The year 1995 was pivotal for me as well. By then I was a self-employed single parent with a ten year old daughter who was just then approaching her prime "consuming" years. In 1995, Armani and Nike were still only names to her and had not yet become consuming passions, but I realized that they soon would be. Clothes buying would have to be a very different experience for her than it had been for the ungainly Long Island adolescent I had been. I sensed that Mike Harris would not be a booster of my consumption goals, even though I was an honest to God entrepreneur. In other words, I knew hard times were ahead.

A strong argument can be made that the mid-1990s were the years when the modern, post-World War II social order that sought economic development for all ripped completely apart. Political and economic changes during the previous twenty years had badly disheveled that order, but it was not until the mid-1990s that the change became permanent, seemingly irreversible, and obvious to everyone. In North America, the radical shift became apparent partly in election results and in the popularity of right wing legislation. In New York, Republican Governor George Pataki replaced liberal Democrat Mario Cuomo. In New York City, Republican Mayor Rudolph Giuliani replaced Democrat David Dinkins. In Ontario, the right wing Progressive Conservative government headed by Mike Harris swept out a New Democratic Party government in 1995. Harris brought a radical rightist stridency to Ontario politics which previously had been absent, even from Conservative governments. The Harris government proceeded immediately to cut welfare checks by one-fifth and to introduce a previously unthinkable work for welfare program. In the United States, President Bill Clinton signed a social security reform law that gutted the country's welfare system. The message coming from North America's legislatures and media was that taking income and benefits from the poor was acceptable, even laudable.

As candidates, Harris, Pataki, and Guiliani made it clear that they wanted to change everything and stand the old social order in its head. Harris said that his mission was to foment a "common sense revolution" to "re-invent the way it [government] works, to make it work for people."[2] The inescapable assumption is that previous governments had somehow been profoundly mistaken in their actions.

The World as a Whole and the U.S.

Radical right wing change was high on the agenda in most of the world's countries during the 1990s. The totality of change shaking up our world has broad political, technological, economic, and ideological as well as legislative aspects. On the political front, the biggest recent change was the dissolution of the Soviet Union and the switch to capitalist liberal democracy in the nations of Eastern Europe. Much of the world watched with astonishment as first the Berlin Wall crumbled and then the U.S.S.R. deflated as quickly as balloon falling on a pin. These change were thrilling no doubt, but they also had many negative consequences. The first was incorporation of formerly Communist nations of the East into the world economic system at a very low level. Their status as a "second world" lost, they were rapidly but informally relegated by G8 leaders to third world status.

Henceforth the governments of the formerly Communist East would be seeking economic support for themselves instead of dispensing it to less developed countries. U.S. political commentator Noam Chomsky predicted this development in a 1991 interview. "Frankly, I think the prospects for Eastern Europe are pretty dim. The West has a very clear plan. They want to turn it into a new, easily exploitable part of the Third World."[3]

The transformation of Communist nations into aid consumers has generated competitive jostling among aid-receiving nations. Advocates of the "old" third world, for instance, expressed anxiety when it was reported that "traditional recipient countries in Africa, Asia, and Latin America will be getting a smaller share of the aid pie."[4]

After the first bloom of publicity about the fall of the U.S.S.R. and the desperate need for aid there, Russia and the other nations of the old Communist bloc faded from public attention as they settled at least temporarily into the status of what Chomsky calls a "colonial hinterland." The authors of *Global Dreams*, a 1993 update of 1974 Simon and Schuster book on corporate power, *Global Reach*, reported that investors were attracted to the former U.S.S.R. "by the lure of Russia's mineral-rich expanse, cheap wages, and an educated work force hungry for consumer goods. But conditions have remained so unsettled that foreign companies have concluded very few deals to produce goods in the former Soviet republics for either the domestic or global market."[5] *Global Dreams* also reports that 4/5 of all economic activity on earth is generated in two dozen countries, not one of which is a former Communist nation of the Soviet bloc.[6]

The near disappearance of Communist ideology has been less publicized than the "big fall" taken by the U.S.S.R.'s economy, but its consequences for the world as a whole have been at least as important. What is now lacking is are political or economic systems that present alternatives to market oriented capitalism. Two partially elaborated and still possibly viable systems from our modern era—dependency theory and liberation theology—do try to unite economic reality with the goal of social justice. The Universal Declaration of Human Rights and other UN based human rights declarations also provide at least a piece of a world view which is different from and in some ways opposed to the capitalist reliance on the free market to sort out the world's winner from its losers. These fragments of a world view may provide guidance to today's theorists and activists.

In *Global Dreams*, authors Barnet and Cavanagh conclude that "the world faces an authority crisis without precedent in modern times," partly because corporate leaders "do not accept responsibility for the social consequences of what they make or how they make it." What transnational business now presents as an substitute for ideology is a host of one liners—new age proverbs they might be called—about how the world operates. Who's got time for ideology anyway, these days? The developed world seems to operate well enough without belief systems more complex that of Forrest Gump's mom: "Life is like a box of chocolates. You never know what you're going to get." This and comparable sayings such as Apple's "Think different" seem to plumb the depths of post-millennial philosophy. "Empowerment" has been another favourite postmodern touchstone. Many current one liners appropriate the vocabulary of the 1960s and convert it into the free market lingo of the 1990s: in Ontario Mike Harris launched, not a "crusade" but a common sense "revolution."

Wolfgang Sachs of Germany's Institute for Advanced Studies laments the wealthy world's impoverishment in ideas this way: "Now captives of competition, these countries long ago destroyed not only much of their precious natural resources but also those treasures of meaning that could have given them peace of mind off the development track."[7]

The nearly universal disintegration of left-wing forces (and the discarding of the term left wing itself) came during the same era as—but has not always been caused by—the collapse of Communism. The breakdown of the Soviet bloc resulted in the demoralization of the world's Communist parties. In North America, Communist party members had in the early and middle twentieth century provided a lot of the legwork for the organization of trade unions and other progressive social organizations, so the demise of world Communist parties was not an unmitigated blessing for progressive groups, even those who completely rejected a Moscow oriented line.

The 1990s also disheveled many of the world's social democratic and other progressive movements. In Nicaragua, important differences surfaced among member of the FSLN (Sandinista Front) in the wake of the 1990 electoral defeat which overturned the Sandinista revolution. In Canada, the New Democratic Party suffered major setbacks at both the federal and provincial levels. These losses must be contrasted with the electoral wins scored by conservative minded social democrats such as Tony Blair in the U.K. who have delinked themselves from the demands of trade unions.

Trade unions around the world were also under attack in the 1990s. In the U.S., union membership dropped to about 15.8 percent of the work force, and the 1994 U.S. Commission on the Future of Worker-Management Relations stressed that cooperation rather than conflict should predominate in the workplace of the future. Canadian did much better, with a drop from 40 to 37.6 percent of the workforce during the decade.[8] In Canada, trade unions have been under attack from right wing, deregulating ideology which depicts the union as an interference in the operations of the free market. A *Toronto Star* article prophesied: "Labour's traditional methods have been torn to pieces by a high-tech revolution and a gale-force recession. Its future: evolve or die." Third world trade unions are contending with even worse problems: unemployment and underemployment rates that so high that union membership is not an option for a large percentage of the workforce, fierce government repression or government cooption of trade unions, and great difficulties in organizing in export processing zones.

The reactions of the worlds' progressive, left wing groups to the rout they suffered in the 1990s included depression, denial, and vehement assertions that their values and goals could not just disappear from the world overnight. And yet, it seems, they did; it turns out that Forrest Gump's mom was right after all. Despite this debacle, citizens' movements opposed to regional integration and a host of alternative institutions in both the G8 world and the less developed work have proceeded apace.

Beyond the retreat of the left, another major upheaval that has rocked our world is an economic downturn that started in 1990 according to the world media, or even much earlier in the opinion of more unconventional thinkers. This lack of buoyancy is pervasive, unyielding, and long-term in its consequences. One very important cause of the post-1990 recession—and of previous economic contractions during the past 25 years—is that there is no longer much demand in the world for basic consumer goods such as houses, furniture, TVs, non-designer clothing, cars, and even basic personal computers. Those who can afford have them already do, and there is little expectation among world business leaders that people who don't now have them will ever be able to afford them. Consumers who are provided with these goods do have to replace them from time to time, and this need does generate some economic activity, but not enough to keep corporations producing at the pace they would like.

Business leaders' response to the saturation of traditional consumer markets is described by sociologist Maria Mies in *Patriarchy and Accumulation on a World Scale.* "In the 1970s, however, the managers of the big national and multinational corporations in Europe, the USA, and Japan, realized that the boom period which had followed the end of World War II was over, that continuous growth, which had been preached to the people in the industrialized countries as a dogma and had thus become for them something they took for granted, had come to an end."[9]

A number of initiatives were launched to counter this trend. The first, according to Mies, was a new international division of labour, which shifted many labour intensive production processes to the third world and at the same time modernized third world agriculture to make it into an export industry. Export production plants soon multiplied in Mexico, the Philippines, South Korea, Singapore and a number of other third world countries. Mies asserted in 1986 that the shift of production to low wage areas meant that "in spite of rising unemployment and a decrease in real wages, the new IDL (international division of labour) guaranteed a level of mass consumption in the rich countries which helps to prevent the outbreak of social unrest."[10] For third world peoples, the new organization of labour meant they seldom used the goods they assembled or ate the food they grew. Yet in the 1990s, prolonged recession broke down this new social contract; people in the developed world knew that their consumption levels were no longer guaranteed.

Corporate mergers and takeovers have since 1970 have been a second major tool used by transnational business to counter chronic economic sluggishness. These deals are producing megacompanies:

> ...the wave of global mergers that began in the late 1970s and peaked in the mid-1980s consolidated horizontal competitors from different countries, and created pyramids of capital that today dwarf in size the firms produced by the three previous merger waves of 1900, 1920 and 1970. At the same time, managers initiated a plethora of contractual arrangements and joint ventures that now fuse them into strategic constellations, shifting the basis of competition from the traditional industry level to that of the alliance network.[11]

This pervasive merger mania is blurring the traditional national identification of companies which operate globally and is at the same time creating monopolistic enterprises that totally dominate world production in their fields. Riccardo Petrella predicted that, by the second decade of the twenty-first century, there may be "only eight to ten large world consortia in telecommunications, five to eight in the automobile industry, three to five in tire manufacturers [sic], and so on." According to Petrella, the factors propelling this globalization are: "high R&D costs that must be shared, the limited pool of high quality, skilled scientists and engineers, and the multinational corporate system itself, which requires telecommunications, organized research, coordinated production, and financial infrastructure on a global scale."

The triumph of American popular culture accompanied the consolidation of corporate power. This Americanization of much of the world's entertainment and culture has been a fact of life for some years, but globalization, merger mania, and the rise of designer labels have since the 1980s greatly accelerated that process. One of the crowning moments of this renewed U.S. cultural dominance was the takeover of Capital Cities\ABC by Disney on 31 July 1995 in the second largest takeover in U.S. history. The merger created what the *Globe and Mail*[12] called "the world's largest entertainment empire." Financial gossip columnists were all agog again the very next day, when Westinghouse Electric Corp. struck a $7.4 billion deal to buy CBS Inc. Edward Atorino, a Dillon Read analyst, enthused: "Entertainment assets are highly prized because of the almost unlimited future for entertainment products with satellites, telephones, television and computers—all these new avenues—on a global scale."[13]

In 1995, Disney earned a new superlative when it brought to the stage the $17 million production of Beauty and the Beast, which was the most expensive live show ever presented in the world. Disney chairperson Michael Eisner had twigged to the fact that, in a 100 channel universe, people "will hunger for live entertainment."[14] One painful paradox of Americanized global culture is that some of the most widely admired U.S. based cultural phenomena originate in the black communities of New York, Chicago, Los Angeles, and other U.S. cities. African-American clothing and music, which get raves when labeled "Made in the USA," usually merit little attention if their African roots are too evident.

Another big and still accelerating global change during the past decade is the drive to push up productivity by steadily increasing the technological sophistication of productive machinery. A number of different names have been coined for this ceaseless quest to be more productive: total quality management, continuous improvement, lean production, agile production, and the virtual corporation. The drive to maximize productivity is both a cause and a consequence of prolonged recession. Employers want to produce more commodities with fewer costs and less human labour because of the downward squeeze on their profits.

At the same time the tendency of high technology to make human labour unnecessary dispatches high numbers of people to the unemployment and welfare rolls, thus making the recession worse. The unemployed do not buy high tech goods, and, as sales go down because people can't buy, business is driven to cuts its costs by becoming more productive. And so the cycle goes.

In today's world, relentless technological change is wiping out whole economic and social sectors. Information consultant Stan Sam Sternberg told a 1995 Ontario Federation of Labour conference that "this time it's not just workers who are going to disappear. It's employers who are going to disappear as a result of the information highway." One technical term for what's happening is "disintermediation." What happened to Wal-Mart as it became the largest merchandiser to the general public in world is now happening to other companies, according to Sternberg. "Wal-Mart does not buy any production at all from distributors," he said. "Every purchase Wal-Mart makes, it makes from the factory." Wal-Mart and other retailers are using information automation systems to eliminate the need for wholesalers and their employees.[15]

Making production of all kinds smarter all the time is just one way to obtain regular productivity improvements. Another is constant encouragement of the survivors of downsizing and the high tech revolution to work harder and more effectively. Human resources managers in Canada and other industrialized countries try to find out how to do this at conferences organized by management consultants. The firms' ads promise improvements in commitment, teamwork, and creativity.

A third change currently shaking our world is a transformation in the meaning and the uses of money. Half a century ago, money was widely assumed to be a medium of exchange for goods and services that could be issued by governments because it was "backed up" by gold reserves and ultimately could be exchanged for

gold. A world monetary system to ensure the orderly exchange of national currencies and goods across borders after World War II was approved at a 1944 meeting
attended by 44 countries in Bretton Woods, New Hampshire. The Bretton Woods
system established the International Monetary Fund to ensure the convertibility of
currencies and to help nations experiencing short-term balance of payments problems. Bretton Woods set up a system of fixed exchange rates for the world's
money, with the U.S. dollar serving as the standard setter for other currencies. It
also guaranteed the convertibility of the U.S. dollar to gold.

The assumption of the Bretton Woods system that the world's financial systems can be neatly managed seems almost quaint today, when speculative hijinks
hold sway over world financial markets. This transformation of world financial
markets started with the 1971 U.S. decision to let the dollar float in relation to
other currencies and has been greatly accelerated by computer technology, which
allows the transfer of huge sums to occur with just a few keystrokes. At the time, of
course, no one—and almost certainly not Richard Nixon, who announced the
break with the old system—realized that the floating of the dollar would unleash a
genie of such titanic proportions.

An account of the breakdown of the world's fixed exchange rate system by
analyst John Barrados says that originally there had been a widespread feeling that
"fairly quickly, a new exchange rate arrangement would be agreed upon, incorporating the principle of fixed exchange rates albeit in a more flexible form than under the Bretton Woods system. Concern with such matters faded into the
background as countries were faced with the oil crisis of 1973 and subsequently, a
severe recession and inflation."[16] Then, at the end of the decade, the tightening of
U.S. monetary policy and rise in the U.S. dollar put an end to any further interest in
developing a global exchange rate system. The dollar's strengthening also led to
abandonment of a possible initiative to make wider use of IMF Special Drawing
Rights (SDRs) as an international currency.[17] Barrados recounts how currency
speculation started to become a prominent feature of the world's financial systems. "Severe currency speculation began...encouraged by the emergence of substantial interest rate differentials in favour of many European countries."[18]

The mushrooming of international financial markets as an important economic force in the world has had numerous consequences for governments and
peoples. One is that governments either are or feel themselves incapable of con-
trolling the worldwide rush of money seeking the highest rate of return. This lack
of control causes lots of jitters among legislators and money managers. According
to Stephen Neff:

> The worries arise directly from the general cosmopolitan nature of this
> 'floating world.' On the one hand, the Euro-currency system is blissfully
> free from such humdrum inhibitions as reserve requirements, interest-rate
> ceilings, or exchange controls...[it is feared] that, because of the high de-

gree of integration of global financial markets, any loss of confidence, any-where in the system, can have world-wide repercussions with lightning speed—a fact graphically demonstrated by the truly global stock market crash of October 1987.[19]

The helplessness of governments also breeds fatalistic acquiescence to the de-mands of those who are seen to be in charge of the financial system. Neff calls the lawyers, financiers and accountants keep international financial systems moving "latter-day Confucian literati, learned in the arcane and abstract wisdom of loan agreements and balance sheets, spot markets and forward markets, and many other mysteries of modern financial alchemy…Governments, to them, are clients or borrowers rather than masters."[20]

During the past two decades, the world's money markets have also denation-alized currencies to a great extent. This new statelessness of the world's money is indicated in the use of terms like "petrodollar," "Eurodollar," and "European cur-rency units." This use of language does not, however, indicate that the world is moving toward the creation of a truly international currency such as an IMF-minted special drawing right, which might be used to stabilize the financial situation of third world countries. The U.S. dollar is the world's increasingly domi-nant medium of exchange. One new development is that the U.S. dollar can be readily swapped for other kinds of financial instruments and hard currencies on world money markets. This swapping happens in the brave new world of "deriva-tives," where the return on a nonmarketable Canadian debenture, for instance, can be traded in for stock market returns. In Canada, even once stodgy organiza-tions like the Ontario Teachers's Pension Plan Board started using derivatives, the financial instrument which became famous in 1995 because of Nick Leeson, the trader who brought down a British bank at least partly through his use of deriva-tives.

A separate but related problem is the enormous mushrooming of national debts in countries around the world, wealthy and underdeveloped alike. From 1980 to 1990, this debt became a topic of intense public discussion as it spiraled at a dizzying pace. The debt crisis statistics are by now well known; by the end of the 1980s, countries of the third world together owed $1.3 trillion to banks and public agencies in the developed world. Developed countries have also been piling up big debts; Canada's total gross owed to foreign creditors and investors was $540 bil-lion at the end of 1992.

Disagreement is rife around the world about the causes of the debt and how it should be managed. Many analysts point to the 1979 U.S. decision to hike interest rates as a key cause of mounting debt. Heavy borrowing by third world countries is also seen as a critical factor. One incontrovertible fact about world debt explosion is that loans were peddled to the less developed world in the 1970s because inter-national financiers needed places to invest money—as much or more than the third world needed the financiers. The third world at that time seemed a good bet, much the same way takeovers and derivatives have appeared to be good bets at a slightly later date. Barnet and Cavanagh describe how finance ministers in Washington for meetings of the International Monetary Fund "were literally accosted on the street by loan hawkers. On the short walk between the Shoreham and Sheraton hotels, the finance minister from one poor Latin American republic was stopped by five of them."[21]

Another sure fact about the debt crisis was that, during the 1980s, it was scary to financiers, politicians and the general public alike because no one had experienced anything quite like it before. In *Friends but No Allies*, Stephen Neff briefly sketches a few world debt doomsday scenarios. In one, the withdrawal of funds from the Eurocurrency system by nervous investors drives banks "to compete with one another for a dwindling supply of funds." In such a panic, "it is easy to imagine, though frightening to contemplate— that interest rates might be driven to alarming levels in extremely short periods of time, perhaps within hours or even minutes."[22] For Neff, another nightmare is the use of "cross default clauses," which "serve to chain the mass of lenders together, since a borrower's default against any one creditor immediately becomes, under these clauses, a default against all others as well. These clauses, then, operate rather like financial suicide pacts."[23]

After a decade or so of living with the threat of financial apocalypse, the world's money managers figured out a number of ways to avert it indefinitely. One such tool is the debt-equity swap, which enables debt holders to trade their debt for pieces of the debtor nations' economies. Another tool used to keep the wolf of default from the bankers' door is the imposition of seemingly permanent structural adjustment programs on the people in the third world and in many wealthy developed countries too—though G8 finance ministers seldom apply the term "structural adjustment" to their own countries. In the third world, structural adjustment set up the specter of permanent austerity without any prospect of relief.

The *Human Development Report 1992* described how third world efforts to repay the debt through increases in exports of primary commodities were doomed to failure because the prices of the commodities dropped as the volume of exports increased. This drop effectively increased the interest on their debts. "For developing countries, the relevant real interest rate on their foreign debt is the nominal interest rate adjusted by the rate of change in their dollar exports. As a result primarily of the fall in their export prices, developing countries paid an average real interest rate of 17% during the 1980s compared with 4% paid by the industrial nations."[24]

In the U.S. and some Canadian provinces, permanent structural adjustment is taking the form of anti-welfare, anti-unemployment insurance, anti-tax measures, and expressions of dislike for people who use government social assistance programs. It has also led to the scrapping of government-led national industrial strategies (in Canada and in Mexico) and their replacement with free trade "open for business" signs. Government itself is treated as a nuisance which must be assiduously downsized. In Ontario, Mike Harris won a big majority by telling voters that "Canadians are probably the most over-governed people in the world...It's time to stop government growth once and for all."[25]

The mushrooming of international financial markets and of international debt, together with permanent structural adjustment, are important factors in another change which is noticeable everywhere around the world, i.e., a loss in power as well as in prestige for governments around the world.

There is a good foundation in fact for governments to suppose that they can no longer control the value of their own currencies or many other aspects of their economies. In addition, governments everywhere are being exhorted to slash their expenses as a way of to lower their overall indebtedness. That governments are insatiable cash hogs has become a truism. "The first place the government has looked to satisfy its appetite for money has been your pay cheques...This has to stop," Mike Harris told the Ontario electorate in 1995.[26] In the U.S., governmental cash hogs have become about as popular as suspected Communist sympathizers were in the 1950s.

So shredded is the prestige of government that no concerted opposition was mounted in August 1996, when Clinton signed the welfare reform law. During the Congressional debate on the law, welfare recipients were compared to ravenous wild animals and reviled in many other ways. During the mid-1990s, the U.S. social security system set up during the long presidency of Democrat Franklin Delano Roosevelt was discarded and repudiated through a number of other measures as well. There was a dismantling of the system set up through the Housing Act of 1937, which "created the basic structure for the nation's system of public housing. Local housing authorities, chartered under state enabling laws [built and administered] their own housing projects, using the proceeds from sale of their own tax-free bonds, while receiving additional federal moneys."[27] A different order was introduced through the Quality Housing and Work Responsibility Act of 1998. The new law allows local housing authorities to skip over some of the poorest families and choose to house families of somewhat higher income instead.[28]

Drastic job cutting at the federal Department of Housing and Urban Development (HUD) was another setback. In 1997, HUD Secretary Andrew Cuomo, son of Mario Cuomo, announced that a quarter of the agency's jobs would be cut. The *San Francisco Chronicle* reported that "HUD has been frequently cited as one of the most mismanaged agencies in the federal government." Job cuts were seen as "a crucial first step in carrying out reform of HUD and heading off more drastic action by the Republican-controlled Congress."[29] The prestige and funding available for public housing in the United States have never been high, and there have been constant cutbacks, especially starting in the years of the Ronald Reagan administration. Anti-social welfare measures in the 1990s should be seen as a continuation of the recent erosion of the U.S. social security system rather than the setting of a radically new direction.

The erosion of public housing programs was coupled the decay or disappearance of a considerable amount of the housing stock available to the urban poor and especially to poor African-Americans. In the Bronx and other areas of New York City, the deterioration abetted by Robert Moses had continued apace in the 1960s and 1970s. This downhill ride was described by Jacqueline Leavitt and Susan Saegert in their 1990 book, *From Abandonment to Hope: Community Households in Harlem*:

> ...from the late 1960s through the early 1980s, parts of New York City experienced a progressive 'dehousing' as landlords abandoned scores of rental property. Whole sections of the Bronx, Manhattan and Brooklyn were devastated. The private real estate market was so weak in some areas that owners preferred to walk away from their buildings rather than attempt to sell them or continue to operate them at a loss...Harlem offered a particularly graphic example of its [abandonment's] effects.[30]

Leavitt and Seagert, who did detailed research on how Harlem residents dealt with this situation, described the eerie, apocalyptic quality of Harlem's landscape.

> Block after block, the landscape of abandonment continues, and empty brick, brownstone or wood shells create an almost separate world...On virtually every block there was other city-owned property, either vacant lots or vacant buildings or both.[31]

The authors also report how "some semblance of a normal life is maintained by those who live in an abandoned buildings whose deterioration invariably means the loss of creature comforts. Plumbing leaks, toilets fall through rotting floors to apartments beneath, plaster peels, carrying with it the threat of lead paint poisoning, and faulty electric wiring routinely short circuits...where outer doors to the street are not secure, urine smells permeate the halls."[32]

During the 1990s, the U.S. poor also kept getting poorer than ever as wealth became more concentrated and government withdrew from responsibility for social equity. The Washington, D.C. based Center on Budget and Policy Priorities found that, in 1994, the after tax income of the richest 2.6 million Americans, the top one percent, was equal to the 88 million who constituted the bottom 35 percent. Two decades earlier, in 1977, the bottom 35 percent had twice the after tax income of the richest one percent.[33] The statistics for just New York City are just as disturbing, the poverty level there rose from 11.5 percent in 1970 to 16.3 percent in 1990, while, at the same time, it lost almost half of its low rent housing.[34]

The slide in the U.S. toward greater poverty and income inequality occurred also in the world as a whole. Statistics on the yawning gap between the world's rich and poor appeared in the United Nations Development Program's 1992 *Human Development Report*, which noted that, in 1960, the richest 20 percent of the world's population had incomes 30 times greater than the poorest 20 percent. By 1990, the richest 20 percent were getting 60 times more.[35] In addition many regions have had their share of world trade drop since 1970: sub-Saharan Africa (3.8 percent to one percent); Latin America and the Caribbean (5.6 percent to 3.3 percent); and the least developed countries (.8 percent to .4 percent).[36] These bleak statistics confirm the observation of Gunder Frank, Fidel Castro, and even of W.W. Rostow that the most developed nations started the economic race way out in front and have continued to widen their lead.

In the U.S., exacerbated poverty, wealth inequality, and the dismantling of social programs, which started during the Reagan administration, soon led to a sharp rise in homelessness. The U.S. has not taken a census of its homeless; a reliable indicator is still the observant eye which can spot the homeless in Manhattan's lower East side, San Francisco' Golden Gate Park, and countless other homeless hangouts across the nation. In his book on *The Economics of Homelessness*, economist Brendan O'Flaherty noted that,

> ...in 1990, each of Manhattan's major transportation terminals had the population of a small apartment building...At the end of the longest peacetime expansion in American history, in the financial capital of the world, hundreds—maybe thousands—of people were making the public spaces of these terminals their home, and the benches had been removed to dissuade other from doing the same. It wasn't always like this. In 1964, researchers from Columbia University scoured four of Manhattan's major parks in order to count the homeless people sleeping there: they found one man.[37]

The great increase in homelessness has been accompanied—not by a campaign for social equity and housing for all who need it (though there are some not very noticeable groups that espouse a social justice oriented approach)—but by rigorous capitalist arguments that efficiency, not equity, is society's most important goal and that the homeless are somehow to blame for their condition because they are mentally ill or not ambitious enough to provide for themselves. In a book on New York City's housing problems, Peter D. Salins and Gerard C. Mildner even claim that homeless people are not a group with a shared social problem. "The lack of a home is merely a common denominator among a disparate group of troubled individuals who have shown up at the city's doorstep."[38] In a similar vein of even-handedness, Brendan O'Flaherty argues that "homeless people should get the same treatment as everyone else; they should not get special treatment."[39] He also maintains that "police don't need a homeless policy; they need only an anti-crime policy that recognizes that some people are homeless."[40]

Delinking of the homeless from the fate of the majority in the U.S. has occurred during the same era as a hard headed (but ultimately senseless) delinking of much of the third world from that portion of the earth's people who can expect to enjoy prosperity or adequate social development in the 21st century. This scenario for the third world is very frankly portrayed in the management oriented book, *Globalizing Management: Creating and Leading the Competitive Organization.*

So developing countries naturally find themselves moving towards the periphery of global development, outside the large affluent communities of North America, Europe, and Asia-Pacific. They struggle to attract investors whose outlook is dominated by the need to maintain competitive party [sic], and hence minimize costs. In this environment, Third World nations compete frantically with one another to attract foreign capital, further cutting domestic margins, eroding whatever common bonds might have united them as a community. Insofar as in coming years firms' productivity gains come principally from the development of advanced manufacturing technologies and automation, is seems likely that Third World nations will be spun further out to the periphery, relying ever more on handouts and castaways from the rapidly growing regional communities.[41]

Barnet and Kavanagh are equally candid in their description of the plight of the world's 47 least developed countries, most of them in Africa. "They are so poor that their economic connection with the rest of the world is pretty much limited to cashing relief checks and opening bags of food from government and private relief agencies."[42] Such bleak views were not published or even voiced in official circles 30 years ago, when the future seemed promising for the world's struggling, and in many cases, newly independent nations. Even by 1989, most journalists and politicians expressed a modicum of ambition that at least some countries of the third world might be fully assimilated to the world capitalist system. It was only after the collapse of Communism and the renewal of the post-1970s chronic recession in the G8 countries that the notion of third world "takeoff" was abandoned.

The final global trend to be noted here is a chronically high rate of joblessness. A recent report by the International Labour Organization says that a global crisis of unemployment and underemployment has left one out of every three people in the world without adequate employment. In Canada, the long-term unemployment was for years stuck near the 10 percent mark, while real wages from 1976 to 1990 shrank an average .3 percent annually.[43] As for the U.S., the 1994 U.S. Labour Department report prepared by the Dunlop Commission pointed out that widening earnings inequality and stagnant real earnings "have characterized the American labour market over the past 10 to 15 years." It warned that "a predominantly middle class society" may be turned "into two-tier society." In matter of fact terms, the Dunlop Report suggests a coming apocalypse caused by the "inability of the job market to offer many employees work that pays better than crime."[44]

In addition to unemployment, there was a big surge in underemployment: nonstandard, part-time, low paying work in countries around the world during the late 1980s and 1990s. These nonstandard workers are very often women who work at home in the so-called informal sector. In *Patriarchy and Accumulation on a World Scale*, Mies describes how third world women are increasingly integrated into the global market economy through the "small scale manufacturing of a variety of consumer goods, ranging from handicrafts, food processing, garment manufacture, to making art objects."[45] Low paying nonstandard work increasingly is the lot of women and men in wealthy developed countries like Canada too. A 1993 report by the National Action Committee on the Status of Women noted that 94 percent of all job increases since 1989 were in the low-paying service sector, where women and young people are usually the job holders.[46] In this burgeoning informal work sector, just about anything goes. Workers are often not covered by labour standards or minimum wage legislation, and even if they are, the standards are hard to enforce on a home-to-home basis.

Canadian Trends

In Canada, the trends decried in Marion Best's 1995 letter continued unabated during the second half of the 1990s. The country's church, trade union, and other NGO leaders were kept busy caring for casualties of the right wing revolution and at the same time criticizing state and corporate policy. The two strongest indicators of worsening social injustice during this period were increased poverty and inequality, and sharply rising homelessness.

On the poverty front, Canada had little to crow about when it compared itself with the United States. A Statistics Canada income distribution study estimated that 5.3 million Canadians were living below the poverty line in 1996. The number of poor people in Canada had risen by 40.4 percent since 1989. During 1996, the bottom one-fifth of families had 6.1 percent of the country's total income, lower than at any time in the 1980s or 1990s. The most affluent fifth held 40.6 percent of total income, the highest level recorded in two decades.[47] The churches, trade unions, and other NGOs kept up pressure on governments regarding the poverty issue, but to little avail. Just before the 1997 federal budget, representatives of the Roman Catholic, Anglican, United, Lutheran and Presbyterian churches issued a statement that deplored federal government inattention to the poverty problem. "Nothing is more indicative of this lack of commitment than its total silence throughout 1996, the year designated by the United Nations as the International Year for the Eradication of Poverty."[48]

Homelessness, which had been rising since the early 1980s became endemic, especially in Toronto. During this period, homelessness in Toronto became more difficult to avoid as part of the daily landscape, though it still was not as inescapable as homelessness in either Sao Paulo or San Francisco. It certainly was more dangerous than outdoor living the two warmer cities; every year a few homeless people died because of overnight sub-zero temperatures. Toronto's churches and synagogues tried to meet people's immediate needs by sponsoring Out of the Cold, a shelter program run by about 25 churches from November to April. At the

Trinity-St. Paul's program where I worked for two winters, the facilities were always strained to the limits and many late-coming guests had to be turned away.

In Canada, the view of homelessness held by both governments and non-governmental organizations was somewhat different from the opinion commonly held in the United States. There was less reluctance to acknowledge that homelessness was at least partly a result of increased poverty and not just a result of individual pathologies. In Toronto, a report by a task force on homelessness commissioned by Mayor Mel Lastman decried the facts that "increasingly restrictive income security programs have exacerbated the problem of poverty"[49] and that "during the last six years, public housing support has been undermined by various actions of governments at all levels."[50] The report of the task force chaired by Anne Golden was released in January 1999 with much fanfare, but it was not at all clear that any level of government was prepared to take decisive action on its recommendations.

The 1990s surge of poverty and homelessness in Canada was rooted in global and national trends that also affected people in the United States and third world countries. Chief among these was the drive for regional economic integration and decreased economic independence for individual nations. After 1985, Canada's political leaders abandoned a moderately nationalistic economic development policy (initiated by the Pierre Trudeau government) that included measures to protect the nation's energy supplies, to oversee foreign investment, and to promote economic activity in the country's economic hinterlands. Though Canada's National Energy Program was much less rigorous than, for instance, Mexico's, its goal was roughly similar: to retain some control at home over the production and sale of oil and gas. In 1984, Trudeau's mild "Canada first" policies were supplanted by Brian Mulroney's drive for increased economic and political harmonization with the United States through free trade.

The economic restructuring launched by free trade assaulted Canadians' living standards in ways unprecedented since the 1930s depression. In the early 1990s, the number of Canadian manufacturing jobs lost because of free trade was estimated at over 300,000 (by Liberal finance critic Herb Gray and other sources). At the same time, a wave of corporate downsizings reduced the ranks of the country's middle managers by a still uncalculated number. There can be little doubt that many of these white collar job losses were attributable to free trade. Even the instigators of free trade in this country acknowledged that it would cause suffering by eliminating jobs, but they dismissed complaints about this short-term pain. Some commentators said that it was useless to complain about poverty caused by free trade. McGill University economist William Watson dismissed complainers as selfish: "It is neither surprising nor shocking that people who would lose their livelihood as a result of free trade would propose policies that serve their self-interest,"[51] he wrote in a 1993 C.D. Howe Institute publication. He went on to argue that "no interest group worthy of the name does not argue that the special gift to which it wishes to be entitled is in fact a right."[52]

Deficit slashing is the partner of regional economic integration, and the latter is very often the ultimate good for the sake of which the slashing is undertaken. Deficits and the national debt, which are spurs to austerity in third world countries, are in Canada also treated as obstacles blocking the way to integration. The December 1994 Department of Finance publication *Creating a Healthy Fiscal Climate*, for instance, estimated the federal debt at almost $17,500 for every Canadian. This debt total was said to be 71.4 percent of GDP, compared with 55 percent before the 1990-91 recession. The publication compared Canada's unfavourably with other G8 nations, noting that the country "now has the second largest deficit relative to GDP after Italy among the G8 countries." The publication's inevitable conclusion: the deficit and the debt must both be slashed. "There is no acceptable alternative."[53]

The arguments for slashing have been very convincing to electorates in many countries. George Pataki, Jean Chretien, Ralph Klein, and Mike Harris have won enormous popularity precisely because they are not afraid to take away the social benefits heretofore enjoyed by the minority, have-not social sectors. Poor minorities are treated as fair game for aggrieved majorities in ways that had been off limits in Canada for at least the last three decades— more or less since Pierre Trudeau's proclamation of a "just society." Even a number of poor Canadians have adopted the deficit-slashing doctrine and said that the automatic payment of their social assistance benefits should be replaced with work requirements.

In 1995, a watershed year also on Ottawa's Parliament Hill, the party of Pierre Trudeau brought in a tough-as-nails budget intended to "fundamentally reform what the federal government does and how it does it."[54] Mike Harris and Jean Chretien, leaders of traditionally opposed parties seemed to get along just fine as they agreed on the need to blend the federal goods and services tax (GST) and provincial sales taxes.

The two governments between them promised to cut 65,000 civil service jobs (45,000 federally and 20,000 provincially). Big cuts were projected in the federal transfers to the provinces for social programs. Agency after federal agency was cut: the National Research Council by $76 million over three years, regional development agencies by $562 million over three years, Environment Canada $234 million over three years, Transport Canada by $1,447 billion, foreign aid by $532 million over three years. Women's programs were cut 15 percent over three years,[55] and one major federally funded women's organization, the Canadian Advisory Council on the Status of Women, was abolished.

In Ottawa, one of the chief leaders of the slashing was Intergovernmental Affairs Minister Marcel Massé, twice president of the Canadian International Development Agency (CIDA), advocate of structural adjustment in the third world, and former Canadian executive director of the International Monetary Fund. A 16

September 1995 *Globe and Mail* report headlined "Excedrin headache No 2" noted that Massé's program review committee had met for the first time since the February budget. According to the *Globe*, "the powers that be in Ottawa well remember the harrowing treatment they endured in Mr. Massé's star chamber last fall, when he and his merry band sliced $17 billion out of federal spending over the next three years. Now ministers and deputies will be summoned again."

It is hard to depict adequately the impact of all this fiscal mayhem on Canada's church groups, community based organizations, trade unions and others who think that it is important to ensure that everyone in society is provided with basic necessities, regardless of their income. After the 1995 federal budget, shock, anger, and grief were all evident as community based groups, churches and unions struggled to assess the damage to themselves and to the users of axed government programs. It is important to remember that the 1995 *coup de grâce* was delivered after years of budget cutting at both the federal and provincial levels. The community response was muted and slow in coming partly because the deficit cutting had hit both government programs and the groups which speak for, develop, and monitor those programs. The 1995 cut in the foreign aid program hit both overseas programs and the Canada-based NGO community which keeps the nation informed about the concerns of the less developed world. After a series of cuts starting in 1991/2, the Official Development Assistance budget as a whole got a further 20 percent cut over three years in 1995. Within the whole ODA package of cuts, the voluntary NGO sector took an 18.5 percent or $45 million cut. (The cuts for bilateral and multilateral aid were 21 percent and 17 percent respectively.)

Within the overall 18.5 percent cut to the voluntary sector was a 100 percent cut to CIDA's Public Participation Program (PPP), which had provided funding to do development education to a network of groups across the country. The elimination of the PPP meant "an end to funding for more than 80 global education centres and groups, seven provincial councils for international cooperation, and 15 national and provincial development education programs including the schools program of provincial teachers' associations."[56]

The NGOs' perception of themselves and their relationship to government were totally skewed by these cuts. During the previous two decades, some experienced NGOs had become increasingly confident about their expertise as aid deliverers and their right to be consulted by government about aid-related matters. During that period, some NGOs started to take a role in delivering government-to-government bilateral aid through programs such as country focus. Any illusion NGOs may have had that they were valued partners of government was shattered by the recent cuts and especially by the 1995 budget. An April 1995 paper by the Canadian Council for International Cooperation (CCIC) noted with consternation that "there was no prior consultation with the community (despite repeated requests by CCIC to discuss with CIDA and the government alternatives

for implementing the 18% percent cut to the voluntary sector), nor has any rationale been provided after they were announced at the end of March."[57]

The decline and fall of the PPP and most of the Canadian development education community is a Canada-made difficulty with consequences at home, but it is
also problem for the poverty-stricken people of the third world, who rely at least
partly on NGOs and global education centres to made their concerns known in
Canada and other G8 countries. According to the CCIC, Southern partners had
been calling upon Canadian organizations to make policy advocacy one of their
primary activities."[58] Aid and global education cutbacks eroded Canada's communication with and ability to assimilate information about the less developed world
just when the relationship needed strengthening because of Canadian absorption
in free trade with the United States, which tends to minimize the nation's awareness of events and trends in the third world.

Programming related to women is another area where a group that needs
protection and its guardian angels have both been felled by recent deficit slashing.
An analysis of the 1995 federal budget prepared by NAC pointed with particular
alarm to the government's elimination of the Canada Assistance Plan. CAP was a
vitally important program to retain, argued the NAC analysis, because it was "the
only piece of federal legislation which protects the right to an adequate income in
Canada."[59] The rights protected by CAP included the right to receive an amount of
income adequate to meet basic budgetary requirements and the right of an individual not to be forced to work as a condition for receiving social assistance. What
NAC correctly saw was that the elimination of CAP signaled the end of the era of
entitlement to basic sustenance, just as the 1996 welfare reform act did in the
United States.

At the same time that NAC was trying to make sure that women's interests
were not damaged by federal budget cuts, it was struggling to cope with federal
cuts of its own. Federal funding to NAC dropped from $540,000 in 1986-87 to
$300,000 in 1991-92 and then to a new low of $256,000 in 1995-96. NAC's vicissitudes have made it much harder for Canadian women to defend their rights to
basic income support, daycare, and other necessities.

One paradoxical result of deficit-slashing is that it has seriously weakened
Canada's volunteer sector, which right wing governments expect to fill the holes
left by government program cuts. The notion that good works should be left to individual initiative is a theme of laissez-faire capitalism which is now all the rage in
the United States and enjoying a more limited vogue in Canada. The CCIC has
noted that,

> ...here and there within the [Canadian] Federal Government, at both the
> political and the administrative level, there is interest in expanding the so-
> cial role of organizations in civil society. There is particular interest in the
> concepts of Harvard professor Robert Putnam regarding the vital impor-

tance of 'social capital' generated through 'networks of civic engagement' by people and organizations in civil society.

(The CCIC also points out that this "free trade" in the idea of volunteerism is a bad idea because the voluntary sector here is more dependent on government support than it is in the U.S.)[60]

The end to new coop housing commitments decreed by the federal government under Mulroney in 1992 and the Harris government in Ontario is another example of self-sabotage in the effort to promote volunteerism. In putting the kibosh on new moderately priced coop housing, Canada's governments also put an end to a form of social organization that is especially effective, because it involves people who all live in the same neighbourhood. The boards of housing coops have invariably been positive forces because they take a role in numerous community matters such as prevention of family violence, promotion of good policing, fire safety, and gardening. It makes no sense to slice the economic support from under coop housing and then urge its occupants to be neighbourly and do more volunteer work.

The defunding of programs like CIDA's Public Participation Program (PPP), the Canadian Advisory Council on the Status of Women, and coop housing have also intensified the dishevelment of progressive, so-called "left-leaning" political parties and coalitions in Canada. Many of the forces that have demoralized political progressives in Canada and elsewhere are very same ones that have contributed to the growth of rejuvenated right wing capitalism around the world: lack of material resources and of a shared, viable program for social change. There are some peculiarly national ingredients, however, in the "left's" troubles in Canada.

The first is that progressive forces were hard pressed to come up with something concrete to do after it became clear that the Canada-U.S. Free Trade Agreement was here to stay. During the late 1980s, progressive Canadians put nearly all their eggs into the basket of fighting free trade, and they lost. After the ratification of first free trade agreement and then of NAFTA, the anti-free trade coalition of trade unions, church based organizations, and community groups that spearheaded the anti-free trade campaign toiled to fine new goals and strategies for its anti-globalization mission. The onslaught of job loss and deficit slashing in the years after 1989 (the year that inaugurated free trade) left millions of Canadians preoccupied with personal difficulties. These difficulties were experienced especially by holders of "soft" jobs that attract progressive people, such as community development and global education.

During the same period, Canada's major social democratic party, the New Democratic Party (NDP), fell into disarray both nationally and in most provinces. The national and provincial parties were victims of the zeitgeist and also of their own inability to propose attention-grabbing alternatives to free trade and deficit-slashing. In the 1988, Liberal leader John Turner managed to snatch the anti-free trade banner from NDP leader Ed Broadbent. On the provincial level, the NDP was riven with dissension about whether and how governments should exercise fiscal restraints.

At the same time, the Canadian trade union movement has been hard pressed even to maintain itself, led alone provide vigorous leadership on broad social issues. Some unions, such as the United Steelworkers, had to cope with a recession caused fall in membership. The International Ladies' Garment Workers' Union (ILGWU) suffered precipitous membership loss as unionized, factory based workers were replaced with home based workers who earn the minimum wage or less. Civil service unions lost members by the tens of thousands because of government cutbacks.

Beyond the problem of falling membership in individual unions, the trade union movement as a whole has had to confront the specter of lost membership and diminished power because of technological innovation, the tremendous growth of the nonstandard work force, and the anti-union offensive mounted by the Canadian Manufacturers' Association and other business oriented groups. The movement has also been beset with internal disagreements over matters like support or not for the NDP, and conciliatory versus confrontational approaches to bargaining. Some unions have responded to the challenge of recession and economic restructuring by merging with other unions; the Communication, Energy and Paperworkers' Union (CEP), for example, is the product a merger.

An end to the long deficit-slashing, post-NAFTA slump for Canadian progressive forces seemed to come in the late 1990s, as a new anti-globalization coalition emerged at events like the battles of Seattle and Quebec City. The long-term objectives of this new movement, which is powered at least party by very young people, are still being shaped.

The Third World
Events of the mid-1990s in Latin America and the third world as a whole had many parallels with those in the United States and Canada. There was a swing toward deficit-slashing right wing political leaders. In Mexico, moderately nationalist PRI presidents such as Luis Echeverria who held office in the 1970s were replaced by free trade adherents Carlos Salinas de Gortari and Ernesto Zedillo. In Brazil, former dependency theorist Fernando Henrique Cardoso in October 1994 became Brazil's second directly elected president since the 1964 military coup. (The first, Fernando Collor de Mello, was impeached on corruption charges in 1992.) By the time he ascended to the presidency, Cardoso had become a rightist democrat.

These two big Latin American powers, which in the early 1990s were the most heavily indebted third world nations, continued to endure the poverty, homelessness, and other consequences of botched economic development which had been manifest since the 1960s and even earlier. Structural adjustment and chronic economic crises made even worse the daily deprivation that was the lot of the majority.

In 1994, Mexico was rocked by crises of truly titanic proportions through the Zapatista uprising at the beginning of the year and the peso crisis at the end of it. The financial package then assembled to rescue the nation's economy only put it more deeply in thrall to IMF and other international financial authorities. The 1994 IMF peso-crisis loan to Mexico was $10.1 billion; in fiscal 1995 Mexico was the second largest borrower from the World Bank.[61]

The bailout package included a policy of wage restraints. Increases were "capped at seven percent, plus an additional three percent for the very lowest wages." Since inflation would be at least 19 percent, according to a conservative IMF estimate, there would be a massive drop in Mexican workers' incomes, on top of the real wage loss they experienced during the last decade.[62]

The purchasing power of the minimum wage dropped drastically—to just 39 percent of minimum daily requirement for survival from 94 percent in 1987. The level of extreme poverty rose by 6.4 percent, with 16 million persons counted as extremely poor and a further 28.7 million considered just "poor," according to official statistics.[63]

Worst of all, there was no end in sight to the free fall of the economy. Economic analyst Carlos Heredia reported in August 1995 that "no one is servicing their debts. Industry is running at 40% of its capacity, inflation in the first semester of 1995 was 32.9% (only nine points less than the rate predicted for the entire year), and over 4 million credit cards (out of a total of 8) are in default…As interest rates quadrupled (from 20% to 80%) almost overnight, people are unable to meet payments for their car loans, their mortgages, and their direct credit."[64]

This kind of economic havoc has been driving more Mexicans to try to enter the U.S. and at the same time exacerbating the xenophobia of right wing Americans. The Mexican paper El Financiero reported that, from December 1994 to November 1995, there was a 30 percent increase in the apprehension of Mexican immigrants. The paper also reported on a U.S. contingency plan to construct concrete barricades along the borders and detain immigrants at military bases. The same article quoted a migration specialist at the University of San Diego who speculated that violence in Mexico could soon escalate to levels not seen since the revolution.[65]

As the Mexican economy was devastated, ever more Mexicans crossed to the U.S. Mexicans left at home then become more dependent on money sent to them by U.S. based relatives. If you go to the little towns outside Mexico City, you can see how dependent people are on the U.S. dollars sent to them, according to Teresa Gutierrez-Haces, President of the Mexican Association of Canadian Studies. You can see people waiting for the money on the 15th and the 30th of the month. Gutierrez-Haces told me that the Mexican economy is "in the process of dollarization."

The poverty and other kinds of deprivation suffered by Brazilians because of globalization are, though less publicized internationally, as acute as the hardships of life for Mexicans. The United Nation Development Program reports that "Brazil has the world's highest degree of income concentration. Today, 32 million people face hunger on a daily basis, in a country that is one of the world's leading grain exporters."[66]

Until his death, Betinho was one of the leaders of the struggle against globalization induced poverty in Brazil. On current conditions there, he commented in a 1990s interview that,

> ...the struggle against hunger and misery in Brazil is the struggle against the model of development currently on offer. The current model is gaining ground for a kind of social 'apartheid' in all of the countries of Latin America in which it exists...The model of life for the poor majorities in our countries is comparable with Somalia, Biafra, and other places considered to be examples of extreme misery.[67]

In the 100 or so other countries of the third world, the questions: the questions "who controls development" and "who benefits?" were posed more starkly than ever before in the 1990s. During the final decade of the twentieth century, capitalist economists no longer tried to put forward the thesis that growth based development oriented to the needs of the majority was possible in the third world, or that a regime of budget-cutting and debt repayment would lead to widespread prosperity either. In Washington, Ottawa, and other G8 capitals, little was said at all about how third world economic development might occur. At the same time, there were regular cutbacks in development assistance budgets.

By then, it was undeniable that no third world country—big like Brazil or small like Cuba, near the U.S.A. like Mexico or far from the U.S.A. like Brazil—had been successful in implementing a long-term national economic development strategy based mainly on savings and investment done at home, or on any other kind of economic development strategy either. This has been true since the start of the postcolonial period, in the 19th century in Latin America, and in the mid-20th century in most of Asia and Africa, right up until the present day. Instead the extraction of these countries' resources continued to be done by multinational companies based in Europe, later in the United States and Japan, and, in some cases, by Canadian companies. The result of this foreign investment was seldom widespread well being among the host country's citizens.

The early transnationals and their successors have presented themselves as using savings, investment, and profits earned at home to start and maintain production abroad. For transnational corporations, "a conventional starting date is sometimes given as 1867, when the Singer Sewing Machine Company of the United States established a factory in Glasgow...[then after World War I, the big oil companies] established significant overseas operations in Latin America and the

Middle East, stimulated by fears of a coming oil shortage in the United States. The presence of Firestone Rubber Company in Liberia and the large-scale operation of United Fruit Company in the banana-producing areas of Central America also date from the inter-war period, as do the activities of ITT in a host of countries."[68] Dependency thinkers such as Gunder Frank and Eduardo Galeano have disputed this version of events and asserted that corporations based in the developed world have often used capital accumulated in the host country to further their investments.

Whether or not third world countries have had their resources and savings appropriated by foreign business is a still a moot point to many analysts. What has become indisputably apparent everywhere is the failure of any third world country to maintain a modicum of control over its own resources and at the same time accumulate resources for long-term development. The exceptions to this iron rule of "non-accumulation" in the third world have been few and transient. For a while in the 1970s, oil-producing third world countries appeared to be candidates for independent accumulation of investment capital. During the 1970s, Mexico, with its abundant oil and its nationalistic political tradition seemed to be an oil-producing third world country that might well "take off"; these dreams of national glory were short lived.

By the 1990s, hopes for sales of high priced commodities on world markets had vanished. Import substitution, too, seemed like yesterday's development recipe. Import substitution, which was recommended by Rostow (under his prescription for at least one strong manufacturing sector) and moderate leftist thinkers alike, has been tried by some non-oil producing third world countries and some oil rich ones as well, like Mexico. Mexican President Luis Echeverria extended import substitution into industries producing capital and intermediate goods, increased exports, and "was also active in the international political sphere, calling for the creation of trade conditions for underdeveloped countries that would, among other objectives, expand the international markets for manufactured exports."[69]

Brazil's recent development history has been quite different from Mexico's, partly because it is basically a non-oil producing country and partly because the country had an extremely repressive military government from the mid-1960s to the mid-1980s. Yet there are also similarities: a moderately nationalistic government in power during the early part of the period—that of João Goulart (1961 to 1964) and a spurt of economic growth driven partly by a surge in manufactured exports. In Brazil, rapid growth from 1967 to 1973 was promoted by harsh military governments such as that of Arthur da Costa e Silva in the late 1960s.

By the early 1970s, Brazil's manufacturing output was falling, principally because the internal domestic market was not growing rapidly. (In Mexico during approximately the same period domestic demand for manufactures was quickly increasing.) After the mid-1970s, growth was sustained mainly by state investment in high priority import-substitution projects.[70] This strategy then led to a steep increase in the country's foreign debt. Its 1978 debt service was $8.1 billion or 64.2 percent of its merchandise exports. Then "the second increase in oil prices in 1979 marked the breakdown of Brazil's restructuring project. The deficit in its current account increased from $7 billion in 1978 to $12 billion in 1980. Moreover, the country was confronted with increasing protectionist policies in the United States against its exports and pressures to decrease its subsidies to exporting firms.[71]

Import substitution in countries like Brazil and Mexico never changed the old answers to the questions "who controls development?" and "who benefits from it?" (The answers were still "primarily foreign companies" and "foreign companies and a privileged minority at home.") In addition, it had only very limited success in increasing domestic demand or generating overall growth in the economy. Even by the 1970s, import substitution was exhibiting "clear signs of exhaustion."[72]

Some big and/or populous third world countries have tried to overcome the weaknesses of import substitution by increasing their exports of manufactured goods. This strategy has had quite limited success, especially in the 1980s, when world recession, the sudden mushrooming of the third world's debt, and the developed world's ever present trade barriers all combined to slow down third world export initiatives. The calculation of third world exports during this period became complicated by the a phenomena documented by Maria Mies and already noted in this chapter: the enormous growth of export processing zones in a host of third world countries including Mexico. In these zones, called *maquiladoras* in Mexico, goods produced by the Fortune 500 companies are assembled (i.e., put together) and sent away from the country, but they cannot truly be called that country's exports.

Figures for the top ten exporters of manufactured goods among less developed countries show a marked decline during the 1980s. The Republic of Korea topped the list in the dollar value of its exports (US$56.4 billion in 1988), yet its annual growth in exports dropped from 23.4 percent in 1970-80 to 13.7 percent in 1980-88. On this top ten listing, Brazil and Mexico were numbers five and six respectively. Brazil's export growth (U.S.$17.3 billion in 1988) dropped from 18.8 percent to 6.0 during the two time spans already named, but Mexico's growth apparently skyrocketed —from 6.3 percent to 19.1 percent. *Maquiladoras*, however, had a large role in this seeming export leap. How third world countries can respond to globalization's current call for export led growth in a way that will benefits their own peoples is a question still to be answered.

For a brief time in the mid-twentieth century, self-reliance, dependency theory, and sometimes even basic needs oriented projects seemed to offer alternatives to development led by transnational companies. The perhaps premature obituary for dependency theory posted at the end of the 1970s has already been noted. Its seeming demise could in some case be attributed to the toppling of governments—such as Salvador Allende's—by external and/or internal political opposition. Some others, like that of Julius Nyrere in Tanzania, were punished by stinging criticism of their failures, even though many of the failures were caused by external rather than domestic forces. A recent *Economist* article, for instance, wrongly dismisses Nyrere as the man who led Tanzania "to independence and preached a form of self-help socialism that squashed its feeble economy and left the state deep in debt."[73] A few African leaders who yearned for independent national development ended up becoming dependent on the Soviet Union, though their dependence was never as extreme as Cuba's. The economic development jury is still out on whether dependency theory and self-reliance could be effectively practiced in a non-hostile international environment. It is doubtful that a friendly environment for self-reliance currently exists anywhere, however.

Beyond dependency theory there is a development scenario which calls for national economic separation from international forces even more drastic than that pictured by most dependency theorists. This strategy is one that focuses on subsistence agriculture rather than industrial development as the key to national economic success. In other words, it favours what might be termed a "Maoist" orientation to how a national liberation struggle should be implemented. This development scenario in fact seemed to fit the realities of post-revolutionary China, where the achievement of agricultural self-reliance seemed absolutely vital to the eradication of poverty (because of the country's large population).

Agricultural development in fact is the other, missing half of import substitution strategies. Economic analysts Diana Alarcón and Terry McKinley analyze the faults of import substitution this way: "One alternative way to generate growth and development would have been to boost the income of the urban working class and build agriculture as an internal source of demand; this would have created a broader market not only for mass consumer goods but also for consumer durables and equipment."[74]

As noted in Chapter Two, a focus on agricultural development as one large portion of a nation's long-term economic development strategy is certainly needed in many less developed economies. An exclusive and permanent attention to it, however, is appropriate only in communities which are satisfied to make a life apart from cosmopolitan comforts and culture. Kampuchea is one country with a recent, very negative experience of a government dedicated to building a country through subsistence agriculture. The terrorist group *Sendero Luminoso* in Peru is an example of a group in Latin America which seemed to abandon the moral scruples usually grouped under the term "common humanity" in its quest for communism based on agricultural production. Any effort to shape a Maoist-friendly strategy for the 1990s would need a very different value system.

So, in the late 1990s, the less developed world was experiencing an unprecedented impasse created by the harsh reality that no development strategy it tried during the twentieth century was really successful. The one development model which both big and small less developed countries—and most developed ones as well—had to adopt in the 1980s and 1990s was structural adjustment. Yet structural adjustment is really an austerity program masquerading as development. It is a regime of belt tightening that now seems likely to last indefinitely in the less developed world and in most of the G8 world as well.

This permanence of structural adjustment is required by the corporate and governmental forces of globalization, whether or not the adjustment even achieves the goals it sets for itself. In a 1994 report on the impact of structural adjustment, Canadian development analyst Marcia Burdette noted that no firm conclusions can be drawn about its efficacy: "Even through the period of their own internal reforms, the World Bank and the IMF continue to support structural adjustment. This constancy seems to stem from firm belief that adjusting countries have done better than non-adjusters. Although that conclusion has been questioned by other sources, the commitment continues, as do the SAPs." Burdette herself is skeptical about the effectiveness of adjustment. "Our observation is that the pain is greater than estimated, the gain is more elusive than predicted, and long-term effects on the social sectors will inhibit true development."[75]

What's in a Name?

The development dilemma currently confronting the less developed world as a whole is exacerbated by the fact that its sense of proud identity as the "third world" of nations has been shredded by the harsh economic conditions it has encountered during the past two decades. Now that the second, Soviet dominated world has disintegrated, even the viability even of the term "third world" is doubtful. To date, no satisfactory substitutes for this admittedly obsolete term have appeared. North-South is inadequate, because geographical terms do nothing to convey the political character of underdevelopment. North-South is also inaccurate; where do Australians, the people "down under," fit in a North-South scheme, for instance? Until a more up do date characterization is found, "third world" is still the most suitable name for the less wealthy countries—formerly colonized by European nations, the U.S., or Japan—now seeking independent economic development.

Many other factors beyond the collapse of Communism have contributed to third world disunity and loss of identity. Many of these factors have already been named here: chief among them are the failures of third world states to make their ways in the world as individual sovereign nations and also to negotiate as a group for a different kind of world economic order through the United Nations and/or other international institutions. (Efforts and negotiations during the 1970s are discussed in Chapter Six.) Another notable reason for lack of solidarity among third world nations is that the reality that the histories of various third world nations have been very different from each other during the past 25 years. During the early 1990s, South Korea won kudos because it had become a donor rather than a recipient country within the World Bank system. Some other very large, populous countries like Mexico, Brazil, and India have achieved lavish lifestyles for a tiny minority, while those nations' majorities are still dispossessed.

Theorists of globalization applaud signs of disunity and competition among the nations of the less developed world. These pundits say that the world's poor countries are in a race with each other to win wages and lifestyles comparable to those in the most developed countries. In this scenario, the environmental and economic victimization of many third world peoples—such as the 1996 gas explosion at Mexico City's Fain Chemical Plant—is seen as an inevitable cost of the race for the "gold." In his criticism of a possible social charter for NAFTA participants, McGill University economist William Watson asserts, for instance, that inequality and discriminatory treatment are necessary conditions of capitalist development. "The main reason Mexican labour is cheap is that it is not very productive. Mexican workers have less education and training than Canadian and U.S. workers and they work with less capital, inferior technology and infrastructure, and under a legal system that has for some time been hostile to capitalism,"[76] he maintains. "The mere fact of low wages cannot be taken as evidence of unfairness or, in economists' terms, failure in the Mexican market for labour. No doubt most Mexican workers would prefer to work for higher wages, but at this stage of Mexico's development that simply may not be possible."[77]

Watson is also complacent about the suffocatingly high pollution levels in Mexico and some other third world cities. In Mexico's capital, "the benefits of a cleanup would not be worth the costs, which might well include reduced exports and all that would be implied by that. If so, then this is simply another case of Mexicans' being willing to endure more than Canadians and Americans to win market share."[78]

The downfall of many third world development efforts during the past decade does not mean that there have been no victories in the fight against world poverty. The 1992 Human Development Report expressed satisfaction about the great recent progress in health and education made in the third world as a whole. In the years 1960 to 1990, for instance, average life expectancy increased from 67 percent of the level in the North to 84 percent; during the same years, adult literacy increased from 46 to 64 percent. Yet these improvements in what the Human Development report calls the world's "human capital" have not resulted in overall economic betterment. Moreover the gains which have been achieved have too often occurred on terms set by the G8 powers rather than by third world governments and peoples.

NOTES

1. Interview with the author in Rio de Janeiro, 7 November 1995.
2. PC Party, "The Common Sense Revolution," p. 1.
3. *Our Generation*, 22 No.1-2 (Spring 91), p. 16 -74.
4. *Globe and Mail*, 25 January 1993, p. 1.
5. 5. Richard J. Barnet and John Cavanagh, *Global Dreams* (N.Y.: Simon and Shuster, 1994),p. 190.
6. *Ibid.*, p. 188.
7. Wolfgang Sachs, "The Third World: A Technophagic Majority?" *New Perspectives Quarterly*, Spring 1990, p. 52-53.
8. *Toronto Star*, 10 July 1994, WS5.
9. Maria Mies, *Patriarchy and Accumulation on a World Scale* (London: Zed Books, 1986), p. 113.
10. *Ibid.*, p. 114.
11. Charles Fombrun and Stefan Wally, "Global Entanglements: The Structure of Corporate Transnationalism," in *Globalizing Management: Creating and Leading the Competitive Organization*, eds. Vladmir Pucik, Noel M. Tichy, Carole K. Barnett (John Wiley and Sons, 1992), p. 16.
12. *Globe and Mail*, 1 August 1995, A1.
13. *Toronto Star*, 2 August 1995, C1.
14. *The Globe and Mail*, 26 July 1995.
15. Sam Sternberg,"Jobs, jobs, jobs," *Technotes. A technology bulletin for Ontario*, no. 10, June 1995.
16. John P. Barrados, *A Key to the Canadian Economy* (Boston: University Press of America, 1986), p. 347.
17. *Ibid.*, p. 351.
18. *Ibid.*, p. 347
19. Stephen Neff, *Friends But No Allies. Economic Liberalism and the Law of Nations* (New York: Columbia University Press, 1990), p. 204.
20. *Ibid.*, p. 206.
21. Barnet and Cavanagh, *Global Dreams*, p. 246.
22. Neff, p. 205.
23. *Ibid.*, p. 206.
24. *Human Development Report*, 1992, p. 4.
25. *The Common Sense Revolution*, p. 17.
26. *Ibid.*, p. 7.
27. J. Paul Mitchell, "The Historical Context for Housing Policy," in *Federal Housing Policy and Programs*, ed. J. Paul Mitchell (Rutgers: The State University of New Jersey, 1985), p. 8.
28. *Christian Science Monitor*, 8 Feb. 1999.
29. *San Francisco Chronicle*, 14 August 1997, A3.
30. Jacqueline Leavitt and Susan Saegert, *From Abandonment to Hope: Community Households in Harlem* (New York: Columbia University Press), 1990. pp. 3 and 4.
31. *Ibid.*, p. 19.
32. *Ibid.*, p. 21.
33. *San Francisco Chronicle*, 14 August 1997.
34. Brendan O'Flaherty, *The Economics of Homelessness* (Cambridge: Harvard University Press, 1996), pp. 133 and 136.
35. UN Development Program, *Human Development Report*, 1992, p. 1.
36. *Ibid.*, p. 38.
37. O'Flaherty, *Homelessness*, p. 1.
38. Peter D. Salins and Gerard C.S. Mildner, *Scarcity by Design. The Legacy of New York City's Housing Policies* (Cambridge, Mass.: Harvard University Press, 1992), p. 145.
39. O'Flaherty, p. 277.
40. *Ibid.* p. 280.
41. Pucik, Tichy, and Barnett, p. 27.
42. Barnet and Cavanagh, p. 191.
43. Jamie Swift, "The Gambler's Society," *Compass* May/June 1995.
44. Commission on the Future of Worker-Management Relations, *Report and Recommendations*, December 1994, p. xxi and p. 3.
45. Mies, p. 115.

46. Canadian Labour Congress, *Women Workers and the Recession*, May 1993, cited in NAC, "Review of the Situation of Women in Canada," July 1993, p. 6.

47. *Canada and the World Backgrounder*, 1 May 1998.

48. *Christian Century*, 12 March 1997.

49. *Breaking the Cycle of Homelessness. Interim Report of the Mayor's Homelessness Action Task Force.* Toronto, July 1998, p. 20.

50. *Ibid.*, p. 29.

51. William Watson, "A Skeptical View of the Social Charter," in *Ties Beyond Trade: Labour and Environmental Issues under the NAFTA*, eds. Jonathan Lemco and William B.P. Robson (Toronto: C.D. Howe Institute, 1993), p. 111.

52. *Ibid.*, p. 126.

53. Department of Finance, *Creating a Healthy Fiscal Climate: The Economic and Fiscal Update* (Ottawa: Department of Finance, 1994), p. 7.

54. *Budget Plan*, Tabled in the House of Commons by the Honourable Paul Martin, 27 February 1995, p. 6.

55. National Action Committee on the Status of Women, There is another way campaign, "A Very Political Budget," p. 4.

56. *Americas Update*, March\April 1995, vol. xvi, no. 4.

57. CCIC, "Implementing the Cuts: The Implications of Budget Cuts to NGO\NGI Programs in the Partnership Branch of CIDA," p. 6.

58. Richard Marquardt, "The Voluntary Sector and the Federal Government: A Perspective in the Aftermath of the 1995 Federal Budget," Ottawa: CCIC, p. 11.

59. Submission by the National Action Committee on the Status of Women to the House of Commons Standing Committee on Finance regarding Bill C-76, p. 2.

60. Marquardt, p. 5.

61. *Globe and Mail*, 25 Sept.

62. *Americas Update*, March/April 1995, vol. xvi, no. 4.

63. ECEJ, *Economic Justice Report*, Vol. VI, No. 3, November 1995.

64. Carlos Heredia, "Foreign Debt: Twelve Years After, It's Mexico Again," *The Other Side of Mexico. Alternative News and Analysis for the International Community*, Number 41, July-August 1995, pp. 4-6.

65. *El Financiero*, 12 November 1995.

66. Maria Clara Couto Soares, "Who benefits and who bears the damage under World Bank-IMF led policies?", in *Fighting for the soul of Brazil* (New York: Monthly Review Press, 1995), p. 13.

67. Interview published in the bulletin of the Latin American Council for Adult Education, translated by Judith Marshall.

68. Neff, p. 199.

69. Diana Alarcon and Terry McKinley,"Beyond Import Substitution: The Restructuring Projects of Brazil and Mexico," *Latin American Perspectives*, Issue 73, Vol. 19, No. 2, Spring 1992.

70. *Ibid.*

71. *Ibid.*, p. 75.

72. *Ibid.*, p. 72.

73. *Globe and Mail*, 25 Sept. 1995.

74. Alarcón and McKinley, p. 76.

75. Marcia Burdette, "Structural Adjustment and Canadian Aid Policy," in *Canadian International Assistance Development Policies: An Appraisal*, ed. Cranford Pratt (McGill Queens University Press, 1994), pp. 216 and 225.

76. Watson, p. 110.

77. *Ibid.*, p. 112.

78. *Ibid.*, p. 119.

5

◆ ◆ ◆

REMAKING DEVELOPMENT: CRITICAL THINKING AND DEEDS

In closing moments of Frank Capra's 1946 movie, *It's a Wonderful Life*, a pledge of $25,000 from the New York based Sam Wainwright is needed to put a decisive kibosh on Potter's evil plan to wreck the Bailey Savings and Loan and the whole town of Bedford Falls along with it. I watch this movie every year in late December, and every year I ask myself, "Why is New York money always needed to bail out the hinterland?"

Despite my complaint about its denouement, *It's a Wonderful Life* is one of my favourite movies. One reason for this is the fact that my mother says that Jimmy Stewart—who plays the hero George Bailey—looks like my father. Another good point about the movie is that it once again demonstrates the truth of the maxim: "That and ten cents will get you a cup of coffee." In addition, *It's a Wonderful Life* is noteworthy because, like "The Girl from Ipanema," it's about economic development. Not only that, it's about affordable housing and also about the need for diversity in the marketplace as a counterweight to monopoly capitalism.

My favourite moment in the movie is the scene of a "run" on the Bailey Savings and Loan during the 1930s depression. George dissuades the crowd from accepting Potter's offer to buy out their shares in the savings and loan by reminding them that, if they go to Potter, "There will never be another decent house built in this town...He's got the bank, the bus line, the department store and now he's after us." The worst thing is that "we're panicking and he's not. Now, we can get through this all right, but we've got to stick together and have faith in each other." Is this just a bit of sentimental rhetoric? I think not; similar injunctions can be found in any handbook on community organizing.

Many other viewers have, over the years, praised *It's a Wonderful Life* extravagantly. Of these, none is more appreciative than film critic Raymond Carney who argues that the movie is about no less than what's wrong with capitalism. "What is wrong with capitalism, according to Capra, is, of course, nothing traceable or localizable in any individual but rather its fundamental repression of our free imaginative energies, its demands that we relentlessly channel then into socially and ethically responsible careers of action."[1]

The origins of *Wonderful Life* can be found in the personal experience of Capra, who was an older contemporary of my parents. As a child in a peasant family in Sicily, Capra had learned that "peasants were poor and had to work like beasts because they were ignorant." In his autobiography, Capra recalled how his family came to Ellis Island, New York, in 1903, much as my own grandparents had. The Capras spent 13 days in steerage on the boat from Italy and then eight days on a train to Los Angeles after clearing Ellis Island. When the family arrived in Los Angeles, "Papa and Mama kissed the ground and wept with joy. I cried, too. But not with joy. I cried because we were poor and ignorant and tired and dirty."[2]

In the chronicles of development, *Wonderful Life* takes its place alongside numerous other exemplary tales about how people build social movements or make their lives worthwhile in other ways. For Canadians, the building of the railroad is an important old story about how our nation came to be; one recent Canadian problem is the country's lack of compelling national stories except ones about personal animosities—between Rene Levesque and Pierre Trudeau, for example or between Brian Mulroney and Lucien Bouchard. U.S. residents treasure stories about the origins of their national life in the Declaration of Independence and the triumph over adversity at Valley Forge. Since the mid-1960s (after the 1963 assassination of John Kennedy), the United States has been suffering from a lack of good yarns about its nationhood. Some of the best new American stories—the acquittal of O.J. Simpson, for example—paint an unflattering or ambiguous picture of American society.

Mexicans have a revolutionary story which still shapes their society, despite recent efforts to recast the country's social order by the globalizing Presidents Salinas and Zedillo. No one who visits the arched dome commemorating the revolution on Mexico City's Avenida Juarez can doubt that Mexicans are extremely proud of their past deeds. Inscribed on the dome are three revolutionary ideals: "Justice, liberty, and democracy."

The 1994 Zapatista rebellion was a further recent story about how Mexicans are still determined to develop their own destinies. In fact, it seems probable that one important goal of the Zapatistas is to act as national storytellers, recounting how *campesinos* have a right to land for themselves and their communities. In a way, the rebellion reenacted some of the deeds of Emiliano Zapata's army of the south. This equating of the Zapatista rebellion with storytelling does not mean the Zapatista actions were just a lark, or a prank done for fun. The revolt provoked bloody retaliation from the Mexican army, caused over 100 deaths, and resulted in ongoing military repression. (It is impossible to provide an exact accounting of the dead, but according to various accounts it adds up to well over 100.)

What the world needs in the 21st century are new chronicles about how justice-oriented social change can happen, such as the story created by the Zapatistas since January 1994. Then action is needed beyond that to make the story an actual physical reality as well as a metaphor. This chapter focuses on some of the critiques, stories, and popular movements needed now to achieve justice and democracy for all peoples.

Critiquing Capitalism

To achieve equitable development in both in the less developed world and the wealthiest nations, new theoretical and story-based critiques of capitalism are needed. These critiques are needed especially because Marxism and early twentieth century excoriations of capitalism have lost much of their factual accuracy and much of their power to convince. At the same time, capitalism has evolved in ways so unexpected that software entrepreneurs like Bill Gates bear no immediate resemblance to the textile mill owners that put Marx and Engels to work penning the *Communist Manifesto*. What has remained constant is the certainty of capitalist theorists that the operation of the free market is always good for the world, whatever temporary or even long-term havoc it may cause.

Contemporary critiques incorporating dependency theory, liberation theology, and social movement theory still need to incorporate some of the truths of Marxism and social democracy that were first enunciated in the 19th century, because these schools of thought are to date the two alternative visions to capitalism that have actually served as foundations for governments and societies. The collapse of worldwide Communism has brought at least one benefit to critics of capitalism: a more freely granted permission to scavenge Marxism for usable ideas, since Marxism is no longer the property of "the enemy," but seemingly a passé belief system now lying inert on the junk heap of history.

There are some real gems to be rescued from the rubble of Marxism. One of Marx's recyclable categories, for instance, is "surplus value," which, briefly stated, is the difference between the price charged for a product and the costs incurred by the capitalist to produce it. "Surplus value" could still be useful to development theorists because it is a concept that helps to explain how and why economic development became so lopsided and uneven within and between countries.

The "reserve army of labour" and a trend toward increasing misery for the working class are two other Marxist ideas which bear reexamination in our times. The continuing relevance of these ideas is evident in a review of the too glib dismissals Western analysts accorded them in 1960 and thereabouts. "Today, only the most fanatical Marxist would argue that an absolute decline in real wages has occurred [in fact, such declines occurred in the 1990s]...a reference to other data, such as the increased leisure through the shortening of the working day, week and year, and the steady extension of state-provided services, merely bears out what common experience and any veteran trade unionist will confirm: the rise in real income and standards of living of the worker in all industrialized countries."[3] There is no comment about the third world, where income and living standards continued to sag during the 1960s, and where Marxism was all the rage.

What is needed now in our post-modern, post-Marxist age is a critique of capitalism which takes into account the needs of the third world as well the most developed industrial countries and the experience of the numerous social movements—third world centred, feminist, anti-racist, environmentalist—which have burgeoned since the mid-twentieth century. New social change theory needs grounding in concrete details and in the enormous complexity of today's social realities. If a strong focus on the outcome of social change detracts from empirical accuracy in carrying out the change, then that focus needs to be set aside temporarily.

This focus on "what is" instead of "what should be" has been noticeable in the work of numerous progressive social theorists in the 1990s. In a 1992 article published by the U.S. based Center for the Critical Analysis of Contemporary Culture, anthropologist Arturo Escobar said that a growing number of third world scholars—including, for instance, Gustavo Esteva and Vandana Shiva—share a perspective which features: "a critical stance with respect to scientific knowledge; an interest in local autonomy, culture and knowledge; and the defense of localized, pluralistic grassroots movements, with which some of them have worked intimately." Escobar then goes on to cite a 1986 article by Esteva which takes the line that social change is "not a teleological project (moving people towards a pre-determined direction) but one which recognizes people's agency and learns how to foster and co-move with them."[4]

Salvadoran political leader Ruben Zamora, who was the Salvadoran left's candidate for president in 1994, struck a similar note in a 1995 article for NACLA's *Report on the Americas*: the critique of right wing ideology "will only be meaningful to the degree that the left is able to propose a viable and real alternative. In other words, the critique has to make practical sense and embody an alternative proposal, no mean feat in today's world."[5]

Contemporary critiques of capitalism need not only to keep their exploratory noses to the ground; in addition, these critiques have to concentrate on cultivating empathetic capacities such those possessed by our American hero, George Bailey. Moral outrage is certainly present in Marx's writing, but ethical judgements are not incorporated into his social change theory, which is instead presented as a matter of science. Marxist political leaders have since the 1960s sustained heavy losses through their neglect of people's desires to goof off and just have some fun.

The development of contemporary critiques of capitalism is important whether or not they immediately lead to action for social change; however, action to overcome the failures of capitalist-based development is the long-term goal. In some cases noted here, (e.g., the drive to organize home based garment workers) community based action to achieve justice even preceded any formal critique of growth oriented development.

What follows here is a brief review of recent social currents which stand as critiques of capitalism, whether intentionally or not.

Dependency Theory

Dependency theory is now usually regarded as a historical curiosity. Escobar relegates it to the past with his observation that "the critiques of development by dependency theorists, for instance, still functioned within the same discursive space of development, even if seeking to attach it to a different international and class rationality...[can't we now establish ourselves as] different from the previous bankrupt order, so that we will not be obliged to speak the same truths, the same language, and provide the same strategies?"[6]

Despite its shortcomings, which in many ways are similar to those of Marxism (too simplistic a diagnosis of capitalism's defects and how the defects could be overcome), dependency theory's analysis of how imperialism keeps less developed countries poor has continuing relevance. Some of the ideas associated with dependency theory continue to show up regularly in third world movements such as the Zapatistas and Sem Terra discussed in this chapter.

Escobar and other social movement theorists are in fact the intellectual offspring of Andre Gunder Frank, Marta Fuentes, Fernando Enrique Cardoso, Raul Prebisch, and other dependency theorists. In fact the first generation has showed a willingness to learn from the second, as well as visa-versa. In a recent article, Gunder Frank took a line very similar to Escobar's. "What is left for 'development' is indigenous self-help on the basis of avoiding the worst and trying to do the best we can."[7] "If there is any hope for 'development,' that is where it is in reality, and that is where it must be developed and later reviewed in 'theory.' Amen!"[8]

Liberation theology

Although liberation theology has dropped out of most North American religious discourse in the 1990s, it continues to provide emotional and intellectual sustenance to social movements in Latin America. Some of its best known practitioners and theorists are based in Brazil; recent exponent include Cardinal Evaristo Arns of Sao Paulo and Samuel Ruiz Garcia, the bishop of Chiapas.

A teaching of liberation theology that remains important in a world where globalization seems to make us all helpless nobodies is that the poor can liberate themselves—and their oppressors too—by realizing their important role in history and taking the space that they need on earth. This notion of self-generated education and liberation, which appears in discussions about community development as well as in theological literature, has helped to generate a a new discipline usually known as popular education. Paulo Friere and Ivan Illich are two of the best known popular education writers. The Austria-born Illich co-founded the Centre for Intercultural Documentation in Cuernavaca, Mexico, and wrote a number of books, including *Deschooling Society*, which unchained learning with by claiming that "rich and poor alike depend on schools and hospitals which guide their lives, form their world views, and define for themselves what is legitimate and what is not. Both view doctoring onself as irresponsible, learning on one's own as unreliable, and community organization, when not paid for by those in authority, as a form of aggression or subversion."[9] This anti-authoritarian, Illichian prescription that "you can be your own doctor and priest" is even more subversive now in the era of globalization than it was when first enunciated.

Critiques Based on Peasants' Experiences

Mexico's Zapatista movement is a well known and innovative initiative to rectify the inequitable land distribution which has become the rule in countries throughout world, as well as in Mexico. These inequities are becoming more acute than ever under the regime of globalization, which treats subsistence farmers are nonexistent or, even worse, as downright nuisances. The Zapatistas brought to national and international attention the harsh repression suffered by *campesinos* in the southern state of Chiapas and their opposition to Salinas's reform of the Mexican constitution's Article 27.

A look at some Zapatista statements and actions shows that the group has always intended to criticize and negotiate with the government rather than to overthrow it. In this respect, the movement's strategy suggests that the days are over—at least in most Latin American countries—when an October revolution, a 1 January 1959 in Havana, or a 19 July 1979 in Managua were feasible and effective ways to achieve justice for the dispossessed. Instead, the act of criticism itself is seen as a way to both start making change happen and to give an identity to the *campesinos* who are making the criticism. Public denunciations of tyranny and the development of a revolutionary working class *for itself* (in Marx's terms) were important aspects of previous 20th century armed rebellions, including Russia's October revolution. These consciousness raising activities were, however, seen more as means to an end—the overthrow of the government—rather than vital constituents of social, personal and political change in themselves.

The Zapatista approach is different. A gander at one of its communiques reveals just how distinctive a social movement it is. A June 1995 communique by the General Command of the Zapatista Army of National Liberation (EZLN) includes Hamlet-like conjecture about what its next move should be. Becoming a revolutionary party is not on its agenda, says the statement:

> Until now the EZLN has only called for groups to organize and struggle for democracy, liberty and justice. But as it is a clandestine and armed group, the EZLN has not organized. We are not a political force…Perhaps our role was only to point out deficiencies and open a space for discussion and participation. Maybe that is all our historic role will be. Or maybe, the time has arrived for Zapatista words not only to move people or create consciousness; perhaps the time has come for 'organizing' to be a Zapatista word as well. This is what we are asking.[10]

The EZLN declaration goes on to speculate about its ties with like-minded groups. The ELZN might become "a new and independent political force," or it might "unite with other forces in Mexico, and together form a new political force.

This and other Zapatista communiques are addressed to Mexicans but they also speak to "the people and governments of the world."[11] The movement's goals are stated as broad principles rather than as concrete achievements such as Marx's "dictatorship of the proletariat." The Zapatistas say that what they want for all Mexicans is "democracy, liberty, and justice"—the ideals inscribed on the Avenida Juarez monument to the revolution. In addition, the movement has global objectives: "...we propose a new international order based on and guided by democracy, liberty, and justice."[12]

The EZLN strategy is a new, previously untried approach to winning justice for communities of *campesinos*. For several reasons, it is also possibly applicable to situations of social conflict elsewhere. The EZLN experience could be transferable because it grows out of the life experience of the *campesino* participants in the movement; it incorporates Arturo Escobar's summons to social change based on quotidian reality. The Zapatista example suggests that social change has to start with an inventory of daily life.

The Zapatistas are exemplary also because they respond to intractability and complexity of their situation by using a variety of tools, including appeals to the international media, popular education, and the occasional application of armed force. Though their words are sweetly reasonable, the Zapatistas are still rebels with guns.

The Zapatista unfurling of the anti-free trade banner has won the hearts or at least the respect of most Mexicans who do not benefit from free trade. According to Mexican historian Antonio Garcia de Leon, the Zapatista demands are "closely linked to the demands of many Mexicans...This explains why they have the sympathy of the majority of independent civic organizations in Mexico."[13]

Brazil's *Sem Terra*, another innovative, intrepid initiative to realize true economic development for poor peasants, is in many ways comparable to the Zapatistas. Both the EZLN and *Sem Terra* have built a constituency that includes the worst off people in their nations' rural areas—the indigenous people of Chiapas who are in danger of losing their *ejido* land and the landless of whatever state in Brazil (though much of the organization's activity has been in the southern part of the country).

Like the Zapatistas, *Sem Terra* (MST) tries to win its objective through direct action, mostly through occupations of unused agricultural land. According to the MST, it has pressured the government to give land titles to about 150,000 families. In 1999, MST was supporting the struggles of another 57,000 families who had occupied uncultivated land in 23 states. The families are living in 300 different camps.[14] This action is technically legal in the sense that the Brazilian constitution provides that unproductive land can be expropriated for agrarian reform. Since the government has not complied with this legislation, peasants have implemented it themselves.

Again comparable to the Zapatistas' campaigns, MST's direct action to assert peasants' rights has met with harsh retaliation. In many cases, large ranchers and military police have used force to try to expel settlers; settlers have declined to leave quietly and without resistance. There have been many clashes between military police and landless groups organized under the Sam Terra banner. Numerous deaths resulting from these police attacks have been reported; there has also been limited use of molotov cocktails and other weapons by land-occupying *campesinos*, according to some accounts.

One of these MST-military police encounters was in August 1995 about 800 kilometers from Porto Velho. The toll of the clash was 53 wounded and 11 dead—two military police and nine *campesinos*, including one child of seven years.[15] When I was in Sao Paulo in November 1995, MST occupations were featured in front page headlines. The 10 November 1995 *Jornal do Brasil* featured a front, half page photo of a confrontation between *campesinos* and the military police on land 580 kilometers from Curitiba. On 11 November, the *Folha de Sao Paulo* cited a 71 day struggle near Barriguda which resulted in 10 deaths. These struggles that were wracking Brazilian politics were little reported in the international press. There have also been cases when MST activists not engaged in land occupations were attacked and killed. In the April 1996 Eldorado de Carajas massacre, which was internationally reported, the military police killed 19 peasants during a peaceful march in the state of Para.

Sem Terra does not have the goal of overthrowing or replacing the Brazilian government, but its full program is more inclusive and ambitious than simple redistribution of land. MST has set up 60 food cooperatives and small agricultural industries. The movement has also set up an educational system and that includes eight secondary schools, MST activist Ramos Figuereido told a Toronto audience in 1999. In addition, *Sem Terra* has developed a seed bank of natural seeds with a trademark. In the health sector, "we are not demanding health care; we are putting forward our own health care system; while pharmaceutical companies are stealing our heritage from us, we are working to develop health care with the people."[16] MST, in other works, is starting to have many of the earmarks of a parallel system of government.

Two final points of comparison between Sem Terra and the Zapatistas will be noted here. Sem Terra, like the Zapatistas, has been influenced by the ideas and values of liberation theology and in fact liberation theologian Frei Betto (whose conversations about religion with Fidel Castro have been published as a book) has been an adviser to the MST. MST also tries to develop global relationships; it participates in both a union of Latin American rural workers and a world wide peasants' organization.

Feminist Critiques

By the 1990s, feminism was the inspiration for several different critiques of capitalism based both in the developed world and the third world. These include feminist theories based on the environment (ecofeminism), on women's rights, and on women's work. This chapter will touch on some of the recently enunciated issues connected with women's "reproductive work": having and caring for babies, housekeeping, doing domestic work for pay in other homes, subsistence agriculture, and many other of the world's maintenance tasks such as the fetching and carrying of water.

Neither capitalism nor Communism has accorded more than a very slight monetary value to domestic work. A number of events have generated a growing pressure for greater monetary and social recognition of reproductive work. One source of pressure is the woman's movement, which has enabled women to ask ever sharper questions about why they and their labour are generally so little esteemed. Another is the work of feminist economic theorists such as Vandana Shiva (India), Selma James (U.K.), Marilyn Waring (U.S.), and Maria Mies (Germany), whose book, *Patriarchy and Capital Accumulation* was cited in Chapter Four. The rigours of structural adjustment and deficit cutting have greatly increased both the amount of unpaid care-giving work and women's desire for proper recompense of it. Lobbying on this front was intense at 1995 UN sponsored World Conference on Women in Beijing.

Along with demands for bookkeeping methods that take women's work into account, there has been an increasing amount of consciousness raising—or "conscientization" in 1960s popular education language—done by women who are engaged primarily in domestic work. This self development work is comparable to the popular education done by the Zapatistas and also accords with the Escobar's social movement theory. Escobar cites the work of Alain Touraine to make the point that "...social movements are not 'dramatic events' but rather 'the work that society performs upon itself.' "[17]

One group currently struggling in many countries around the world for a new place in society is migrant domestic workers. One of the most astonishing current world labour trends is the movement of many millions of women from country to country and from rural areas to cities to clean other peoples' houses. Worldwide, the best known of these women are the Filipino nannies who migrate to other Asian countries, the Middle East, and also to Canada. There are numerous other women-exporting countries: India, Sri Lanka, and Caribbean countries. These women can travel halfway round the world to sweep someone else's floor because most people in both the developed and less developed world avoid this low status, low paying work if they can. In Mexico and many other countries, women migrate from rural areas such as Chiapas to Mexico City to work as domestics because lopsided development has pushed them out of their home communities.

Organizations of migrant (and home based) domestic workers have recently come together in a number of countries around the world. For the most part, these are partly pre-trade union groups, partly moral support groups, and partly popular education seminars. Together they are developing a new feminist critique of capitalism based on the value of the labour that they perform for society. They are making domestic workers what Marx hoped the working class as a whole would become: a class *for itself*, a protagonist of history. One of these organizations is the Mexico City based ATABAL, a decade old collective of women committed to promoting the organization of Mexico City's domestic workers.

In a November 1995 Mexico City interview, ATABAL's communications coordinator, Olivia Martinez Morelos, told me that the group's work is vital because a high proportion of Mexico's economically active female population is engaged in domestic labour. Recently, Mexico's economic crisis has swelled the ranks of women forced to work in this sector. Atabal and the Group "Esperanza" together sponsored the first meeting of Mexico City domestic workers in October 1995.

In Canada, INTERCEDE is a Toronto based organization of domestic workers which sine 1979 has provided moral and other kinds of support to some of the 90,000 Filipina and other migrant domestic workers currently in Canada. INTERCEDE also does considerable lobbying on behalf of domestic workers with both the federal and provincial governments. It has, for instance, consistently argued for federal legislation which would lift live-with-employer requirements for foreign domestic workers and make it easier for them to become landed immigrants in Canada.[18] INTERCEDE's issue-oriented work constitutes a critique of Canadian capitalism and an effort to develop a new social ethos.

An Environmental Critique

A strong environmental critique of capitalism has been brewing at least since the publication of *Global Reach* in the mid-1970s, when Barnet and Muller predicted:

> The transcendent debate of the 70s concerns not socialism, but growth. Indeed, it is asserted by partisans on various sides of the debate that all the great social issues inherited from less apocalyptical times, such as justice, democracy, and freedom [the triad inscribed on the Avenida Juarez monument] can be resolved only through a sensible attitude toward the growth of human institutions. The practical problems of politics are thus problems of scale. Humanity must find an appropriate scale for its political and economic institutions, or it will eventually be crowded out of existence of drowned in its own waste.[19]

This practical approach to global environmental concerns predates complexities that have cropped up in environmental discussions during the next twenty years. First of all, environmentalism has started to emerge as a critique of both traditional capitalism and socialism. The environment is therefore not an *alternative* to socialism as a topic of controversy; instead it is a key element in the evaluation of *any* economic system. Environmentalism is a needed new way to deal with a slew of social problems—some recent, but many of them eons old (such as sewage disposal). In addition, it has turned out that environmental issues are connected more to human habits and ways of thinking than they are to the sheer size of our various projects. In the 1990s, environmental discourse has become so complicated that it has sprouted a number of branches with names like "ecofeminism" and "ecotheology." Philosophical ecology has generated a large literature including books like *Close to Home. Women Reconnect Ecology, Health and Development Worldwide*, edited by India's Vandana Shiva and *Ecotheology. Voices from South and North* edited by Canada's David Hallman. In a recent essay on social theology, Latin American theologian Tony Brun says that ecology "is a novelty. As a human science and concern it is relatively new. In theology and ecclesiology, its newness is even more evident as the ecological perspective begins little by little to influence these disciplines."[20]

Recent action on ecological issues is also producing critiques of uncontrolled industrial development and, in some cases, concrete measures to protect or repair the environment. Greenpeace, the best known international environmental organization, has during the past quarter century, performed many feats of daring in defense of our earth; one perhaps intentional limitation of its work has been its failure to mount a coherent theoretical critique of capitalist and socialist industrial development. At the same time, local groups in various countries such as the Toronto Environmental Alliance, the Environmental Studies Group based at Mexico City's Autonomous National University (UNAM), and Salvadoran Centre for Appropriate Technology (CESTA) are developing cures—stopgap or long-term—for local pollution and at the same time exposing the inadequacies of their local development models.

That action on the environment is usually seen as a criticism of the political status quo there can be no doubt. "A lot of confrontation has been building with the government" [because of CESTA's work], CESTA President Ricardo Navarro told a Toronto audience in 1996. To them, "we look like we are organizing against the government...They are trying to find foreigners who are leading our movement."[21] Who could have thought that the effort to rid our earth of poisons would be seen as subversive? It turns out that environmental protection is anti-establishment because it makes governments and corporations change their priorities.

Human Rights Based Critiques

Post-World War II movements to assert human rights have spawned distinctive critiques of capitalism and traditional socialism. A host of national human rights commissions and international groups like Amnesty International have also been spawned. These groups have developed a practice and in some cases a working philosophy of human rights. What these philosophies all tend to emphasize is the complexity and universality of humanity. They assert that humanity has an identity on this earth which is unique, multidimensional, and worthy of protection. Unlike capitalism, which emphasizes the excellence of the market, and also in contrast to communism's assignment of the lion's share of power to the state, recent human rights theory assigns importance to all the institutions which attend to human needs, be they political, social, spiritual, or economic. The backbone of this theory is the 1948 Universal Declaration of Human Rights.

Some recent campaigns to counter the ideology and social consequences of globalization have focused on human rights as a force to countervail the weight of sheer economic necessity. In Mexico, the Citizens Movement for Democracy (MCD) was founded by Dr. Salvador Nova in the early 1990s after an electoral fraud spoiled his run for governor of San Luis Potosi as a candidate for a coalition of organizations. "Writers, artists, people from other political parties, and people of diverse ideological tendencies formed a council to defend human rights and to press for fair elections," MCD representative Elena Enriquez Fuentes told me in a November 1995 Mexico City interview.

In a social climate rife with cynicism and fear, the MCD and like-minded groups are impelled to reassert some basic social values such as honesty and respect for the people's rights.[22] The charter of citizens rights promulgated at the July 1995 national meeting of citizens' organizations goes into a great deal of detail about particular rights and how they should be observed. Just a few of the rights listed in the charter are: the right to democracy and citizen participation, labour rights, economic rights, the right to food and health care, the right to education and culture, indigenous peoples rights, women's rights, the rights of children, the rights of the disabled, the rights of women prostitutes. The awareness of a "new generation" of human rights—the rights of gays and lesbians, children, the disabled, the rights of people with AIDS—expressed in the charter is shared by the Zapatistas. The June 1995 EZLN communique, for instance, declared that "intolerance toward gays and lesbians is an attempt to coverup the government's own hypocritical and corrupt morals."[23]

In Brazil, the campaign for respect of basic human values in politics was organized in response not to military dictatorship but to a botched attempt at a return to democracy. Soon after the 1989 presidential election—the first direct vote for chief executive in a quarter century—Brazilians became indignant at revelations of widespread corruption in the government of Fernando Collor de Mello, former governor of the state of Alagoas, who had defeated working class hero Luiz Inacio da Silva in the balloting. Betinho and many other Brazilians organized the Movement for Ethics in Politics, a coalition of about 900 organizations throughout the country, to press for impeachment.[24] The movement, which reasserted the necessity for honesty and respect of basic human rights in public life, later developed a new identity as Citizen's Action against Poverty and Hunger and For Life, a basic needs oriented popular movement discussed later in this chapter.

The critiques of capitalism that have sprouted since about 1960 are profuse, complex, and sometimes contradictory among themselves. The great strength of Marxism and its offshoot, Communism, was its adherents' agreement on goals and their consistency of purpose—at least some of the time. Now that there is a multitude of critiques, the trick needed to make them stand together where there is a need for unity and go their own ways when they want.

Think Globally, Act Globally

Remaking development will require deeds as well as critical thinking. The focus of much postmodern writing and organizing to achieve social change is on micro-realities such as the neighbourhoods and the daily lives of small groups. There is emphasis on the need for members of a group—tenants, trade unionists, coop members—to stick together, as they did in *Wonderful Life*. This careful attention to detail, praiseworthy and fascinating as it is, obscures the continuing desperate need for radical change in relationships among whole peoples and countries which was so evident in political action during the 1960s and 1970s. Many of the inequities suffered at the neighbourhood level start with decisions taken in governmental and corporate meeting rooms far from the localities where they are implemented. For instance, the pollution and sickness generated by U.S. based *maquila* operators engaged in production along the U.S.-Mexico border, for instance, are not immediate problems to those who control the operation from afar, but instead one of the costs of doing business.

Solutions to international problems will require a thorough reform of international institutions such as the United Nations, the International Monetary Fund, and the international development banks. Some of the needed elements of such a reform are set forward in Chapter Six. One important goal of this reform is to increase third world governments' resources for development and also their power be decision makers on international issues. Another reason (little mentioned in Chapter Six) why the world needs a new way to do global managing is that the power of transnational corporations has waxed greatly since the days of *Global Reach*, when it was already stupendous. So overdeveloped is this power that the recitation of statistics about it tends to throw listeners into a state of paralyzed helplessness. "According to calculations by the editors of the *Economist*, the world's top 300 industrial corporations now control more like 20 percent of the world's $20 trillion stock of productive assets."[25] Yet precisely because transnational corporations try to dictate so many choices about work, consumption, and recreation, people around the world can't give up their efforts to put corporate resources to work for the community as a whole.

No doubt measures are needed to increase the leverage of governments *vis-a-vis* corporations. The efforts of governments to control corporate power have been so rife with problems in the past, however, that reluctance to have government act as a watchdog on corporations has become widespread. Action at the level of the UN and international financial institutions such as the World Bank could also be important, though the chances seem slim the latter would act resolutely to bridle corporate power since the corporate agenda sets their priorities.

Since the early 1980s, ambitious new protagonists—with the hubris to believe that they can take on the transnationals—have arrived on the international scene. These are the NGOs, such as Oxfam, Greenpeace, IBASE and FASE in Brazil, the Maquila Solidarity Network in Canada, and the National Network Against Corporate Secrecy in the U.S. The new ambition of many NGOs since the 1980s is to act more as opinion makers and political leaders rather than as aid dispensers and executors of priorities set by others. There are several reasons why NGOs are presenting themselves as pace setters in international politics.

One factor is change in the situation of NGOS and in the political environments where they dwell. Brazil's IBASE is an NGO that experienced great changes both internally and in its political environment during the past decade. IBASE (the Brazilian Institute for Social and Economic Analysis) was founded in 1981 by people returning to Brazil after exile in Chile, Mexico, Canada, the U.S., Africa, and Europe during the period of military dictatorship. The three key actors were Betinho, Carlos Alfonso, and Marcos Arruda.

From 1981 to 1989, IBASE was a service group that did research for social organizations, IBASE staff person Pedro Dalcero told me in 1995 interview in Rio de Janeiro.[26] Civil society—including a clutch of unions and community organizations—was still very weak. A new national workers' central, the CUT, was founded in 1982 with Lula (Luis Ignacio da Silva) as the emerging leader. In the early years, IBASE did considerable work for and with the CUT, but by the start of the 1990s CUT had its own 15 member research team. At the same time, IBASE was finding it "couldn't answer all the demands from social movements," Dalcero told me.

At this turning point, IBASE started to picture itself and other NGOs as "political actors," instead of as providers of analysis needed by other groups. It was decided that IBASE would adopt a "proactive attitude; we would not wait to be asked. We would have our own agenda as opinion shapers. We tried to transform ourselves into a think tank." By the mid-1990s, IBASE had made considerable movement toward this goal. It had a magazine, *Democracy*, published every two weeks, which was distributed to committees in the Campaign Against Misery and for Life, a social movement closely linked to IBASE which grew out of the Movement for Ethics in Politics. It also had a program on an educational, government sponsored channel that reached 500,000 people. IBASE had a video division which produced features about AIDS, about the campaign against misery, and about indigenous people. IBASE was involved in considerable preparatory work for recent UN conferences in Vienna, Beijing, Copenhagen, Cairo, and Rio. It was a founder of the Association of Progressive Communication (APC), an international e-mail provider for NGOs.

By the mid-1990s, IBASE saw itself as a significant actor in the effort to build a strong civil society, an "actor without a tie to a specific social sector," according to Dalcero. "NGOs can bring a third approach other than government and opposition. Even if Lula were elected, IBASE would remain independent." This vision of how society's progressive forces marshal themselves is a world and well over a century away from Marx's call for the dictatorship of the proletariat. "The proletariat as Marx pictured it is disappearing," Dalcero told me. More and more, "opposition is disconnected from production." As political actors, "we deal with symbols; we struggle in the field of the imaginary." The concept of "democracy" as a notional foundation has become important to to IBASE participants, as it has to Mexico's Zapatistas. To the old, French revolution era, democratic touchstones —liberty and equality—IBASE adds "solidarity, participation, and diversity." All these complicated, hard-to-achieve ideals are integral to "IBASE's definition of democracy," according to Dalcero.

A comparison of IBASE's vision of social change with that of the Zapatistas produces some startling patterns. IBASE sees itself as an political actor on global scale in a way that the Zapatistas definitely do not; still the Zapatistas in their statements portray themselves as a movement with a global consciousness. Even the effort to put the two into the same category as change seekers may seem ill advised at first. The Zapatistas are armed rebels, while IBASE's people use only computers in their drive to achieve democracy. Yet in the millennium, when symbols and virtual reality have become the terrain of struggle, is a computer so different from a gun after all? The comparison breaks down at certain key points—guns kill people while computers do not (not directly anyway)—but still there's something to it.

Closer scrutiny indicates that the resemblances are in fact more than superficial. Neither group sees itself, at least at this point, as an opponent of government which might someday overthrow the government or win an election. They both seem to see themselves, at least for the short term, as some sort of third or fourth estate with a permanent anti-establishment role. This preference for what Americans might call a "Naderesque" role may spring from a realistic assessment of the groups' limitations, or it could be a product of the widespread disgust with political parties of all stripes. Both the Zapatistas and IBASE are concerned about popular education and about making a role for themselves as credible public opinion makers on a world scale. They both declare that "democracy" as their goal. Yet the irreducible difference remains: the IBASE offices look basically the same as those of any other NGO, proactive or not, while the EZLN may be the world's first armed NGO, with no office except Chiapas's countryside.

During the past decade, a number of NGOS have, despite cutbacks, developed the sophistication and technology needed to compete with TNCs and global organizations such as the G8 for the world's hearts and minds. Some NGOs also claim with some truth that they can mobilize forces staunch enough to change the policies and practices of international organizations—both governmental and private. John Clark's 1991 book, *Democratizing Development*, asserts that "throughout the world, from Western to Eastern democracies, from developing to Communist countries, there is a groundswell of popular movements. These movements are often led by, or supported by, voluntary organizations." Clark provides examples of the work of numerous NGOs around the world, including DISHA, a landless workers organization in Gujarat, India, which has "taken action in the High Court, in the state Parliament, and through the media on the behalf of the labourers."[27]

Clark also espouses an NGO based development strategy—for IFIs and governments as well as for NGOs—which he calls the DEPENDS approach. DEPENDS is an acronym for: development of infrastructure, economic growth, poverty alleviation, equity, natural resource base protection, democracy, and social justice.[28] DEPENDS, in other words, is a more complicated and diverse development of the triad "democracy, liberty, and justice."

In a reflection on the future of NGOs, Canada's Brian K. Murphy pictures NGOS as prominent movers in a possible new kind of social change process—a profound, dynamic, and broad-based *open conspiracy* for change—at home in Canada and abroad in the wider world. "A conspiracy, because this vision sees action based in broad coalitions in a movement of people and groups committed to the ethic of mutual support and co-operative action (an ethic largely created and shared in the long struggles of the feminist movement), breathing together, sharing life, action, and hope."[29]

NGO backed coalitions have in fact chalked up a number of successes that have been great media events, but not only that; some of these gains have real differences in peoples' lives around the world. Clarke names the global campaign since the late 1970s against the transnationals' (especially Nestlé's) marketing of infant formula as a great recent NGO breakthrough. "Hence both Northern and Southern NGOs concerned with health have established the International Baby Foods Action Network (IBFAN) and Health Action International (HAI) to expose and combat immoral practices by manufacturers in their marketing of baby foods and pharmaceuticals, respectively. International codes of conduct and controls have been introduced by UN agencies as a result."[30]

A worldwide, NGO-spearheaded boycott (endorsed by the United Church of Canada and a number of other Canadian groups) directed at Nestlé's products was called off in 1984, when Nestlé agreed to stop formula promotion and to abide by the UN World Health Organization code on the marketing of breast milk substitutes. Yet this David and Goliath tale had no once and for all happy ending. The U.S. based group Action for Corporate Accountability renewed the boycott against Nestlé in October 1988 after the group found evidence that Nestlé was still using excessive distribution of free samples as a promotional tool. There were some gains: a 1989 United Church survey of third world medical services where the church had ties showed a 93 to 100 percent breast feeding rate among mothers in African hospitals. In two out of four Philippine hospitals reporting, however, breast feeding rates were just 30 percent and two percent respectively; this resulted from separating the mother and child at birth for longer periods in the Philippine hospitals than in the African ones.[31]

In addition to their modest successes on the transnational corporate front, NGOs have chalked up some gains in the field of international governmental summitry. At various UN meetings, including the 1995 Beijing conference on women and Copenhagen conference on Social Development, the alternative NGO forums generated as much publicity as the official governmental forums. Development-minded NGOs have also used G8 summits to make their own kind of media hay. On the occasion of the 1995 Halifax G8 summit, Canada's churches issued an ecumenical study and action kit that called for action on a number of fronts, including world trade, structural adjustment, high interest rates, and the structure of IFIs.

NGO interventions at World Bank-IMF meetings have also made a splash electronically. A noteworthy claque was made at the 1994, 50th anniversary World Bank-IMF meetings in Madrid. The *Globe and Mail* ran articles headlined "Bankers run into social protest" and "Bankers get lesson in social justice." Development issues writer John Stackhouse reported that, at a Madrid rally, "protestors chanted slogans against the IMF, the United Nations in Bosnia, genocide in Rwanda, the General Agreement on Tariffs and Trade, homelessness in Europe, sterilization campaigns in South Asia and the industrial world's failure to commit 0.7 percent of gross domestic product to foreign aid."[32] Stackhouse suggested that the spectacle was a freak show, but he also made it clear that the NGOs made their points.

So what is the upshot of all this NGO hobnobbing with journalists at meetings of international financial institutions (IFIs)? Certainly there has been a growth in world awareness of development issues such as poverty, desertification, and environmental protection. Still, expansion of one's consciousness is not the same thing as becoming free from poverty; this is the great weakness in a world view which treats culture as the chief development issue. Yet, wait, It's true that NGO pressure has also brought another kind of change to the concrete details of global deal making in the IMF and the World Bank. Pressure from third world governments and NGOS based in both the third and first worlds has changed the development policies and lending processes of both institutions, in strictly reformist but still not insignificant respects (which are discussed in Chapter Six).

In the late 1990s, many third world based and first world based NGOs had more analytical and technological capacity, but fewer financial resources than they had have had in many years to raise issues with transnational corporations and international financial institutions. Lots of NGOs around the world have been hurting, and hurting badly. IBASE, for instance, had to make a major cut of twenty positions in May 1995. The institute has been trying to lessen its dependence on funding outside Brazil through revenue generating projects such as the provision of e-mail services.[33] In Mexico, ATABAL, which work's with Mexico City's domestic workers, told me that it doesn't have the resources to reach women in all parts of the city. "Many organizations left the country last year," Olivia Martinez Morelos told me in 1995. "They said they had to make other areas a priority." The resource squeeze continues on into the millennium.

Our Home and Native Land

Equitable development will require political restructuring at the at the level of the nation as well as of the globe. There has to be a pause in world's mad rush to free trade and regional integration long enough for people to reassert the importance of national governments. This rediscovery of nationality and\or ethnicity is already occurring in many areas of the world, especially the former U.S.S.R. and Eastern Europe. This reassertion of nationality is extremely poignant in lands where people have had their language, customs, and decision-making power wrested from them by imperial powers.

Yet an entirely new kind of nationalism, beyond the rediscovery variety, is needed in the 21st century to help people resurrect the ideals of democracy and liberty in their lives. In the mid-20th century, Marxists and other progressive people tended to downgrade nationalism as a force that was liberating in the 18th and 19th centuries, but retrograde in the 20th, when social action and revolution had to be based on class rather than on nationhood. This thesis, which was somewhat believable in the 1960s has lost some credibility in the 1990s as the notion of "class" takes a beating because of economic restructuring and the wildfire spread of new technologies. The leftist effort to divide nations into categories such as petit bourgeoisie, national bourgeoisie, working class, and lumpenproleriat now seems superceded by history (though these categories still have some continuing relevance.) One Marxist notion which still could still be useful in 21st century discussions about nation and class is "the reserve army of the poor," a group that expanded exponentially under the globalization regime of the 1990s. In countries across the world, G8 and less developed alike, restructuring is creating an army of surplus population—clad in ponchos in Latin America's mountains, in pin stripes on Wall Street, in the spandex of sidewalk prostitutes everywhere. They are sleeping on the sidewalks of Sao Paulo and trudging through deserts as they flee north from Mexico.

Though these people do share an important characteristic—they are all "extras"—they are in most other ways quite diverse and need different kinds of resolutions to their dilemmas. Hence, despite Marx's still stirring call for working people of the world to unite, it is equally sensible to issue first of all a call for them to separate themselves into groups small enough and homogenous enough to agree on some common goals.

The desperate need of so many of the world's people for new ways to stay alive and prosper is the chief reason why the idea of nationhood has to be resurrected in the 21st century; the nation is manageable entity where people may anchor themselves and find ways to work with others. Another reason why the state has to be rehabilitated as a geo-political force is that the role of state as an equalizer of resources, regulator of corporations, and enforcer of some measure of social justice has to be reasserted. In venues around the world, the state is currently in disrepute because of two (completely opposite) bad qualities it is said to have: it is said to be both too strong and too weak. Right wing publications like *The Economist* and right wing politicians like Mike Harris have been quoted several times in this book to the effect that the state is an over-intrusive, domineering nanny.

Then, in practically the same breath, the state is said to be an incompetent bumbler who always gets things wrong and is woefully lacking in the clout to be world class. This view is often shared by friends of the state as well as by its critics. EC futurist Riccardo Petrella, for instance, claims that the new high-tech network,

> ...has eroded the basis of democracy that was associated with the development of the nation-state. Territorial accountability has been radically diminished. City councils may spend weeks debating the allocation of $200,000 for housing rehabilitation, while the British financial houses transfer $120 billion from one market to another within minutes, fundamentally affecting currency balances, exchange rates and terms of industrial finance. Where's the democracy?[34]

Beyond these depressing realities, there is still a need for new ways to make the state act as a regulator and equalizer of a country's resources. A number of citizens' organizations in Mexico, for instance, have since the early 1990s developed a bevy of proposals to awaken the Mexican state from its long snooze of corrupt practices and PRI domination. The wakeup call has come most stridently from the Zapatistas and non-PRI political parties, but the pro-honest-government Citizens' Movement for Democracy described earlier in this chapter has also urged upright people in government to bestir themselves, and advised the non-upright to start worrying.

In 1995, a number of Mexican citizens' organizations joined forces to launch a wake-up-government campaign titled the Liberty Referendum. The referendum's goal was to gather millions of signatures on a proposal for a new economic program to replace the neo-liberal model. The newsprint tabloids distributed by the Liberty referendum campaign called for a detailed economic and political program which would require forceful action by an activist, democratically oriented government. The chief elements of the program are:

♦ An economic recovery program which would include: the channeling of public spending to provide jobs; tax reform to lighten the burden on the poorest, lowering of the value added tax, and a curb on speculation through a tax on stock market transactions; a new production-promoting monetary policy; lower interest rates; the financing of economic development with domestic savings.

◆ Measures to strengthen the domestic market including: a boost in the minimum wage; resolution of the problem of overdue loans through negotiation; suspension of privatizations; redirection of agricultural policy, adoption of an industrial policy which would place performance requirements on investors.

◆ The reshaping of international relations especially through the renegotiation of NAFTA and the renegotiation of the foreign debt.

The tabloid decried how "For years, the government directed all economic policy toward an increase in exports and an opening to foreign capital to modernize the country and lift it into the first world." An appeal is issued for all Mexicans to take a hand in putting together another model: "We need the participation of this country's women and men, without distinction as to their employment, unemployment, or disposition. Welcome, business people, merchants, workers, rural people, housewives, professionals, students."

The referendum's sponsors—including the Action Network on Free Trade and associations representing small and medium businesses, coffee growers, peasants and bank debtors—made a broad appeal to all but the most privileged Mexicans because the economic crisis posed an unprecedented threat to the PRI and to the Mexican government as a whole. From the referendum materials, it can be inferred that referendum supporters want political changes so drastic that they would create a state quite different from the one that has been run for many years by the PRI and more recently by the PAN government of Vicente Fox. No one yet knows how that renovated state would operate, but there can be little doubt—either on the left *or* right in Mexico—that an able, honest, strong national government is required.

Regulating Trade

In the 21st century strong states will still be needed, not only as inventors of broad economic strategies, but also as the chief makers and enforcers of rules regarding a nation's trade. This role will in fact become increasingly important, both in the developed world and the third world, as the pressure for regional trade agreements continues to build. There are a number of forces pushing a worldwide regional integration agenda now more than ever before. Regional integration is first and foremost the goal of transnational corporations, which see free trade areas as vital to their globalized business ventures. For the world's lead trading nations, such as the United States and Japan, free trade is an advantage they want to secure the widest possible markets for their goods. In the case of the United States, NAFTA is needed also to compensate for the relative economic decline which the country has experienced since the late 1960s. Nations with less powerful economies have their own reasons for seeking free trade. In a 1993 book published for the GATT Secretariat, analysts T.N. Srinivasan, John Whalley and Ian Wooton say that regional integration is driven by "the search for safe haven trade agreements by smaller countries, which now, more than ever before wish to secure access to the markets of large neighbouring trading partners because of their fear of higher trading barriers in the future."[35] Another force propelling integration is "the desire of developing countries to lock in domestic policy reforms by signing international agreements."[36] The authors see an inexorably negative dynamic for less developed countries in the charge to free trade.

This fatalistic view of free trade is one which condemns most less developed countries and some G8 countries to what some analysts call a "race to the bottom," which basically means that governments see themselves as forced to accept any terms whatever in the effort to stay competitive and be part of the global trading club. Indeed this grim view of modern global trade is partly accurate; poor nations can't win and they can't not be in the game either.

In the 2000s, trade unionists, progressive social activists, people who benefit from national social programs, and, indeed people everywhere who have been hurt by free trade and globalization have to get national governments to buck up and believe that they can take some action to regulate their trade. In Mexico, the fight against free trade has been bound up with the larger campaign to free the country from PRI dominance and to concoct an entire national economic development strategy. Still specific measures are needed to deal with the impact of NAFTA on the Mexican economy. The renegotiation of NAFTA called for in the Liberty referendum is said to be needed especially to save economic sectors which are about to disappear, with the goal of improving their competitiveness. Referendum architects emphasize that this action is not meant as a return to protectionism or as a support for inefficiency.[37]

In Canada, the free trade issue has been more separated from the issue of overall national economic development than in Mexico. As noted in Chapter Four, trade unions and other progressive groups were in the mid-1990s left searching for a new agenda after going through their entire repertoire of talk and action to oppose free trade. Their problem of developing a strategy on trade was compounded by the newly intensified dustup over Quebec. Since free trade was no longer a compelling public issue, trade unions and other progressive organizations shifted much of their trade related work to the sphere of lobbying. As in Mexico, attention was focused on renegotiating NAFTA—through charters and side agreements on justice related issues— rather than abrogating it.

In Brazil, the state's situation is quite a different one *vis-a-vis* international trade. Brazil is the leading power in a regional customs union, Mercosur, which went into effect at the start of 1995 and includes Argentina, Paraguay and Uruguay as well as Brazil. The formation of Mercosur does not, however, mean that the

Brazilian state has take on the job of lessening the impact of globalization and promoting social justice. In fact, it seems to signify that the strongest participants in the country's capitalist system will gain a new measure of dominance.

Some progressive analysts are in fact extremely negative about Mercosur and see it as divesting the Brazilian state of regulatory powers which were already weakened by 1990s privatizations. "Contrary to the European process, where the state carries fundamental weight in regulating and implementing integration, in Mercosur the national states have renounced their role in regulatory intervention, thus denying evidence that the state is still the main agent in the international economic process," writes IBASE staffer Maria Clara Couto Soares. Couto Soares concludes that "considering that integration in the Southern Cone is occurring in a context of deep economic crisis, the absence of strong state intervention is even more serious, since the market logic that will direct integration is not that of expansion and incorporation of new sectors and consumers but that of economies that are deepening their mechanisms for exclusion in recessionary contexts."[38]

Couto Soares calls on what she calls "the popular sectors" to push for acceptance of another agenda for regional integration by the Brazilian state. "This agenda would include a Social Charter to guarantee the preservation of and expansion of gains obtained by rural and urban workers, consumer and environmental protection, public investments, and programs for training and relocating segments of the working class affected by integration."[39]

It is clear that the unions and other workers organizations in Mercosur's member countries need to push a social justice oriented agenda. In fact, some initiatives have been taken on this front. A letter questioning the Mercosur goals and process, signed by representatives of six labour centrals in the four countries, was delivered to the nations' presidents in Montevideo, Uruguay at the end of December 1992.[40] In the end, the country's political leaders have to make the right decisions about trade, however.

There is at least one more reason why a strong nation state is needed even and especially during the reign of globalization. The state is the indispensable provider of social programs such as health insurance, unemployment insurance, and family benefits. These social benefits were relentlessly pared away in both developed and third world countries during the 1990s.

In Canada, the cutbacks have been in publicly funded health care and unemployment insurance; in Mexico the reductions have been in basic social safety provisions such as the minimum wage (which has been eroded through currency devaluations and a host of other social ills such as work in the informal sector). NGOs in Canada, Mexico, and the U.S. too, and such as various anti-NAFTA groups and the coalition that put together the Liberty Referendum, have emphasized their belief that social welfare is a responsibility of government.

Political Parties Outmoded?

Like national governments, political parties suffered substantial losses of prestige and power in the 1990s. This shrinkage has hit parties of both the left and the right in this hemisphere. Within some parties on the left, the decline is prompting many party activists to call for a broadening of party organizations so that they better incorporate the concerns of a wide number of social movements. (Many right-wing party strategists, in contrast, have tended to sharpen their parties' focus so that their platforms more closely match the agendas of the transnational business community. This trend has been observable in the U.S. Republican Party and Ontario's Progressive Conservative Party).

This movement to new style political parties is also being fed by dissatisfaction with old party models. On the left, dissatisfaction with Moscow-led Communist parties, which had been brewing at least since the advent of the New Left and Euro-Communism during the 1960s and 1970s, climaxed in the late 1980s with the collapse of the U.S.S.R. and Warsaw Pact governments. Now the universally accepted wisdom is that Communism is synonymous with a tightly centralized, hierarchical party structure. History suggests, however, that other kinds of organization are compatible with Marxism and Communism (if not with Leninism). "The First International of the 1860s, in which Marx played a large part, was also not a party but a weak federal organization loosely united around the Marxist philosophy."[41]

Socialist and social democratic party structures have fared little better than the Communist models. For them, the loss of prestige has been a product of party failures to juggle successfully the demands of the business community with the requirements of social justice. The 1973 toppling of Chile's Salvador Allende government was the most dramatic and, to leftists, painful proof that an unarmed, third world government led by a socialist party cannot escape defeat.

Three decades after Allende, methods other than military coups are usually used to deter social justice-seeking parties and governments, but the memory of Allende's experience remains a strong bridle on Latin American nationalist ambitions. In these times, a social democratic government can in fact be sent scurrying for cover by the simple act of brandishing of a bad mark by Moody's or Standard and Poor's bond-rating squads. This certainly was the experience of the New Democratic Party government of Bob Rae in Ontario. The Rae debacle only intensified many progressives' post-Allende conclusion that social democratic and socialist parties and governments will be thwarted no matter what they do.

An issue separate from the continuing utility of traditional party structures and practices is the recent negative experience of many of this hemisphere's progressive political parties at the polls. Especially galling for the Workers' Party (PT) in Brazil and the Party of the Democratic Revolution (PRD) in Mexico have been the victories that were seemingly snatched from them in two recent national elections—in 1988 and 1994 for the PRD and in 1989 and 1994 for the PT. The first loss was especially bitter for the PRD because it is widely believed in Mexico that the party in fact won that election but was prevented from claiming the win because of fraud committed by Mexico's ruling party since 1929, the PRI (Institutional Revolutionary Party.)[42] In the PT's 1989 loss, in contrast, the enmity of Brazil's big media—TV Globo—toward the PT and its leader, Luis Ignacio da Silva, is thought to have been a decisive factor.[43]

In the wake of maddeningly frustrating defeats, the PT and the PRD were left searching for a role and a renewed belief in their futures. The PRD's difficulties were compounded by the 1994 transfer of the mantle of progressive leadership to the Zapatistas (the EZLN), which did not forge an alliance with any political party.

Even more paralyzing than the electoral setbacks of this hemisphere's progressive parties has been the moral or political discrediting of large numbers of this hemisphere's political parties and elected leaders. In the U.S. and Canada, one strong contributor to this sullying has been negative political advertising that depicts candidates of all stripes as venal, incompetent, or self-deceived. In Mexico, lack of confidence in the PRI and in all aspects of political life reached catastrophic proportions, especially after more and more evidence of wrongdoing during the Salinas administration has been unpacked in public view.

As political parties have lost their luster, enthusiasm has surged for and within the host of new social movements already cited in this chapter: environmentalist, feminist, third worldist, human rights oriented, and other movements. A line of thought has developed which holds that social movements are in many ways incompatible with the fixed structures and programs developed by nation states and their parties. Arturo Escobar, the anthropologist already quoted in this chapter, has propounded this "social movementalist" line.

> Social movements may actually make difficult the consolidation of extra-social bodies such as the State. If the State implies an arborescent structure (i.e., unity, hierarchy, order), that of new social movements might be rhizomic: assuming diverse forms, establishing unexpected connections, adopting flexible structures, moving in various dimensions (the family, the neighborhood, the region)...Social movements are defined more in terms of change and becoming than as fixed states, structures, and programs.[44]

Despite the fact that social movements afford more space for spontaneity and maybe for fun than most political parties, as already noted in this chapter, there remains a need for permanently established political parties which take as their territory an entire nation-state. Without political parties, there is no chance that peoples will develop schemes for social betterment which encompass everyone in their society. Without political parties, social action remains just the preserve of a gaggle of sometimes competing social movements, who at their worst, can be (and frequently are) dismissed by right wing governments as "special interest groups."

A great problem for social democratic and populist parties in government is that, after they take power, they have to take into account the demands of all social sectors. This process almost inevitably sparks a falling out with the parties' pre-election supporters. This has happened so often to provincial New Democratic Party governments in Canada that some might conclude that the estrangement is well nigh inevitable.

Yet people who seek distributive and other kinds of justice cannot remain stuck in a position which promotes political bitterness. Surely it is not too late to establish workable party structures suited to our times. A few generalizations can be ventured about the specifications required for a socially progressive, twenty-first century party. First of all, such a party will have to welcome and incorporate a variety of tendencies and social currents, unlike Communist parties and also unlike the New Democratic Party, which has strongly discouraged left wing ginger groups within the party. One big reason why a new looseness is needed in party tenets is that a great many people around the world now decline to adhere to a set of sharply defined beliefs, be they political or religious.

The progressive party of the future may in fact lean toward socialism or even communism, but it will have to welcome a great number of new human rights oriented groups—feminists, anti-racists, and gay and lesbian rights advocates—as well as a new ideological diversity. Trade unions and "trade unionism," formerly the mainstays of labour oriented and social democratic parties, will be one of the important groups or tendencies within such a party, but trade unions will have to move over to make psychological and organizational room for newer and often less well funded social movements.

A second caveat about the structure of new progressive parties is that some provision has to be made for a powerful executive group to lead the party and for the party majority to rule on some key issues. Anyone who has been involved in a progressive social movement knows that the imperatives of strong leadership and of majority rule on some issues very often cause the organization's downfall. It seems a classic no win situation: you can't get anywhere without strong leadership, but strong leaders arouse resentment. Yet solutions can be devised: frequent changes in leadership and the installation of strong mechanisms to keep leaders accountable to the membership. These kinds of solutions are more apt to be successful within neighbourhoods or other small communities than at the level of the nation state or continents. Yet accountability mechanisms are need in these big arenas too.

Are there any examples in this hemisphere of a progressive mass party which combines strong national leadership with a willingness to incorporate diverse ideological tendencies and social groups, or is such a political force only a chimera? In this hemisphere, Brazil's PT is the party that comes closest to being a party for the twenty-first century. The PT provided a platform for the long pent up discontent of Brazil's impoverished majority. It took root in neighbourhoods and in base communities inspired by liberation theology and in the robust new union movement that became the powerful CUT.

The PT has incorporated a number of diverse leftist and/or progressive tendencies and also managed to develop some local accountability structures in venues where it governed, such as the participatory budget in Port Alege[45] and health councils in Sao Paulo.[46] In the early 1990s, the party as a whole started to identify itself more distinctly as an election oriented political party rather than as a collection of movements. This development in the party precipitated debate but not a fracturing. "Radical leftists factions of the party interpreted increased stress on political institutions and elections as reformist, as an abandonment of the working class and of the PT's mission. The party's majority faction, *Articulacao*, viewed this emphasis instead as an effective use of available political opportunities."[47]

Then came the two defeats of the PT's presidential candidate, Luis Ignacio da Silva, the charismatic leader of Brazil's main trade union confederation, the CUT. These setbacks have confronted PT members with hard questions about where to direct their energies in the future. In a 1995 interview in Sao Paulo, CUT staff person Alexandre Barbosa talked about "a great feeling of angst on the Brazilian left."[48] Still Barbosa expressed pride in the PT's achievements to date. "Brazil did create a mass party, the PT. No other Latin American country has done this. The PRD's power can't compare to the PT's. Other countries use the PT as a model."

A final word needs to be said about another kind of party which has the potential to become a major force in hemispheric politics: these are the Green parties which are currently active in Canada, the United States, and some European and Latin American countries. The great strength of Green Parties is that they can focus sharply on earth-saving issues because they lack the ponderous vote-winning mechanisms of traditional parties. In the United States particularly, where there has been no mass social democratic or socialist party, the Greens are an attractive alternative. The Green Party there has in fact been able to attract credible, high profile candidates like Ralph Nader. France's Green Party attracted international attention when it chose as its leader the now middle aged Daniel Cohn-Bendit, the famous "Danny the Red" of the massive 1968 protests in France.

To date no Green party has been able to attract a membership large enough to make it a consistently influential political force in any country, except in Germany where, in the late 1990s, it forged a coalition with the ruling Social Democrats. Green parties are still new actors in hemispheric and world politics.

Renovated Trade Unionism Needed

Another requirement in the new millennium is for a new kind of trade union, different from those that developed in this hemisphere during and after the 1930s depression. The U.S. based unions which grew up under the aegis of the Wagner Act became the prototypes for post-World War II unions in this hemisphere. The characteristic features of this type of unionism have been the union shop (all employees have to join the union), the compulsory dues check off (the Rand formula), and engagement in collective bargaining to obtain the best possible contract for members. The prototypical worker under what has been called this "Wagner Act regime" of unionism has been the male worker in an auto or steel plant. This trade union model has been challenged by the regime of globalization described in Chapter Four.

In virtually all countries, trade unions have been struggling to deal with the financial and other losses inflicted by declining membership. During the 1990s, trade unions in most countries remained on the ideological defensive when they tried to make a case against privatization, social program cutting, and deficit slashing. In a Sao Paulo interview, the CUT's Barbosa said of the Cardoso government's privatization drive: "the government is winning almost everything. It has sixty percent of the Congress with it, and it can approve what it wants. You think, we have to show up to make an argument against it, but after a while you start to think, why even show up?"[49]

Despite the gloom and doom scenario that bedevils trade unions, unionists and their allies have developed initiatives to reverse the damage done in the 1990s by globalization and its concomitant phenomena. One is a push to replace workplace-by-workplace or even industry-wide bargaining with sectoral or broad based bargaining for some kinds of workers: those who work at home or in small workplaces where they generally lack the protection of employment standards legislation or the support of collective bargaining mechanisms. In Canada, Quebec already has a sectoral bargaining system which was patterned on a European model. Quebec's sectoral bargaining "operates by ministerial fiat to extend the terms of a collective agreement across a sector so that unionized and non-unionized workers alike share the same basic employment standards."[50]

Unlike many of the other development-promoting strategies cited in this chapter, sectoral bargaining does not involve the self-activation or realization of its beneficiaries. Yet this kind of bargaining, plus improvements to employment standards legislation, has been advocated by unions in the needle trades to improve the situation of garment workers and other home based workers. A 1993 brief submitted to the Ontario government asserted that "province-wide mandatory broader-based bargaining is a necessary requirement if the women employed in precarious, non-standard jobs are to benefit from collective bargaining."[51] The unions' thinking in this instance is that the installation of a collective agreement and basic labour standards will enormously improve garment workers' prospects.

Another measure to deal with downsizing and membership loss is union amalgamation. This merging of unions is occurring in both Canada and the United States, in some cases even among unions with workers doing completely different kinds of work. In Canada the Communications, Energy, and Paperworkers Union was formed in 1992 through the merger of the Energy and Chemical Workers' Union, the Communications Workers of Canada, and the Paperworkers' Union. Since then the Southern Ontario Newspaper Guild and the Broadcast Employees' Union (NABET) have also joined the CEP. The most ambitious recent trade union unification is joining three of the continent's largest unions: the United Steelworkers of America, the United Auto Workers, and the International Association of Machinists (IAM). The unified union should have about two million members, making it the world's largest union outside Germany.

A trend related to shrinking membership and union amalgamation is the occurrence of union organizing drives in sectors previously untried by them, and sometimes fierce competition among unions for new members. The United Steelworkers in Canada, for instance, launched drives to unionize retail workers, including those at Wal-Mart, after it merged with a retail workers union in the 1993. No less than three unions—the Canadian Auto Workers, the Ontario Public Service Employees' Union, and the Culinary and Casino Workers Union of Ontario—tried to sign up members at a Windsor, Ontario gambling casino which opened in the mid-1990s.

The trend toward larger, multi-sector unions has the potential to increase the clout of working people vis-a-vis globalized corporations. It also could help replace traditional craft and sectoral loyalties with a broad, global working-class consciousness of the type envisaged by Marx. (A concomitant disadvantage is that the personal identification of union members and staff with their union may diminish.) Boosts in unions' international contacts, shared strategies, and coordinated action are other initiatives which could increase their effectiveness in the twenty-first century. Global communication among unions has already been occurring through organizations such as the UN's International Labour Organization (ILO) and the International Confederation of Free Trade Unions, which includes the Canadian Labour Congress, the AFL-CIO and Mexico's major trade union central, the CTM. In the future, more attention needs to be focused on specific joint efforts to enhance workers' ability to negotiate with transnational enterprises. This local to local and even person to person cooperation among unions has in Canada and the United States very often been sparked by union activists and unions with left-wing roots such as the United Electrical Workers (UE), rather than by the directors and governing bodies of major unions.

Since the approval of NAFTA, there has been some intensification in efforts to build relationships among Mexican, Canadian, and U.S. workers. One recent examples involves person-to-person contacts between U.S. and Mexican unions. In this instance, a joint effort between the U.S. based UE and Mexico's Authentic Labour Front (FAT) to organize workers in Mexico's *maquilas* took an unexpected twist when FAT organizer Robert Valerio was asked to go north to help with an union organizing drive at AceCo, a Milwaukee aluminum foundry which has "a reputation as a low-paying and dangerous workplace. Because of high turnover, it is always hiring. The company employs mostly Hispanic workers, most of whom are Mexican."[52] Valerio came to Milwaukee to talk to Mexican workers about their fears as immigrants. He was able to deal with their concerns, and, in addition, "Valerio's presence alone gave the feeling that what was happening to AceCo had real significance."[53]

A very drastic change needed to ensure the continuing success of this hemisphere's trade union movements is a move to what some of its supporters call "community unionism," a way of organizing workers that includes more participants than just the bargaining unit members and covers issues not traditionally handled through a collective agreement. This new method of workers' organizing is to trade unions what Brazil's PT is to old style political parties: it is a new "take" on the traditional model. Like the PT, the community-oriented union encompasses groups and social agendas which may appear—and sometimes really are—incompatible with each other in some way. The trend to community unionism is part and parcel of the new academic and popular preference for non-dogmatic social movements over rigidly structured parties and unions.

Community unionism is needed at this juncture because it is very well suited to organizing home workers or employees in small workplaces. Though sectoral bargaining can be an effective way to deal with pay and working conditions in small workplaces, it does nothing to engage the workers who benefit from it in consciousness-raising or other self-development activities. Community unionism as a vehicle for social change could achieve maximum effectiveness when it is used in conjunction with sectoral bargaining.

In Canada, an outstanding example of community unionism to date is the campaign launched by the needle trades' unions and their allies to improve the wages and working conditions of garment workers in Ontario and elsewhere: primarily Mexico and Central American countries. In Ontario the protagonist union is UNITE, a union formed from the 1996 amalgamation of the International Ladies' Garment Workers' Union (ILGWU) and the Amalgamated Clothing and Textile Union.

In many countries, the garment industry is particularly ripe for community unionism because it is a truly globalized industry which is aggravating the impoverishment of many already poor women workers around the world. Now that the whole world is a manufacturer's bailiwick, fifty percent of a Canadian manufacturer's production, for example, may be "done off-shore in countries where labour costs are significantly lower. Manufacturers design the garment in Canada, buy the fabric here or abroad, and (perhaps) cut the garment in their own shops. The pieces are sent to Taiwan, the Philippines, Mexico or Malaysia to be assembled and then shipped back to Canada for sale. The other half of the manufacturer's line is completed by home workers close to the large retailers for just-in-time production."[54] Strategies far beyond simple collective bargaining are needed to deal with such a complicated production network.

In Canada the ILGWU got started on a home workers' organizing campaign when union membership sharply declined as Canadian retailers struggled to keep costs down by switching to homework. This campaign has had two major thrusts: first, a concerted effort to locate home based garment workers and involve them in the ILGWU sponsored Homeworker's Association, a pre-union grouping of women home workers, many of them immigrants of Chinese origin.

Energy has also been put into building the Labour Behind the Label Coalition, which includes representatives of numerous women's and other social action groups. The coalition's purpose is to develop a high public profile for the union's organizing efforts and to press for legislative improvements such as sectoral bargaining and higher employment standards.[55]

The great strengths of community unionism practiced by UNITE and the Labour Behind the Label Coalition, and by comparable organizations such as the National Labour Committee in New York, are that they include goals and community groups that are much broader than those encompassed by traditional collective bargaining. The ambitious objectives of the ILGWU drive, for instance, which include the curbing of corporate power, make it comparable to the Nestle infant formula campaign and other NGO efforts to bridle corporate power. This widening of agenda and constituencies makes community unionism very compatible with social movement theory.

Community unionism has distinctive shortcomings as well as strengths. It may proceed much more slowly than a classical union organizing drive because it usually seeks to organize workers who are poorly paid, often scattered in small workplaces, and in lots of cases uninformed about their rights as people and workers. Consciousness raising may be the first activity workers—like the domestics in ATABAL—need to undertake, and this self-development may go on for months or even years. The trick is to combine this consciousness raising with activities to achieve concrete social goals. A second weakness is that unions and their allies in these situations usually lack the money and clout enjoyed by industrial workers such as those in auto or by public sector workers. This lack has to be overcome through support from other actors in society, such as NGOs or progressive governments.

Mobilizing in the Cities

One further field where new organizations and strategies are needed is in the mobilization of people around basic needs at the level of neighbourhoods and municipalities. Work is needed at this level especially because it is in neighbourhoods that the caring of people for each other is most likely to be exercised or not. The experience of Brazil's PT party and of the neighbourhoods Santa Marta, Rio de Janeiro, and Corpus Christi, Mexico, (described in Chapter Three) has shown that this caring is valuable in itself and also has the potential to become a political force. In the 21st century, work in cities and particular neighbourhoods will assume a new importance as fewer people have full time jobs and more people join the ranks of part-time home workers or of the world's unemployed reserve army of labour.

One of best known grassroots basic needs oriented movements in Brazil is Brazil's Citizens' Action Against Poverty and Hunger. Citizens' Action developed out of the momentum generated by the anti-Collor Movement for Ethics in Politics. After 1993, Citizens Action attempted to mobilize all Brazilians in a campaign to feed and provide other necessities to the country's 32 million people who lacked the means to purchase a monthly minimum basket of food. The imperative driving the movement has been the need for people to stick together in adversity, as enunciated in *Wonderful Life* and other stories about the political potential of neighbourliness. According to one historian of the movement, Carla Rodrigues, Citizens' Action was inspired by three concepts: partnership, initiative and decentralization.[56]

Citizens' Action eschewed techniques like telethons and simple check writing. Instead it attempted to awaken individual people's affective solidarity with people who lack basic necessities. The movement's goal has been to start bridging the great divide between the country's social classes. According to Rodrigues,

Brazilian social apartheid has divided the country in two. What Citizen's Action managed to do was bring together and break the mutual indifference they displayed. It is not by chance that of the 20 publicity films produced for Citizen's Action by volunteer professionals, the one that called the most attention depicted the driver at the wheel of a luxury automobile rolling up his window in front of a homeless child who is asking for money at a traffic light.[57]

Though Citizens' Action succeeded in mobilizing people around basic needs, it has been criticized by many Brazilians on the left for concentrating too exclusively on basic social welfare issues. In fact the organizers of the movement, including Betinho and others from IBASE, have been aware of its limitations, according to Rodrigues. The result of the movement's emphasis on decentralization, for instance, is that Citizens' Action is "incapable of demonstrating to the public what has been accomplished."[58]

In fact Citizens' Action has from the first tried to raise issues like employment and land reform together with the urgent necessity to nourish hungry people today. Land democratization became a chief focus of concern starting in 1995, according to Rodrigues. Somehow Brazilians have to come to understand that land concentration is causing not just hunger, but poor distribution of society's other resources; Citizens' Action has made such education its job. The point is that "Better utilisation of land would benefit many besides those directly involved in working the land."[59]

In Mexico, numerous self-help and political protest organizations have developed in Mexico City to help people deal with the financial hardships generated by the 1994 peso crisis. El Barzon is a movement which has been highly effective in calling attention to the credit squeeze on small businesses, consumers, and farmers. Interest rates in the country have in many cases become murderous rather than simply punitive.

El Barzon's tactics in fighting high interest rates have been bizarre, funny, and very media friendly (something like the attention-grabbing activities favoured by Greenpeace). One Barzonista tactic has been the nude-in; groups of Barzonistas arrive at banks, take off their clothes, and instead wear placards with slogans like "We want to pay but there's no money." Sometimes they are armed with paper bags full orange peels, and other food scraps. "This is all we have to deposit," they say to the tellers.[60] On one day in 1995, the Barzonistas staged their takeovers in three different Mexico City banks, in the neighbourhoods of Perisur, Nuevo Leon, and Queretero. They were greeted with laughter and applause and pursued by photographers and other journalists.

The Barzonistas are not just jokers; in fact, they have won important successes in their dealings with government. A November 1995 occupation of a floor in the Bank of Mexico by seven Barzonistas ended in an agreement to set up a national dialogue on the issue of credit card debt. The Barzonistas were greeted by 300 people waiting outside when they left the bank.[61]

The Barzon is a social movement that bears watching because it has all the earmarks of a movement which can succeed in our "post-Leninist" era: a knack for inventing forms of social protest that are different from traditional letter writing campaigns and street demonstrations, and a talent for appealing to peoples' emotions and not just their sense of abstract justice. The Barzon has engaged in talks and offers of mutual support with the EZLN, which, like itself, is a group which has devised innovative strategies to fight for social justice. The Barzonists way of operating, which seems to be by way of "loose association," is in line with the vision of Arturo Escobar and other social movement theorists.

Since the 1960s and 1970s, widespread social protests have not been a prominent feature of U.S. city life. New York City has not, however, lacked community based action to remake development in its less affluent quarters. Some of that action has been in Harlem, the neighbourhood where landlord flight became endemic during the 1960s and 1970s. Sixty percent of Harlem's land came to be owned by the city during that period. Leavitt and Seagart chronicle how buildings may have been bought and resold by speculators a number of times before being abandoned. The choices facing African-American residents of the buildings were extremely restricted.

Instead of trying to move away from Harlem, many residents banded together and asked for resources to buy and operate their own buildings as cooperatives. In response to tenant demands, the city government devised a unique set of ownership transfer programs; the first building returned to the market by 1979. The authors see this initiative as a protective measure that helped to stem the tide of homelessness in New York. "Had the city done nothing to save landlord abandoned buildings, the homelessness problem would have occurred much earlier."[62]

Leavitt and Saegert also emphasize throughout their account that Harlem was saved (at least partially) and given the opportunity to regenerate because of "people's care and commitment to place and community."[63]

Extensive interviews revealed that the tenant movements in most of the successful coops dated back to rent strikes and other struggles with landlords during the 1960s. It also became clear that "in each building, older people, sometimes in their eighties, played a critical part in saving the building." The social networks that helped to build the tenants' organizations were not best friend relationships. "To some extent, these histories of mutual aid arose out of insufficient resources, as an alternative to the money economy."[64] (Much like the networks in the marginal neighbourhoods of Latin American cities, as described in Chapter Three.)

What Can People Do?

A chief argument of this book is that the trajectory of development has been quite different in the developed countries with the most powerful economies and in the 100 or so nations of the third world. This had to be so because they came at modern development from very different starting points: England and the United States had an imposing head start, while many third world countries remained colonies without the ability to set their own economic courses throughout the nineteenth century.

Still the weaknesses and results of that development were not so different in the developed and less developed worlds, because the goals of development were similar in both spheres, that is, growth and the strengthening of the already strongest sectors of the economy. Environmental protection, human rights, and the allocation of resources to people living at or below the level of bare subsistence were all neglected. This is why New York seemed so familiar to Paulo Freire when he visited there in 1967. It has already been noted Chapter Two how Freire "saw and heard things in New York that were 'translations'—not just linguistic ones, of course, but emotional ones as well—of much of what I had heard In Brazil, and was hearing more recently in Chile."

Social organizations in the developed and less developed world have been discussed together in this chapter because their needs and goals are often similar; this is so because they are both affected by the weaknesses of growth oriented development. Unions, political parties, and NGOs in all parts of the world can learn from each other, and, indeed, they often do. The learning very often has gone from the developed to the less developed world, but it might equally well be transmitted in the opposite direction.

For the immediate future, our most pressing task is to deepen and extend the new critiques of capitalism which have been generated by the events of the past half century. We especially need narratives which evoke in their hearers and readers strong willingness, desire, and resolve to change the world. Latin American countries can make an especially strong contribution to critiques of capitalism that include story and song. More than one commentator has noted that Latin America has "a culture of playful and festive creativity. Work, production, productivity, and efficiency are not the bottom line on our continent. To learn how to enjoy, live and play is a desirable attribute in any society, and it becomes essential in a society that needs to share work and to work less, that all may live without seeking to accumulate once basic needs are satisfied."[65]

Humour like that of the Barzonistas will be an important feature of social critiques which can take us forward to a terrain where a new kind of justice oriented social change is possible. It is no surprise that "creaming," that is, sticking cream pies in the faces of objectionable religious and political leaders has in Europe and Quebec become a form political expression frequently used by people who have few other means to make their views known. The relationship of a cream pie to a hypothetical gun that might be used instead of a pie is somewhat similar to the relationship of IBASE's computers to the Zapatistas real guns: the pie is used to perpetrate symbolic rather than real violence on the creamer's "target." Public figures who have become extremely irate about being "pied" are quite right in their perception that the creaming is funny, but not at all friendly. What is rejuvenating and positive in the work of the creamers is their irreverence toward the people and institutions now in control of our economic futures.

Humour is needed in critiques of capitalism not only because it ridicules pretensions of those in charge; it also points toward a happier future. "This 'liberating element' of humour ferments the creativity to criticize the violence of the present and sigh for a different tomorrow...As a divine grace that anticipates liberation, humour is a powerful protest and also a powerful consoler."[66]

Critiques of capitalism based on human emotions have to be complemented by continued enunciation of broad political principles like the Mexican revolution's triad of justice, liberty, and democracy. IBASE's other touchstones, "solidarity, participation, and diversity," and John Clark's DEPENDS approach should not be forgotten either. Widespread disillusionment with the failures of both Communism and social democracy should not lead us to throw out the babies of political parties, trade unions, and Marxist theory along with the bath water of dogmatism, authoritarianism, and political terror. With the mechanisms of globalized capitalism are as vast and intricately linked together as they are, there is a corresponding need for justice oriented social movements to develop structures strong enough to control those mechanisms and make them accountable.

NOTES

1. Raymond Carney, *American Vision: the Films of Frank Capra* (Cambridge: Cambridge University Press, 1986), p. 379.
2. Frank Capra, *The Name Above the Title* (New York: Vintage Books, 1985), p. 5.
3. Henry B. Mayo, *Introduction to Marxist Theory* (New York: Oxford University Press, 1960), p. 106.
4. Arturo Escobar, "Imagining a Post-Development Era? Critical Thought, Development and Social Movements," *Social Text*, 31\31, pp. 27-28.
5. NACLA, *Report on the Americas*, Vo. XX19, No. 1, July/August 1995, p. 8.
6. Escobar, p. 26.
7. Andre Gunder Frank, "Latin American Development Theories Revisited: A Participant Review," Latin American Perspectives, Issue 73, Vol. 19 No. 2, Spring 1992, 125-39.
8. *Ibid.*, p. 137-8.
9. Ivan Illich, *Deschooling Society* (Harper and Row Publishers, 1970), p. 2.
10. EZLN, "Democracy or Authoritarianism: the choice for Mexico's Future," reprinted in *The Other Side of Mexico*, Number 41, July-August 1995, p. 1.
11. *Ibid.*, p. 1.
12. "The EZLN's National and International Consultation," *The Other Side of Mexico*, No. 41, July-August 1995, p. 3.
13. Antonio Garcia de Leon, "Chiapas and the Mexican Crisis," NACLA, *Report on the Americas*, Vol. XXIX No.1, July-August 1995,p. 12.
14. *Sem Terra* literature dated 8 April 1999.
15. *Jornal do Brasil*, 9 Nov. 1995.
16. Speech at meeting in Bloor St. United Church, 18 April 1999.
17. Escobar, p. 36.
18. Ontario District Council of the International Ladies' Garment Workers' Union and INTERCEDE, *Meeting the Needs of Vulnerable Workers: Proposals for Improved Employment Legislation and Access to Collective Bargaining for Domestic Workers and Industrial Homeworkers*, Toronto, Ontario, February 1993, p. 7.
19. Richard J. Barnet and Ronald E. Muller, *Global Reach* (New York: Simon and Schuster, 1974), p. 334.
20. Tony Brun, "Social Ecology. A Timely Paradigm for Reflection and Praxis for Life in Latin America," in *Ecotheology. Voices from South and North*, ed. David Hallman (Geneva: WCC Publications, 1994), p. 79.
21. Riacrdo Navarro, talk at York University, 19 March 1996.
22. *Juego Limpio*, p. 5.
23. Cited in *The Other Side of Mexico*, p. 2.
24. Carla Rodrigues, "Citizen's action, an exemplary history," unpublished paper, p. 2.
25. Richard J. Barnet and John Cavanagh, *Global Dreams* (N.Y.: Simon and Shuster, 1994), p. 285.
26. Interview in Rio de Janeiro, 10 November 1995.
27. John Clark, *Democratizing Development* (London: Earthscan Publications Ltd., 1991), p. 6.
28. *Ibid.*, p. 25.
29. Brian K. Murphy, "Canadian NGOs and the Politics of Participation," in *Conflicts of Interest. Canada and the Third World*, Jamie Swift and Brian Tomlinson eds. (Toronto: Between the Lines, 1991), p. 204.
30. Clark, p. 6.
31. United Church of Canada, "Summary of United Church Monitoring of Infant Formula Protection," 14 November 1989.
32. *Globe and Mail*, 3 October 1994.
33. Interview with Pedro Dalcero, 10 Nov. 1996, Rio de Janeiro.
34. Riccardo Petrella, "World City States of the Future," *New* Perspectives Quarterly, Fall 1991, p. 62.
35. T.N. Srinivasan, John Whalley, and Ian Wooton, "Measuring the effects of regionalism on trade and welfare," in *Regional Integration and the Global Trading System*, eds. Kym Anderson and Richard Blackhurst (Hertfordshire: Harvester Wheatsheaf, 1993), p. 73.
36. *Ibid.* p. 73.
37. *Vamos al referendum*, p. 12.
38. Maria Clara Couto Soares, "Mercosul: Neoliberal Integration," p. 4. (unpublished)
39. *Ibid.*, p. 7.
40. Hector Alimonda,"Mercosur, Democracy, and Labour," trans Bill Steiger, *Latin American Perspectives*, Issue 82, Vol. 21, No. 4, Fall 1995, p. 30.

41. Mayo, *Introduction*, p. 132.
42. *The Globe and Mail*, 23 August 1994.
43. John Powers, "Fighting for the Soul of Brazil," in *Fighting for the Soul of Brazil*, eds. Kevin Danaher and Michael Shellenberger (New York: Monthly Review Press, 1995), p. 215.
44. Escobar, "Imagining a Post-Development Era?"
45. William R. Nylen, "The Workers Party in Rural Brazil," *NACLA Report on the Americas*, Vol. XXIX, No. 1, July/August 1995, p. 27.
46. Margaret E. Keck, "Brazil's Workers' Party: Socialism as Radical Democracy," in *Fighting for the Soul of Brazil*, eds. Danaher and Shellenberger (New York: Monthly Review Press, 1995), p. 237.
47. *Ibid.*, p. 233.
48. Interview in Sao Paulo, 6 November 1995.
49. Interview in Sao Paulo, 6 November 1995.
50. Ontario District Council of the International Ladies' Garment Workers' Union, *Meeting the Needs of Vulnerable Workers: Proposals for Improved Employment Legislation and Access to Collective Bargaining for Domestic Workers and Industrial Homeworkers*, Toronto, February 1993, p. 35.
51. *Ibid.*, p. 71.
52. *Labor Report on the Americas*, #12, May-June 1995, p. 1.
53. *Ibid.*, p. 2.
54. Jan Borowy, Shelly Gordon, Gayle Lebans, "Are These Clothes Clean? The Campaign for Fair Wages and Working Conditions for Homeworkers," in *And Still We Rise*, Linda Carty ed. (Toronto: Women's Press, 1993), p. 304.
55. Virginia Rose Smith, "A Union for Homeworkers," *Compass*, May/June 1995, p. 23.
56. Carla Rodrigues, *Citizen's Action, An Exemplary History*, unpublished, undated paper written in Rio de Janeiro, p. 4.
57. *Ibid.*, p. 4.
58. *Ibid.*, p. 6.
59. *Ibid.*, p. 13.
60. *La Jornada*, 16 November 1995, p. 49.
61. *La Jornada*, 17 November 1995.
62. Jacqueline Leavitt and Susan Saegert, *From Abandonment to Hope: Community Households in Harlem* (New York: Columbia University Press, 1990), p. 9.
63. *Ibid.*, p. 4.
64. *Ibid.*, p. 39.
65. *Latin American Agenda 1996*, p. 7.
66. Brun, "Social Ecology," p. 84.

6

◆ ◆ ◆

NOBODY'S HAPPY: INTERNATIONAL INSTITUTIONS

George Bailey never made it to Ipanema Beach, but I did, during my Rio visit in 1995. As I swam in the beach's clear blue waters, I remembered how much George wanted to see the world. In *Wonderful Life's* "lasso the moon" scene, George tells his future wife Mary, "I'm shaking the dust of this crummy little town off my feet, and I'm going to see the world." George never did see the world, but he remained an internationalist at heart. Like George, I favour an international approach to the world's great political issues. The New York City excursion I most enjoy, both in my teen years and at the present day, is to the United Nations headquarters, which is situated on the East River in mid-town Manhattan. The sight of the flags of all nations lifted by the breeze into an uncommon unison of motion is stirring. I always take time too for a protracted viewing of the East River. Sometimes I even spot a oily looking duck or two paddling gamely through its murky waters, but I don't try to heave bread to them from my great distance above the river. Instead I regard them as symbols of the natural world struggling to survive in a great flood of unsustainable development. I wish them well on their trip to cleaner waters.

What I did not know during my teen years was that the United Nations was, like the Long Island Expressway and the Cross Bronx Expressway, a development project put together by Robert Moses. During a few days of intense negotiating in 1946, he managed to edge out San Francisco and Philadelphia, cities that also wanted to host the UN. Moses convinced John D. Rockefeller to put up $8.5 million to acquire a seventeen acre tract bounded by 42nd and 49th Streets.[1] Moses biographer Robert Caro noted that some community minded politicians objected "to a city unable to provide the necessities of modern life for its people spending millions on the UNO and giving tax exemptions on real estate that could bring the city millions more." What Moses could not have guessed at the time was that, by the 1990s, the UN would be such an unpopular institution in the United States that its relocation to Paris or even to Rio de Janeiro—if such a move were feasible—might cause little grumbling among American political leaders. This widespread discontent with one of pillars of the post-World War II world regime is a strong signal that the international order (if in fact there ever really had been an agreed upon order) had, like the postwar domestic consensus, broken completely to pieces during the middle years of the 1990s.

It is to the UN and the other chief international institutions that my consideration of economic development now turns.

The point has already been made in Chapter Five that caring communities with courageous leaders of the George Bailey stripe will be needed to remake development in the post-modern world; all the efforts of NGOs, trade unions, church based and other groups will not be enough to create whole societies that are committed to realizing equitable development. National governments, too, need to be enlisted in the campaign. One key role for world governments in this regard is to establish, and continually adjust, institutions of world governance and finance to the changing needs of all the world's peoples.

Many pressing problems of development can be solved only at the level of global negotiations and cooperation: the tendency of the strongest economic sectors to grow ever stronger at the expense of the weaker ones has to be corrected on a worldwide as well as a national basis. Likewise the problems of huge debts and low commodity prices, both of which are great obstacles to third world development, require solutions at the international level. The policing of corporations like Nike and the Gap, which extract a great deal of cheap labour from third world peoples, likewise requires action by international organizations as well as by determined NGOs. The issues of agricultural reform and bloated cities need to be dealt with by international organizations.

The unhappiness of just about everyone under the sun with the UN and other global institutions was on conspicuous display at the UN's 50th birthday party for itself in 1995.

The first big flaw in the proceedings was that a large fraction of the 190 world leaders who flew to New York for the festivity were in the midst of major authority crises on the home front. Canada's prime minister, Jean Chretien, was just days away from a stinging near defeat in a referendum on Quebec independence. At a special session of the UN General Assembly, Chretien sat directly in front of Cuba's Fidel Castro, who was natty in a dark blue suit, but still struggling hard to turn around his country's embargo-ridden economy. President Bill Clinton was facing a six-day shutdown of the whole U.S. government,[2] while his southern neighbour, Ernesto Zedillo, was being lambasted at home for his lack of credible leadership. In South America, Brazil's new president, Fernando Henrique Cardoso, a social democrat and former dependency theorist, was politely denounced by old colleagues as he privatized large chunks of the country's economy.

The manifest discomfort or disrepute of many of the leaders assembled in New York was by no means the only curious feature of the UN's half century birthday party. An equally prominent oddity was the UN's cash shortfall of U.S.$2.52 billion; by October 1995, only 68 members had paid their 1995 assessments, which were due on 1 Jan.[3] Almost half the overdue amount was owed by the

United States, the UN's biggest financial backer and also its most severe critic. U.S. delinquency drew criticism even from some of its G8 allies.

The really embarrassing side of this UN spectacle was a very public group gripe about the organization's shortcomings. Calls for UN reform were rife, with third world leaders such as Nelson Mandela asking: "(Why do) many in positions of power and privilege pursue cold-hearted philosophies which terrifyingly proclaim 'I am not your brother's keeper'?" G8 powers, in stark contrast, stressed the need for the UN to pull up its socks and be fiscally responsible; British Prime Minister John Major said that there must be a "new focus on efficiency."[4] The complaints were similar to grievances often voiced at the United Nations during the past 25 years. The dissatisfaction expressed was, however, more intense than usual, as if the last two decades of North-South discussions had exhausted everyone's patience. French President Jacques Chirac, for instance, talked about threats "to the very existence of the United Nations." Still there was a ray of hope in the form of the Carlsson group, a lobby of 16 nations, including Canada, organized to press for reform in the institution. The point that the great conclave on the East River made most graphically was precisely that there is exigent need to remake the world's international institutions, and that middle power lobbies, such as the Carlsson group, have a key role to play in the process.

How the System Works

The current world multilateral system includes a by now diverse array of organizations: the United Nations, the Bretton Woods Institutions (the World Bank and the International Monetary Fund), and the International Trade Organization (formerly the GATT). These three sets of institutions are those formally constituted after World War II as authorities to oversee the world's political and financial fortunes. At a slightly later date the regional multilateral development banks were set up, e.g., the Inter-American Development Bank and the African Development Bank. Each of these organizations includes a number of special facilities set up for specific purposes, such the World Bank's International Development Association (IDA), which provides low interest loans to the most badly strapped third world countries. The International Monetary Funds has opened so many different loan windows at various times that it has become a kind of international greenhouse for greenbacks. There is the standby arrangement, the general arrangements to borrow (GAB), the structural adjustment facility, the enhanced structural adjustment facility (ESAF), and a systemic transformation facility (STF). As if that weren't enough, there are also the Special Contingent Accounts (SCA-1 and SCA-2)! The IMF's bewildering variety of acronyms reflects the drastic ways its mandate has shifted over the years. The IMF now has tools for every third world problem, which have been applied so often and so indiscriminately to countries such as Brazil and Mexico that these IMF patients could in the 1990s have been said to be on their 19th nervous breakdowns. A major problem with both the IMF and the

World Bank is that they are currently serving a host of different purposes, some of which are quite different from those set out in their original mandates.

In addition, a whole crop has come and gone of informal global clubs, which supplemented or in some cases overshadowed the official international institutions. These groups have included at various times the Nonaligned movement, the Organization of African Unity, the Organization of American States, the Group of 77, and the Group of Seven. Most recently there is the Group of 15, a new association of third world countries launched in 1990. At a November 1995 meeting in Buenos Aires, the group approved a document which criticized the social impact of globalization.[5] The informal global groups tend to be more openly devoted to regional or group interests than the Bretton Woods institutions or the UN. The communique from the 1995 summit of G8 countries in Halifax, Nova Scotia, for instance, said that "the central purpose of our economic policy is to improve the well being of our people, allowing them to lead full and productive lives."[6] The clear meaning of "our people" in this context seemed to be "people of the G8 world" and not of the entire world. Remaking the more informal groups such as the G8 would be a harder job than tackling the official international institutions.

To determine whether and how the global institutions may be remodeled, it is first of all necessary to determine what the world's most developed countries (especially the U.S.), Canada, and various third world countries have at stake in these organizations and discover the reasons they might have for seeking to change the Bretton Woods agencies and the United Nations.

The United States
The government of the United States, which includes the world's most powerful critics of the UN, is assessed to pay 25 percent of the UN budget.[7] The U.S. has become chronically in arrears on its payments. In 1994, for instance, the U.S. was the biggest delinquent ($687 million), followed by Russia ($597 million).

The U.S. exercises influence the UN also through its permanent seat and veto on the Security Council, which has held along with China, France, the United Kingdom, the United States, and the Soviet Union. The report of the Global Governance Commission, which was chaired by Ingvar Carlsson (of the Carlsson group) and Shridath Ramphal, calls the council "the key institutional arm of the system, specifically charged with ensuring peace and security in the world. It was the only organ of the UN with power to take decisions that bind all member-states and to authorize enforcement action."[8]

The permanent seats and veto power were both contested by some UN members at the organization's founding conference in San Francisco, but "a few months earlier, Churchill, Roosevelt, and Stalin had already made up their minds on this issue…unless other countries accepted the permanent membership of the five with their right of veto, there would have been no Charter."[9] Its permanent seat on the Security Council has given the U.S. a great deal of leverage to secure its global political and military goals, especially since the demise of the U.S.S.R.

U.S. leaders conducted the Korean War and the Persian Gulf War under the UN mantle; the lack of UN legitimation for the Vietnam war is one of the reasons for that conflict's continuing worldwide unpopularity. The U.S. has also been involved in some UN peacekeeping operations, but has been generally unenthusiastic about UN military ventures where it is not clearly in charge. The traumatic Somalia peacekeeping mission in the early 1990s "contributed to a loss of faith in UN-led operations among some members-states, not least of which was the United States."[10]

U.S. leaders have generally been critical of UN organizations other than the Security Council. The one nation, one vote General Assembly where members are allowed to debate but not to decide has sometimes—with its famous "Zionism is racism" resolution, for instance—been a nuisance to the United States, but never a serious threat. The UN's specialized agencies—the World Health Organization; the Educational, Scientific and Cultural Organization (UNESCO); the International Labour Organization (ILO); the Food and Agriculture Organization—which also adhere to the one country, one vote system have from time to time been targets of U.S. ire. The U.S. and the U.K. in fact withdrew from UNESCO in the mid-1980s.

The organization and purposes of the World Bank (IBRD) and the International Monetary Fund are very different from those of the United Nations. Briefly stated, the main difference between the UN and the IMF is that the former's goal is a broad and nonspecific (i.e., the promotion of peace and cooperation throughout the world), while the IMF is mandated to perform a very particular function—the maintenance of an orderly and stable flow of currencies across borders. The World Bank has always focused on development tasks; its original mandate, to support economic development first in war torn Europe and later the third world, resembles that of some UN agencies. Recently, it took on some of the jobs that formerly were shouldered mainly by the IMF: financing structural adjustment and debt management programs.

Both the IMF and the World Bank were brainchildren of U.S. officials. "The IBRD, like the IMF, was designed primarily by officials of the U.S. government, notably Harry Dexter White, working under Secretary of the Treasury Henry Morgenthau, with a minor input from Lord Keynes of Great Britain...At the time of its founding the United States held over 37 percent of its voting power. Its headquarters were located in Washington, its charter providing that the 'principle office of the Bank shall be located in the territory of the member holding the greatest number of shares.' "[11] Though U.S. voting power has since been considerably diluted, the voting percentage of the top five members (all G8 participants)—at 38.82—equals almost exactly the original U.S. voting share. This combined voting power ensures that the economic development theories favoured by the world's greatest capitalist powers will continue to control the bank's practices. The custom that the World Bank president is a U.S. citizen continues to this day.

Almost exactly the same configuration of voting power holds sway at the International Monetary Fund. The same top five members—the United States, Germany, Japan, France, the United Kingdom—hold almost exactly the same voting share (38.9 percent) that they do in the World Bank. The usual practice has been to appoint a European as chairperson of the IMF. This practice leaves only the post of UN Secretary-General—a global booby prize of sorts—as an office which a third world candidate might hope to attain.

The weighted voting system at the World Bank and IMF is much more congenial to the U.S. and the other largest G8 powers than the U.N.'s mixed system. The U.S. and the other most powerful G8 members also are steadfast in their support for the World Bank and the IMF because the IMF especially and secondarily the World Bank are essential to the practical, day-to-day work of keeping the world economy functioning. Short of an outbreak of total war, they are much more important to the maintenance of the new world order than is the United Nations.

Although the U.S. could not get along without the IBRD and the IMF, American leaders have displayed an increasing amount of displeasure with two institutions during the past 15 years.

This dissatisfaction has been evident especially when U.S. legislators debate replenishment of the IDA, the World Bank's soft loan arm. U.S. reluctance to fund the IDA, which started during the Reagan years, has been chronicled by Canadian aid analyst David Protheroe. In 1987, "American insistence forced IDA-7 to $9 billion, the first-ever drop from one IDA replenishment to the next."[12]

In the 1990's, the anti-cosmopolitan, anti-IDA attitudes displayed by Republican Presidents Ronald Reagan and George Bush were adopted and in some cases intensified by a Republican Congress. In 1995, the U.S. was in arrears on its 1994 commitment and still due to pay $1.7 billion on its 1995 commitment. The *Toronto Star* reported late in 1995 that there were "growing fears the conservatives in the U.S. Congress will refuse to support an IDA 11."[13]

Conservative U.S. leaders' attitudes toward the IMF are not all that different from those directed toward the IDA. They are well aware, especially since the 1994 Mexico peso crisis, that they need the fund to rescue and supervise cash-strapped third world countries. IMF deputy managing director Stanley Fischer said at a 1995 meeting that "history will probably regard the Mexican crisis as a defining moment for the fund."[14] The IMF's problem is with its prestige, which is low. To those accustomed to doing their business in the gleaming towers of Citibank or the Royal, the IMF is the banker on the wrong side of town. The IMF provides is what a recent Canadian analysis calls "short term funds on very hard terms."[15] Recipient countries tend to think that IMF managers are tight-fisted usurers, while the managers reciprocate by considering their clients deadbeats (not in so many words, but the message is clear through their actions).

An analysis written in the late 1980s by Irving S. Friedman, one of the Fund's founders, speculated that "as a consequence of its preoccupation with the problems of developing countries, the Fund may well find that the industrial countries will become more reluctant to substantially increase their financial support for the Fund in the future. In a sense, the Fund could find itself faced with the same reluctance as now exists to increase ODA."[16]

Friedman's prediction became true during the decade after he uttered it. In 1998, the U.S. House of Representatives voted not to authorize $18 million in new funding for the IMF. House speaker Newt Gingrich opposed the fund with an argument that sounded strangely similar to that of the IMF's leftist critics. "I hear people come to this floor who claim they represent workers, who say they are for an international bank institution that is totally secret, that is run by a bureaucrat whose major policy is to raise taxes on workers in the Third World to pay off New York banks...That does not sound like populism to me."[17] The U.S. and other great powers have also been unwilling to consider measures which would make the IMF a stronger positive force in world economic affairs. One such third world proposal—to increase international liquidity through a large issue of Special Drawing Rights (SDRs)—got a cool reception when it was floated at the 1994 IMF meeting in Madrid.[18]

The dislike of right wing U.S. politicians for international institutions is usually not shared by other G8 powers. The G8 Halifax communique, for instance, includes a firm statement of support for both the IDA and the United Nations. "IDA plays an indispensable role in helping reduce poverty and integrate the poorest countries into the global economy. We urge all donor countries to fulfil promptly their commitments to IDA 10 and to support a significant replenishment through IDA-11."[19]

The right-wing, U.S. based critique launched especially against the UN and the World Bank in the 1980s and 1990s has complicated the role of third world and other observers of those institutions who also voice their dissatisfaction, but from a left or progressive perspective. *Globe and Mail* financial columnist Peter Cook has written of the World Bank that "it has too few friends. Those most interested in what it does—non-governmental organizations in the aid field—have often become fierce opponents, claiming that the bank's grandiose projects harm the environment and the poor. Those whom it most needs to influence, such as U.S. politicians who are now being asked to vote on replenishing the IDA's coffers, are also hostile."[20]

At least some third world development analysts regard the World Bank, for instance, as their ally. A 1990 book published by New Delhi's Research and Information System for the Non-Aligned and Other Developing Countries, for instance, proposes that "the coordinated lobby of the IMF-World Bank-IDA should bring about pressure on the developed countries for suitable modifications in their monetary and fiscal policies as also the exchange rates so that the effectiveness of the resource transfer to the developing countries could increase."[21] Even a half-hearted and authoritarian ally is better than no ally at all, according to this line of thinking.

The truth is that no amount of negative talk, by U.S. leaders or by anyone else, is going to bring down the world's multilateral institutions. During the past twenty-five years United States leaders have felt a need to export as acute as the export-need experienced by third world countries. The North American Free Trade Agreement (NAFTA) is the chief current manifestation of the U.S. push to expand its trading borders, but the Bretton Woods institutions and even the much maligned United Nations are equally vital to the satisfaction of this requirement to export. No matter how much U.S. politicians dislike their overseas obligations, they are very likely to keep on fulfilling them. The more important question is whether the U.S. and other wealthy powers will be willing to share their power with other nations (third world nations and middle powers such as Canada) in the interests of achieving a more equitable, and ultimately more workable global order.

Canada

Canada is a middle power that has a place at the G8 table despite its relative lack of economic and military wallop.

Canada's voting share in international institutions such as the World Bank is small; this relative lack of power does not, however, mean that Canada is necessarily excluded from taking an important role in the Bretton Woods institutions and the United Nations.

Canada's main problem in international organizations is that it has identified itself with the most powerful group of nations. By joining the G8 and later the free trade agreement, Canada has tied itself closely to the world view of the world's other wealthiest countries. Canadians could find other congenial international partners among the middle powers of Europe or Latin America. This would be an improvement on Canada's current method of acting as a bridge between the large and small powers. This method involves staking the Canadian position in many disputes right at some hypothetical middle, but still with a noticeable tilt toward the U.S. position.

Canada's tendency to stick to the dominant free world consensus was evident in the United Nations especially during 1970s discussions in the UN Conference on Trade and Development (UNCTAD) about a New International Economic Order (NIEO) and a Common Fund to support and lift the prices of third world commodity exports. The campaign at the UN for an NIEO was closely tied to calls for just prices for third world products made throughout the world at that time by leftist organizations, popular movements, and dependency theorists. On the NIEO, Canada consistently took stands which political scientist Cranford Pratt called "defensive and negative," despite the fact that Canada had a lot in common with third world producers of copper and iron ore.[22]

Canada's position on the NIEO contrasted sharply with that of a number of European powers who supported the third world position and tried to make a case for it to the world's other industrialized countries. These countries were Norway and Holland, together with Sweden and (to a lesser extent) Denmark.[23] There was, in other words, a "third option," beyond the third world and the dominant Western power stances, but Canada chose not to adopt it.

Canada's history with multilateral institutions such as the World Bank has been chronicled by David Protheroe. In the late 1960s and 1970s, Canada's official target for multilateral aid was 35 percent of the Canadian total, considerably higher than the norm of 20 percent noted in the 1969 report of the Commission on International Development. In fact, "targets were exceeded in practice, peaking at 44 percent in 1976-77, though in large part for the accidental reason of under-disbursement of bilateral targets."[24] Protheroe praises Canada's support for concessional lending through the soft loan funds of regional development banks, especially the Africa Development Fund. He concludes that "the period 1968-78 was a near-golden age in Canada's multilateral aid diplomacy, a worthy companion to the better-known pinnacle of Canadian foreign policy in the 1940s and 1950s, which culminated in Lester Pearson's Nobel Peace Prize (1957)."

The multilateral share of Canada's aid program dropped, but stayed fairly stead during the first years of the 1990s—at 33 percent in 1991-92 and 34 percent the following year. What changed significantly during this period was the total amount Canada devoted to its foreign aid program, which was pared back year after year. Then in the watershed 1995 federal budget multilateral aid sustained an overall cut of 21 percent.[25]

Canada's steady participation in the work of the world's international institutions has won the country a smidgen of influence within them. In the United Nations, Canada's power is strictly speaking no different from that of any other nation that is not a permanent member of the Security Council. In fact Canada's middle power status and history with the organization have made it a candidate for some special jobs, such as its chairing in 1983 of a committee which tried to solve the United Nations Development Program's perennial financial problems.[26]

The character of Canada's participation in weighted voting institutions like the World Bank and the IMF is different from the input it makes at the UN. Though Canada's voting share at the World Bank is small, it has its own executive director—one of 24 who sit on the Bank Group's executive board, which meets two or three times a week to review IBRD loans, IDA credits, IFC investments and MIGA guarantees.[27] (In 1994, the Canadian executive director cast a vote for a group of 12 countries with a combined voting power of 4.28 percent.) At the IMF likewise, Canada has an executive director, who represents the same group of 12, for a combined voting total of 3.72 percent.

The jobs of the directors at the two institutions have been quite different, primarily because the institutional functions are completely distinct. Yet in the 1990s, the distinction between the two institutions is growing smaller. Contributions to the IMF's enhanced structural adjustment facility (ESAF), for instance, became eligible to be counted as Official Development Assistance (ODA) in 1988. (The ESAF is the principal mechanism for IMF provision of financial support on concessional terms to low income countries facing protracted balance of payments problems.)[28] At the same time, the World Bank has become more and more embroiled in the work to help the IMF fulfill its mandate through structural or sectoral adjustment lending. According to the Canadian Council for International Cooperation (CCIC), an umbrella group for Canadian NGOs, "IDA funds were seen as the most suitable vehicle for this kind of lending to low income countries because of its highly concessional nature. The primary feature of this kind of lending was to restore a troubled economy's debt servicing capacity by urging indebted countries to adopt major economic reforms."[29] In practice, it is hard to distinguish this kind of adjustment-focused IDA lending from the IMF's ESAF lending. There is overlap among people as well as tasks at the world's financial and aid giving institutions. Marcel Masse, a former IMF executive director as well as a two-time CIDA president, is a notable Canadian example of this human linkage.

There has been less polarization and therefore a less sharply defined dominant position in the World Bank and IMF than in the UN because they deal with issues that are less overtly political than the UN's concerns and also because the world's Communist states did not participate in these organizations. Still, in a quiet and informal way, Canada has supported the dominant Western consensus about the ways that multilateral aid money should be used: in the World Bank and regional development banks such as the Inter-American Development Bank. This informal acquiescence with the preferences of the U.S. and other biggest powers happens on a daily basis, because the practice of voting is frowned on in these institutions. Canada's Department of Finance reported in 1995, for instance that "since most decisions at the World Bank are taken on the basis of consensus, Canada rarely exercises its influence through a formal vote at the Board."[30]

History supplies examples of Canada's failure to question U.S. use of multilateral institutions to enforce its political preferences. During the early 1970s, for instance, Chile's socialist government headed by Salvador Allende obtained no loans from the World Bank and had three loan applications turned down by the Inter-American Development Bank. After the 1973 coup which toppled his government, both banks soon approved loans to Chile. On the occasion of the approval of a 1976 World Bank loan to Chile's dictators, nine of the board's 20 directors abstained or voted against the loan to show their disapproval of backing for the coup makers. Canada was not among the loan opponents. At the Inter-American Development Bank, Canada approved even a $22 million loan hurried through the bank just after the coup.[31]

During the 1980s and 1990s, Canada also went along with the dominant view of the chief issues facing the World Bank and the IMF—debt management, structural adjustment, and concessional funding through the IDA and soft loans arms of the regional development banks. On the issue of structural adjustment, Protheroe portrays Canada in its classic bridging role as an interpreter who adds nuances to the stances taken by the wealthiest G8 nations. He calls Canada's position on structural adjustment "pragmatic and ideologically middle of the road"; our leaders have tended to favour continued lending for social services as well as for adjustment. Canada has sided with "the majority of donors, disagreeing with the American tendency to support only lending for policy change." In the IDB, Canada's views on structural adjustment "fell between those of the United States and the Latin Americans and reflected a desire to be a bridge-builder."[32]

Protheroe's depiction of Canada's attitude to structural adjustment differs somewhat the view presented in the 1991 report *Diminishing Our Future* prepared by two Canadian church groups—the Interchurch Fund for International Development and the Canadian Council of Churches. *Diminishing our Future* depicts the Canadian International Development Agency under President Marcel Massé as a wholehearted and even enthusiastic adherent of structural adjustment. "CIDA has in recent years embraced this particular analysis (i.e., adjustment oriented) of Third World poverty, and, in close alliance with the IMF, is seeking to ensure that Third World countries follow the policy prescriptions that are so easily deduced from this analysis." The country case studies presented in the church report make it clear that, if Canada's aid agency has not been the world's most zealous in its pursuit of structural adjustment, it has nevertheless been a loyal and disciplined adherent to that strategy.[33]

On the now highly contentious question of funding for the IDA and the soft loan windows of the regional development banks, Canada has generally showed itself to be a conscientious supporter of concessional lending to the world's most disadvantageously positioned countries. Yet there have been at least two downward pressures on Canada's contributions to these funds during the past 15 years: cuts to the aid budget as a whole, and gamesmanship with U.S. leaders, who have taken the lead in making funding a tortuous and never straightforward process.

In 1980-81, Canada for the first time asked for a lower share of an IDA round—down from 5.83 percent to 4.3 percent in IDA 6. Canada's share of IDA 10 (1994-96) was its lowest ever—4.0 percent.[34] These decreases were dictated by budget pressure at home. The need to compensate for U.S. cuts or else punish the U.S. (and the third world) for American delays or nonpayment first surfaced over IDA 6, when most donors retaliated against the U.S. by reducing their own contributions. "Some countries soon repented and joined in a $500 million rescue package of voluntary contributions for 1982, but Canada did not, because of limited budgetary leeway."[35] Canada's record on concessional international lending, while somewhat different from that of the U.S., does not constitute a breach of the great power consensus.

One of the chief arguments for the realigning Canada's chief friendships in the international sphere is that Canada has a tradition of what political scientist Cranford Pratt calls "humane internationalism." Pratt says that "at the core of a humane internationalist world-view is the proposition that Canadians (and of course citizens of other countries as well) have obligations toward those beyond their borders."[36] During the years after World War II, these cosmopolitan values were bolstered through a number of forces. "First the primary values of this culture, a belief in equality, in personal freedom, and in political participation, are felt to be universal in their validity." A second factor has been Canada's own social welfare culture which has abetted the building of a network of legislation to protect society's most vulnerable members. Factors three and four are: the influence of Canadians who have worked overseas for organizations like CUSO and the recent social teachings of Canada's Christian churches.

Canada's humane internationalist tradition stands in sharp contrast to the isolationism which wracks U.S. society periodically. Canada's behaviour over the years has usually reflected its commitment to the values of humane internationalism. Canada's is one of a small number of fully paid up members at the United Nations, and from time to time it fields high quality, pro-U.N. ambassadors such as former New Democratic Party leader Stephen Lewis. Its participation in the UN has been unwavering despite the fact that Canada has never been offered plums such as a permanent seat on the Security Council. It has not backed away from its commitments to multilateral institutions even though multilateral aid, unlike much bilateral aid, is not tied to procurement in Canada. In the 1980s and early 1990s, Canada was in most years the world's fourth or fifth largest multilateral donor.[37]

Reformers Gather

Canada's "business as usual but with cutbacks" policy toward the World Bank, the IMF, and other multilateral institutions has come under fire from Canadian churches, unions, and other NGOs precisely because these financial institutions' practices have at least arguably hurt the countries of the third world more than helped them during the debt ridden, crisis plagued years of the 1980s and 1990s. Reformers have usually focused on changes they would like to see made at the World Bank and the United Nations.

Improvements called for at the World Bank are meant to increase the democracy, openness, and quality of its work. At the UN, the desired reforms are intended to open up the Security Council to participation by other nations and to strengthen the financial and other capacities of the organization as a whole. Reformers have often devoted less positive attention to the International Monetary Fund and simply called on it to stop what its doing: structural adjustment. The possibility has to be seriously considered that the IMF could play a useful role in the world.

Canadian NGOs and other reformers have called for a number of specific changes which they hope can be implemented in the near future. One is to root World Bank/IMF operations more firmly in the Canadian democratic system. A delegation from the Canadian Catholic Organization for Development and Peace (CCODP), for instance, met in 1995 with Secretary of State for Financial Institutions Douglas Peters to present him with cards from 70,000 Canadians asking for action "to make Canada's representatives to the IMF\World Bank more accountable to Parliament."[38] A 1994 report by the Canadian Council for International Cooperation called for a number of changes at the UN: the inclusion of Germany and Japan as permanent Security Council members and the expansion of the Security Council.[39] Regarding the World Bank, the CCIC recommended that "the Canadian government explore ways of removing the IDA from World Bank management and establish a new mechanism of international cooperation which could manage these funds in a more open, democratic, and ecologically sensitive manner." In addition to this and other very specific proposals, CCIC made two sweeping recommendations about the Bretton Woods institutions: "that the Canadian government undertake a full review of the World Bank and IMF with a view to democratizing their structures and operations" and "that Canada freeze any new ODA commitments to the World Bank and IMF pending a full review of Canada's participation in these institutions."[40]

Canada's response to outcries for reform has been conscientious but unenthusiastic. The actions of our leaders on this front manifest a belief that the old, post-World War II international institutions will suffice in the new world order, with just a bit of fixing here and there. The chief step the government has taken to date is to supply more information to the public about its role in various global organizations. Financial institution minister Doug Peters wrote to CCODP that "one way we have responded is to prepare an Annual Report to Parliament on the Operation of the Bretton Woods Institutions...In addition, Executive Directors appear before various Parliamentary Committees, most recently the Standing Committee for Foreign Affairs and International Trade." The 1994 annual report to Parliament includes information on a number of items—such as activities of Canada's office at the IMF and World Bank borrowing in Canada—which were previously little known to most Canadians.

Another way Canadian leaders have responded to public pressure is to act as advocates within the World Bank or other institutions on issues which have recently gained new importance as development related concerns —especially women in development (WID) and the environment. The World Bank executive director, for instance, has reported in 1994 that "that the bank adopted a new policy that promotes gender equity in economic development. The Canadian Executive Director's Office was closely involved in formulating this first-ever policy on gender."[41] On the sticky structural adjustment controversy, the Canadian executive director asserts, "Canada has pushed the Bank to ensure that social sector issues are increasingly considered in adjustment loans and has argued that the Bank should have a poverty focus in all of its operations."[42]

A final measure taken to satisfy World Bank\IMF reformers here and around the world has been the release of some information regarding projects to recipients. Peters' letter to CCODP reports that "the World Bank has recently created a public information centre in Washington." In addition, measures have been introduced to involve those affected by a project in its design, according to Peters. "In fiscal year 1994, more than 40 percent of Bank operations benefitted directly from beneficiary participation."

The Canadian government's greater distribution of information about its global role and its effort to make some adjustments in the Bretton Woods institutions don't come close to addressing the concerns of people who are concerned about realizing greater justice in communities around the world. Unfortunately there are lots of reasons to believe that most Canadians' interest in making international organizations work is actually declining. In a report on the state of "humane internationalism," Cranford Pratt concluded gloomily that "as Canadian society becomes less caring towards its own poor, it is likely that it is also becoming less concerned about those beyond its borders."[43] Protheroe seems to confirm this pessimistic analysis when he comments on Canada's recent participation in multilateral institutions: "But now there was a more hard-nosed and unsentimental edge to this participation."[44]

Despite the undoubted decline of humane internationalism, there are still grounds to suppose that Canada might shoulder the job of global institutional reform, if the job as a whole were conceived differently. Ours is an era of radical restructuring, after all, so why not turn the renovating tools onto the likes of the United Nations, the World Bank, and the International Monetary Fund? The main obstacle to any thorough reform is the deep polarization about how such a change should proceed. The U.S. and most other G8 powers want to make these institutions more efficient, not more democratic, and the only shifts they want to discuss are financial and logistical ones. International affairs specialist John P. Renninger reported in 1989 that "…the study of structural and institutional [UN] issues has become somewhat unfashionable, particularly among scholars from the United States." By the mid-1990s, lack of interest in broad institutional issues had hardened into a fierce G8 determination to discuss only dollars, and how to spend less of them.

The world's less developed governments are the ones who most want to change the world's supranational institutions to make them more democratic and more helpful to peoples still struggling for equitable economic development. Since the final gasp of NIEO and other North-South negotiations at Cancun in 1980, they have been unable to find a firm material foundation to support their argument for a more equitable world order. Between the G8 and the less developed world, there are a number of middle powers who are sympathetic to the complaints of the third world and possibly able to act as a new "third force in world politics." The identity of these pro-third world nations varies from election to national election, of course, but their numbers often include Sweden, Norway, Holland, and Belgium. In the future, their ranks could be swelled by Canada, Australia, Ireland and other nations which are not the world's most powerful and not the world's least developed either. This group could be the world's development fixers, acting in the international arena (if not at home), with the UN Declaration of Human Rights and not narrow economic self-interest as a guide. Indeed this group could be the new "second world" of the 21st century—a new ethical force in a universe where belief in the inevitability of globalization's capitalist excesses has taken a strong hold. Now that the competition between capitalism and Communism is over, there is a need for some person or philosophy or group of nations to proclaim a new dichotomy, that is, the one between the need of the many to live in dignity and the drive to make the world's most powerful economic entities even more powerful than before. This is a job that would suit Canada fine, if its leaders would consider shedding their identification with the G8 and instead search for a home within another grouping of nations.

The Third World

For the nations of the less developed world, the UN and the Bretton Woods institutions have a different reality than they do for the nations of the G8. Many of the world's less developed countries were not present at the 1944 Bretton Woods conference, and great many were not present either at the 1945 UN founding conference in San Francisco. Many current UN members were not even independent nations at the time. Kenya, for instance, did not join the UN until 1963; for Barbados the membership date was 1966. The category "underdeveloped," "less developed," or "developing" did not even exist at the time, let alone the name "third world." It was not yet clear that the non-European, non-North American countries of the world might have common goals to pursue in international institutions.

What the world's less developed nations put into both the UN and the Bretton woods institutions is financial contributions and participation. In the UN, the General Assembly determines the assessment of each member, based on a ten year average of the country's GDP and a number of other factors. Since the UN has no way to compel the payment of assessments on time, delinquency has frequently been practiced by third world nations as well as by wealthy developed ones such as the U.S.[45] In the World Bank, all members pay a subscription and have voting power based on their financial contributions. There are enormous differences among countries in the amount of their subscriptions; in 1994, for instance, Canada's subscription was about five and one half million U.S. dollars. The subscription for the U.S. stood at $30 billion, while Brazil's was $3 million. In the day to day governing of the bank, executive directors such as Canada's have the principal role. Of 24 executive directors serving in 1994, eight were from the third world.

(There was also one from the Russian Federation.) These directors were elected, in contrast to the directors representing the big five (U.S., Japan, Germany, France, U.K.) who were appointed. The combined voting power of the eight is only about half of the big five, and, in any case, it would be hard for the third world to try to muster support for a particular vote, since decisions are usually made by consensus rather than voting.

An alternative forum to raise third world issues would be the bank's board of governors, which includes the finance ministers or other representatives of participating countries. The less developed world has a clear majority on the board, but this representation does not deliver a lot of clout, since the board meets on the occasion of the bank's annual meeting, but not often otherwise. At these meetings, third world representatives do raise their concerns, and are rewarded with media attention. The unequal distribution of decision-making power remains constant, however.

A comparable but much more complicated arrangement holds sway at the International Monetary Fund, where all members are assigned quotas, which , as in the World Bank, are in many cases greatly divergent from each other. Again like the World Bank, there are both appointed and elected executive directors. Of 22 directorships, third world representatives held nine in 1993.

In addition, the IMF has a board of governors, an interim committee, and a development committee. The interim and development committees each have 22 members who are "Governors, ministers or others of comparable rank."[46] These committees normally meet twice a year. These committees and boards are all venues where members from less developed countries can present their arguments, but not very often with great success because of the system of weighted voting and consensus decision-making.

It should never be said that the less developed countries have always been poor victims of imperialist greed; up to 1980, the year when North-South negotiations decisively failed, the less developed world did achieve some notable successes within international institutions, if only because of the audacity of some of its leaders, including Julius Nyrere and Fidel Castro.

The two chief third world successes in the 1960-80 period, according to development analyst Muchkund Dubey, were the formation of the group of 77 and the launching of the now much maligned International Development Association (IDA) within the World Bank. "When the Group of 77 emerged on the scene in 1964, it was hailed as one of the most important phenomena of the postwar years."[47] A perhaps tragic irony of the Group of 77's history is that it set out to change the distribution of material resources in the world, but in the end changed mostly the world's consciousness. During more than a decade, the Group of 77 gave a name and identity to the third world and, through its lobbying for an NIEO, named the some of causes and consequences of underdevelopment in the world's poor countries. The Group of 77 is now dead as a doornail, even if a few persist in using its name, but it did have undeniable achievements, mostly of a metaphysical kind. In his account of North-South negotiations, Dubey asserts that the creation of the IDA was a result of third world initiatives.

> It is now generally recognized that the struggle the developing countries waged for the establishment of a Capital Development Fund in the UN led to the creation, not only of the special fund within the UN, but also the International Development Association within the World Bank. Similarly, the pressure that the developing countries mounted within UNCTAD to get a Supplementary Financing Facility created, was, in no small measure, responsible for the improvement of the IMF Compensatory Financing Facility and the establishment of the Extended Fund Facility.[48]

These past victories are sources of hope that there may be some triumphs ahead for less developed countries acting in concert; these, however, are all still to be won.

Benefits Conferred

What the less developed world now receives through global institutions is some limited real clout (beyond the token authority conferred by World Bank\IMF directorships) in the conduct of the world's affairs and some fairly hefty sums of money, which was paid out in the early post-World War II years to do development, but more recently simply to keep some countries afloat and help them pay the interest on their bloated debts. The power of the less developed world is exercised mostly in UN bodies and especially in the General Assembly. U.S. and sometimes other G8 spokespeople heap on the assembly an opprobrium they wouldn't dream of visiting on the U.S. Senate, where (like the General Assembly) small states have voting power equal to that of the largest and wealthiest. American author Wendell Gordon is one who continues to belittle the assembly. He complains: "The one-country, one-vote system prevailing in the General Assembly might be acceptable if the countries were around the same size, but a situation in which five countries represent half of the population of the world and half of the countries represent only about 4.5 percent of the total population makes such a procedure a bit undemocratic."[49] He goes on to assert that "the General Assembly may sometimes appear as a forum in which most of the time is devoted to emotional speakers from underdeveloped countries who are bent on denouncing the Western temperate-zones powers." Yet Gordon admits that the assembly gets some important work done. Finally, it is hard to deny that the assembly's inclusion of nearly all the world's countries makes it the authentic global village of the world's peoples, with a unique authority to speak and vote on the great issues of the day.

There are other sections of the UN where the one nation, one vote holds sway—the United Nations Development Program, which has considerable resources ($1.5 billion in 1991) for the provision of technical assistance on projects undertaken by the World Bank or other agencies. Unlike the World Bank and the

IMF, the UNDP does not have continuing revenue sources, a limitation which puts it in a position somewhat like that of the IDA: perpetually asking for provisions. The fact that the UNDP is so fettered is what prevents it from becoming a powerful Capital Development Fund.

The UNDP does work closely with the World Bank on many matters, with the UN agency in a "second fiddle" capacity. The World Bank reported in 1994 that many borrowers use UNDP services to implement technical assistance financed by the bank. The UNDP is important to the third world because it an arena where less developed countries have initiative on development matters.

Less developed countries can also command a majority in several of the specialized agencies which operate under the aegis of the UN's 54 member Economic and Social Council. It should be noted that the World Bank and the International Monetary Fund are also technically specialized agencies of the UN.

The UN specialized agencies have been a focus for conflict between the less developed nations and the G8 powers. The third world clings to these organizations because its representatives are able to take the lead in setting the agenda there. The International Fund for Agricultural Development (IFAD), which was launched in 1978 (later than the other specialized agencies), "was intended specifically as a rival lending institution controlled by developing country members."[50] The U.S. and sometimes other G8 governments have countered third world initiatives by accusing these organizations of mismanagement and ideological excess. As already noted, these charges were made especially about UNESCO, but also about the FAO. The Canadian analyst characterizes the dustup at FAO this way: "At the Food and Agriculture Organization (FAO), the same issues—politicization, chaotic management, and personal empire-building by the director-general— surfaced. Uncharacteristically, Canada campaigned openly for the ouster of the director-general, and when the West's favoured candidate in the election of 1987 lost to the incumbent, it unprecedently delayed payment of its annual assessment and again considered withdrawal."[51]

The money received by the third world for development comes from a number of sources including the World Bank's International Development Association (IDA) and the UN agencies.

The analysis by Bajaj and Panchamukhi indicates why the IDA is so important and why its current situation is unsatisfactory to the third world. The first problem is that "the amount of IDA [funding] has either remained stagnant or declined in real terms in the period of the 80s."[52] The replentishment for IDA 7 was actually lower than that for IDA 6, for instance. The second chief complaint is that the per capita IDA commitments have not compensated the world's less developed countries for declines they have experienced in their terms of trade. In Asia, for instance, which as a whole suffered deteriorating trade terms during the mid-1980s, there was at the same time a fall in per capita IDA commitments. "In other words, at a time when the countries of the Asian region require much more concessional assistance to revitalise their economies in the context of growing adversity of the external factors, such assistance was not forthcoming."[53] Bangladesh, for instance, experienced a 13.6 percent decline in trade terms from 1985 to 1987 and at the same time had its IDA per capita commitment take a fall. Still the IDA has some good points; "it is commendable that concessional aid is moving towards the social welfare sector which helps in the promotion of long-term sustainable development."

Third world governments most trying relationships have been with the International Monetary Fund. A decade or so ago, IMF dictated austerity programs were often the occasion for outbursts of social unrest. In Brazil, for instance, the country's 1983 IMF approved program required a revision of the Brazilian wage adjustment law.

Although the Brazilian Congress objected, the military government then in power reduced the wage adjustment from 100 percent to 80 percent of the inflation rate. Resultant social pressures arising from the very stringent wage adjustment pressure, in the face of continuing high inflation, led to rioting. In May 1984, sugarcane workers burned crops in one town, and were eventually given an increase in their piece work rates.[54]

In the late 1990s, violent explosions of discontent about IMF programs on the whole gave way to dickering about stabilization prescriptions contained in IMF Policy Framework Papers, which are prepared for all countries eligible for the IMF's structural adjustment facility or enhanced structural adjustment facility.[55] These PFPs, though supposedly prepared jointly, show a high degree of standardization."The issue which is frequently posed is whether the policy content of PFPs is unduly uniform across countries."[56] When the targets of these IMF programs made the point over and over that austerity programs aggravate poverty, a limited amount of "poverty reduction" was added to the structural adjustment recipe.

It is a curiosity of the 21st century that the IMF, which has been a scourge to the third world, could finally turn out to be one of the poor's allies in the world. One reason for this possible change is that the IMF does not have much prestige in the G8 world. Another is that, coercive and mean minded as its policies have been, the IMF has been a source of money countries needed to stay afloat. By the mid-1990s, at least some spokespeople for less developed countries and for "middle power" countries had developed proposals for how the fund and the world's poor countries could develop more constructive ties. Some of these are presented in *Our Global Neighbourhood*, the report of the commission on global governance. The report noted "it is to the credit of the IMF that it has managed to transform itself from an intimidating ogre to a welcome source of concessional assistance."[57] This is quite a compliment for an unpopular banking institution.

Another Outcome

The world's political leaders could have left the UN's fiftieth birthday party with something better than a big photo to show for their work. They could have come to an agreement that world's global institutions are working way below their potential and should be restructured to make them work better. They could have decided to take one or two concrete initiatives in this regard, not as the G8 or the Group of 77, but as the assembly of all the world's people. Scoffers can snicker that this scenario is overly visionary, but these cynics don't have a real answer to this question: why not global reform?

The fact is that there is already an impressive heap of proposals for reform of the UN and the Bretton Woods institutions emanating from thousands of the world's NGOs and governments. Very few of these proposals are radical or utopian; most of them ask for modest measures to make these institutions function somewhat more democratically. To date, they have not been seriously debated, mainly because the governments which control the global institutions don't want to loosen their hold, and the countries of the less developed world feel that it is useless to aim for a big breakthrough such as a couple of seats on the Security Council. Somehow a way has to be found out of this impasse on intransigence on the one hand and hopelessness on the other. This discussion can be started with a brief review of what the main parties to the discussion have put on the table.

The U.S./G8 Position

There is both a right and a left wing inside the G8, despite the fact that the group is like-minded on the most issues. The U.S., is furthest to the right; the European nations, Japan, and Canada, while by no means a monolithic group, are generally more positive about what can be achieved through multilateralism. Like the U.S., however, when they talk of reform, they usually mean change to achieve more efficient use of money, not to promote democracy. A G8 agenda for UN reform was set out in the 1995 communique from the Halifax summit. The recommendations for the UN are to streamline its operations and eliminate duplication. The UN is to "develop a more effective internal policy coordination role for the Economic and Social Council; encourage deeper cooperation between UN and specialized agencies both at headquarters and in the field; consolidate and streamline organizations in the economic and social fields, such as humanitarian relief and development assistance; and encourage the adoption of modern management techniques."[58] On the question of duplication, the communiqué points to the possible overlap between the new World Trade Organization (WTO) and the United Nations Conference on Trade and Development (UNCTAD). There is no acknowledgment of the reality that it would be good sense to maintain the two institutions simply because UNCTAD has always been regarded as a third world forum, while the WTO (successor to the GATT) is certainly a great power- dominated organization.

There is no mention whatever of a possible change in the composition of the Security Council.

On the World Bank, the Halifax summit has little to say except that its decision making could be improved through changes in the operations of its committees. No particular committee is named and no specific change recommended. This minimalist approach to World Bank reform is comparable to the G8's strategy on the UN: to advocate only efficiency-promoting, administrative changes and to shun revisions to weighted voting like the plague.

In its June 1995 statement (which came after Mexico's peso crisis), the G8 line on the IMF was anything but complacent and minimalist, as it was with the UN and World Bank. Instead the great powers made a number of detailed proposals to beef up the fund's job as world financial police officer. The recommended changes to the IMF include:

◆ The provision of "sharper policy advice to all governments" and the delivery of "franker messages to countries that appear to be avoiding necessary actions";

◆ The establishment of a new Emergency Financing Mechanism which would provide faster access to the fund in crisis situations;

◆ The doubling as soon as possible of the amount available for emergencies under the General Agreement to Borrow.

This prescription for the IMF indicates that the G8 insists on a makeshift, ad hoc approach to world crisis management, because a more thorough strategy would necessitate a remodeling of the whole world financial system.

Canada

On questions of reform to global institutions, Canada is situated at the middling left of the G8 (but not as far left as France). Canadian leaders shun the extreme positions espoused on the right by the U.S. and on the left by some third world nations, by many NGOS, and occasionally by other big powers such as France.

Within the UN, the most recent Canadian position is that reform of some usually unspecified kind is needed in the Security Council. The Canadian Committee for the 50th Anniversary of the UN proposed that our government should have "guidelines" rather than a "fixed position" on the issue of council reform. These guidelines are: an increase in the number of Security Council members, up to 21; reduction in the significance of the veto power; support for the principle of assigning a fixed proportion of council seats to less developed countries.[59] This rather fuzzy Canadian committee position is in fact notably strong and clear compared to the Chretien government's position, which is enunciated in its 1994 foreign policy review paper. There Canada's ambitions for the Security Council are only that: "there is greater consultation between Council members and those non-members who have a particular interest in issues considered by the Council"; and that "relevant regional players participate in Council debates."[61]

In its discussion of UN matters, the 50th anniversary committee does recognize the second burning issue (other than political control) currently facing global institutions: determination of the amount and control over money for third world development. The committee's recommendation for the creation of a Sustainable Development Security Council is, however, so sketchy that it is impossible to say whether the Council's main purpose would be to tighten the bridle on the specialized agencies, or instead to make available on third world terms a new supply of development money. On the development funding issue, the Canadian Council for International Cooperation (CCIC) is also somewhat nonspecific in its previously cited proposal to remove the IDA from World Bank management. The CCIC says nothing about whether the UN should be involved in this new funding endeavour.

With regard to reform of the World Bank and the IMF, Canadian politicians and even NGOs are, if anything, even more cloudy that they are on UN-related issues, possibly because these organizations are huge, solidly entrenched, and not subject to defeat in elections the way national governments are.

The special joint committee that reviewed Canadian foreign policy for the Chretien government recommended that "any review of the operations of the international financial institutions should be comprehensive" and also called for yearly appearances before parliamentary committees by the Canadian executive directors at the IMF and World Bank. In its response to the special joint committee, the government agrees with the committee that a review of IFI operations must include "all relevant aspects of governance and portfolio management." The call for annual appearances by executive directors in parliament is, however, politely declined.[61]

Some NGO oriented development analysts have been tentative in their recommendations for IFI reform. African-Canadian writer James Busumtwi-Sam, for instance, talks about needed changes. One of these changes could be "reducing the intrusiveness of conditionality by creating a truly multilateral framework that involves LDCs in the setting of standards and objectives."[62] The CCIC was considerably more resolute in its already cited proposals on this matter, with its call for a full review of Canadian participation in the World Bank and the IMF for a freeze on new ODA commitments to the World Bank and the IMF, pending the review.[63] Unfortunately, not a single stone has been turned by the Canadian government since all these brave statements about IFI review were uttered. The IMF and IBRD have continued inexorably in their former courses.

The route Canada has taken in lieu of a thorough review of IFIs is to be an advocate for the already mentioned limited adjustments in IFI programs and practices regarding women's rights, the environment, and structural adjustment. The government describes Canada's role in the World Bank this way: "We project Canadian values into the international system by building alliances with other 'like-minded' countries and by encouraging the development of policies and projects that are consistent with Canada's international development policies."[64] It cannot be denied that this circumspect nudging of the world's financial giants does have positive but very limited results.

The Third World

There currently is no single agenda for reform of global institutions which is comparable to the NIEO mounted by the Group of 77 in the 1970s. There is also no currently viable theory comparable to dependency theory, which provided the NIEO with its intellectual sinews. This lack of a both a theory and a platform is a further sign of the disheveled state of third world oriented political forces in this era of right wing mastery. Yet all the elements of a coherent reform program can be found in a number of recent reports, especially in *Our Global Neighbourhood*, the report of the Commission on Global Governance. This report lacks a strong theoretical foundation, but it is replete with specific initiatives for reform that stand a chance, albeit a small one, of being approved and adopted.

The commission's reform program focuses on two main issues: the need to democratize international institutions, including the UN, the IMF, and the World Bank; and the need to provide a stable source of development funding for the third world. Its recommendations for democratizing the UN's operation focus on the Security Council and especially on two aspects of the council's operations: the assigning of permanent seats to five great powers and the provision of veto power to each of the five. (The agreement of all five permanent members to UN actions is not necessarily needed. The Soviet Union was absent for the vote which made the Korean War a UN action, and China abstained on some votes pertaining to the Persian Gulf War.)

People in the third world are well aware that the "big five" are unlikely to welcome curbs to their power. Security Council revisions advocated by the commission are sensible measures which ask only for great power recognition that the world has changed greatly since 1945. The commission's program calls for the creation of a new class of standing members, including two from industrial countries and three from the larger developing countries. Then a full review of the council membership should be done during "the first decade of the new century." The commission also wants the veto phased out.[65]

Commission members realize that discovering an acceptable way to change G8 dominated decision-making processes in the World Bank and IMF will be as difficult as Security Council reform. The commission's approach to the system of weighted voting is very moderate. It proposes that, in the IMF, quota weights should be based on GDP figures which look at purchasing power parity rather than at conventional GDP. This change would "generally benefit developing countries. At present, the new GDP and GNP per capita measures are being used by some to argue that certain countries are not poor enough to qualify for aid."

Over the years, many commentators have noted that a shift in the weighted voting systems, though badly needed, is itself not enough to make the IBRD and

IMF more democratic, because voting seldom happens within the two institutions. The great powers have a big edge because they have the habit of dominance. Analyst Sidney Dell has observed that "formal challenges to the dominance of the major powers have been rare, and even though the developing countries could, in principle, muster a collective veto on many of the Fund's decisions requiring qualified majorities, in practice issues are never allowed to reach that stage. Instead negotiations continue until the requisite degree of consensus is achieved."[66]

One way to break the habit of great power dominance is to strengthen the role the two institutions' various boards and committees, e.g., the IMF Board of Governors, which, like the UN General Assembly, includes one representative from each country. These more politically representative bodies of the IMF and IBRD generally meet only occasionally and don't get involved in the day functioning of the organizations. One body that has received considerable attention in this regard is the IMF's interim committee, an advisory body of 24 fund governors, ministers, or others of comparable rank. The committee normally meets three times a year. The need for a fairly small council of elected officials to help direct the fund's operations has long been recognized. In 1973, the U.S. Treasury Secretary said that "the logic is strong that for the Fund to act effectively, members governments should have available a forum of workable size within the organization at which responsible national officials can speak and negotiate with both flexibility and authority."[67]

A proposal for a Permanent Council never flew, partly because less developed countries were wary of it. They were not prepared to see fund machinery strengthened without an assurance that the new body would be even handed in its treatment of all fund members. The interim committee was considered a better vehicle for the participation of politicians in the fund. Yet in the late 1980s, Dell lamented that "even the opportunities provided by the existence of the Interim Committee have not yet been fully utilized."[68] In the 1990's, some advocacy for IMF and World Bank committees to serve at least sometimes as contervailing forces to the executive directors was revived. The Global Governance Commission, for instance, called both for interim committee reform and for the creation an Economic Security Council which would take on many of the interim committee's functions and add some new ones.[69]

Democratization of the IMF is only one of many changes needed in the fund to turn it from a feared global "enforcer" to a positive force in international affairs—a world banker of distinction. In a 1987 essay, American academic Richard Cooper pointed in this direction with his view of "the possible evolution of the IMF toward the standing of a world central bank as a lender of last resort, a source of international liquidity, as a contributor to global economic stabilization and to the management of exchange rates, and as a provider of an intermediating arrangement for making key economic decisions through a strengthened Interim Committee."[70]

A comparable role is favoured by the commission, which wants to see the IMF take a role in stabilizing exchange rates, in surveying the policies of the world's most developed countries (and not just those of the third world), and in enlarging global liquidity through the issue of SDRs. The commission is resolute that the IMF should keep out of development field, and instead leave it to the World Bank and other development agencies. "Its main long-term role, however, should be what is founders intended: to provide oversight of the international monetary system as a whole, not just of its most indigent members."[71]

The most serious ongoing controversy about funding for third world development projects is that the world's providers of concessional funding for development do not provide a continuous or stable level of resources for this purpose. Instead funding institutions have to go hat in hand to the world's donors every few years. A number of UN based tax schemes have been proposed as alternatives to this sporadic funding. One such scheme, advanced by the American economist James Tobin, is a tax on foreign exchange transactions. This tax would tend to dampen down international financial speculation at the same time that it provided money for development. "The revenue potential is immense, over $1.5 trillion a year for the 0.5% tax," according to Tobin. The Global Governance Commission talks favourably about the Tobin tax and also about some other possible revenue earners, such as fees for the use of some common global resources.

Yet the Commission undermines itself on this matter by mentioning a number of taxing possibilities rather than fixing on one which seems like a good bet. The commission report then goes even further to make a case against itself by dwelling on the bad points of the Tobin tax. "Such a tax faces considerable practical problems, however, not the least being the decentralized, unregulated, electronically mediated nature of foreign exchange markets in most industrial countries, with no paper trails to provide a tax base." The commission's statement on the Tobin tax end lamely with the assertion that "the problems may not be insuperable, but they have to be addressed."[72]

Though this is not ringing statement of certainty that stable funding for development can be found, it is at least a probe sent out in that direction.

The global governance commission does not raise the matter of removing the IDA from World Bank jurisdiction, one of the proposals advanced in the CCIC's agenda and also one of the objectives of negotiators for the third world, who asked for a capital development fund housed in the UN some thirty or more years ago. The main purpose of such a move would be to endow third world countries with a development fund controlled by or at least largely controlled by them. The logical place to house this reborn IDA would be the United Nations. In fact, the rehoused IDA would resemble the fund the third world asked for long ago, when it received the IDA instead.

It is impossible to know for sure why the world's less developed nations are not putting forward a strong petition for an improved development fund. This apparent lack of interest may be a product of discouragement at the failure of the NIEO. Third world leaders are also well aware of the fact that their leverage in world affairs has recently decreased even from its modest levels during the NIEO years because of the collapse of the Communist, second world. So where is the political drive going to come from to get the Tobin tax and new development fund launched?

It is at such a juncture that Canada can offer important support to the less developed world and also help itself in its now-more-than-ever anguished search for a national destiny. Support by Canada and like minded middle powers for a thorough reform of international financial institutions is needed now because the third world will not achieve its goals in global institutions without some high profile, energetic intervention from another group of nations. The job of this new "second" world of nations would be to countervail the force of G8 policy toward the UN, the IMF and the World Bank.

This new second world includes the world's "middle" industrialized, non-G8 nations, such as the Nordic nations or the nations of Eastern Europe. The second world also really includes some misfiled G8 nations such as Canada and Italy. This group of middle powers has reasons for wanting the world's international financial institutions to operate more democratically and justly. International development analyst John P. Renninger pointed to the potential impact of middle power intervention several years ago. He was hopeful that what he saw as "the emergence of a group of middle powers" could cut across the traditional alignment of nations in the U.N. This "middle power influence" has not been very noticeable in recent debates about international institutions, but there certainly steps could be taken to make it more prominent.

Why would Canada shift its allegiance in such critically important matters? One reason could be that the world's middle powers are losing patience with the domination of world politics that the U.S. has exercised since the collapse of the Soviet Union. Another is Canada's wish for a new national identity as it struggles with its great plague of post-NAFTA, post-referendum neuroses. Then there is the need for Canadians to show some fidelity to their humane internationalist traditions. Within the world community as a whole, there is a desire for a renewed sense of purpose at the United Nations. Only a concerted campaign by a whole group of member nations can restore to the organization the luster it had during the early postwar years. Moving the headquarters away from the East River, New York, to a third world country could also help to reinvent the UN's sense of mission.

NOTES

1. Robert Caro, *The Power Broker. Robert Moses and the Fall of New York* (New York: Alfred A. Knopf), p. 774.
2. *Globe and Mail*, 20 November 1995, Al.
3. *Globe and Mail*, 25 Sept. 1995, A10.
4. *Toronto Star*, 24 October 1995, A3.
5. *Folha de Sao Paulo*, 7 November 1995.
6. Halifax summit communique, p. 1.
7. *Our Global Neighbourhood, the Report of the Commission on Global Governance* (Oxford University Press, 1995), p. 300.
8. Ibid., p. 234.
9. Ibid., p. 235.
10. Ibid., p. 108.
11. Cheryl Payer, *The World Bank: A Critical Analysis* (New York: Monthly Review Press, 1982), p. 22.
12. David R. Protheroe, "Canada's Multilateral Aid and Diplomacy," *Canadian International Development Assistance Policies: An Appraisal*, ed. Cranford Pratt (Montreal and Kingston McGill-Queen's University Press, 1994), p. 35.
13. *Toronto Star*, 10 October 1995.
14. *Globe and Mail*, 25 Sept. 1995, B2.
15. Canadian Council for International Cooperation, "Towards a Common Future," January 1994, A discussion paper, p. 20.
16. Irving S. Friedman. "The International Monetary Fund: A Founder's Evaluation," *The Political Morality of the International Monetary Fund*, ed. Robert J. Myers (New York: Transaction Books, 1987), p. 28.
17. *Multinational Monitor*, May 1998, p. 6.
18. *Our Global Neighbourhood*, p. 186.
19. "Halifax Summit Communique," p. 4.
20. *Globe and Mail*, 25 Sept. 1995.
21. J.L. Bajaj and V.R. Panchamukhi, *Aid in the 1990s with Special Reference to the World Bank and the IDA* (New Delhi: Research and Information System for the Non-aligned and Other Developing Countries, 1990), p. 62.
22. Cranford Pratt, "An Eroding and Limited Internationalism," in *Internationalism Under Strain: The North-South Policies of Canada The Netherlands, Norway and Sweden*, ed. Cranford Pratt (Toronto: University of Toronto Press, 1989), p. 31.
23. Ibid. p. 27.
24. Protheroe, P. 29.
25. CCIC, Review of 1995-96 spending estimates for CIDA, p. 6.
26. Protheroe, p. 30.
27. *Report on Operations Under the Bretton Woods and Related Agreements Act*, 1994, p. 30.
28. Ibid., p. 11.
29. Canadian Council for International Cooperation, *Towards A Common Future*, January 1994, p. 18.
30. *Report on Operations Under the Bretton Woods and Related Agreements Act*, p. 30.
31. Robert Carty and Virginia Smith, *Perpetuating Poverty* (Toronto: Between the Lines, 1981), p. 156.
32. Protheroe, p. 38.
33. ICFID and the CCIA of the CCC, *Diminishing our Future CIDA: Four Years After Winegard*, p. 19.
34. Protheroe, p. 35.
35. Protheroe, p. 35.
36. Cranford Pratt, "Canada: An Eroding and Limited Internationalism," p. 24.
37. Protheroe, p. 25.
38. *The Global Village Voice*, Vol. 19, No. 4, Spring\Summer 1995.
39. Canadian Council for International Cooperation, Towards A Common Future, p. 21.
40. Canadian Council for International Cooperation, *Economic Justice. Toward a Just and Sustainable Canadian Foreign Policy*, January 1994, p. 21, 22.
41. *The World Bank. Canada's Role*, p. 13.
42. Ibid., p. 12.

43. Cranford Pratt, "Humane Internationalism and Canadian Development Assistance Policies," in *Canadian International Development Assistance Policies: An Appraisal*, ed. Cranford Pratt (Montreal and Kingston: McGill-Queen's University Press, 1994), p. 336.

44. Protheroe, p. 33.

45. Wendell Gordon, *The United Nations at the Crossroads of Reform* (New York: M.E. Sharpe, 1994), p. 100.

46. *International Monetary Fund*, Annual Report 1992, p. 14.

47. Muchkund Dubey, "The North South Negotiating Process," *World Economy in Transition*, eds. Krishna Ahooja-Patel, Anne Gordon Drabek, Marc Nerfin (Oxford: Pergamon Press, Ltd., 1986).

49. Gordon, p. 16.

50. Payer, *The World Bank,* p. 19.

51. Protheroe, p. 43.

52. Bajaj and Panchamuki, p. 42.

53. Ibid., p. 43.

54. Henry B. Schechter, "IMF Conditionality and the International Economy," in *The Political Morality of the International Monetary Fund*.

55. Bajaj and Panchamukhi, p. 60.

56. Ibid., p. 61.

57. *Our Global Neighbourhood*, p. 187.

58. Halifax Summit, *Communiqué*, p. 6.

59. Canadian Committee for the Fiftieth Anniversary of the United Nations, "Canadian Priorities for United Nations Reform," (Toronto: Dundurn Press, 1995), p. 310.

60. *Government Response to the Recommendations of the Special Joint Parliamentary Committee Reviewing Canadian Foreign Policy*, p. 9.

61. *Government Response to the Recommendations of the Special Joint Parliamentary Committee*, p. 39.

62. Ibid. p. 262.

63. CCIC, *Economic Justice. Toward A Just and Sustainable*, p. 22.

64. Canada and the World Bank, p. 5.

65. *Our Global Neighbourhood*, p. 241.

66. Sidney Dell, "The Future of the International Monetary System," in *The Future Role of the United Nations in an Interdependent World*, ed. John P. Renninger (Dordrecht: Martinus Nijhoff Publishers, 1989), p. 130.

67. "Statement by the Governor of the Fund and World Bank for the United States," *Summary Proceedings of the Annual Meeting of the Board of Governors*, 1973, IMF, Washington, D.C., 1973, cited in *The Future Role of the United Nations in an Interdependent World*, p. 131.

68. Dell, p. 133.

69. *Our Global Neighbourhood*, p. 188.

70. Richard M. Cooper, "The Evolution of the International Monetary System Toward a World Central Bank," in *The International Monetary System, Essays in World Economics*, cited in *The Future Role of the United Nations in an Interdependent World*, p. 109

71. *Our Global Neighbourhood*, p. 187.

72. *Our Global Neighbourhood*, p. 219.

7

◆ ◆ ◆

BRINGING IT BACK HOME

The *coup de grace* to North America's post-World War II economic and social system that occurred in the mid-1990s made the system's inherent deficiencies more apparent than ever. The radical scaling down of social welfare measures and the summary dismissal of the requirements of disadvantaged minorities made the need for authentic economic development more apparent than ever. The tumbling down of the old order also presented the opportunity for new or at least different alternatives, though some pundits—Jeremy Rifkin in his 1995 book *The End of Work*, for instance—said the opposite: that globalization was so pervasive and inevitable that any leftists or even Rooseveltian liberals left in the world had better order Socratian doses of hemlock forthwith.

Development is still seen as a credible goal by many economic analysts. Development proponents usually do not try to define development very precisely, however. Andre Gunder Frank, who was disillusioned about both dependency theory and the prospects for national self-reliance, posed the development question again in his 1991 memoir. "So what are the real alternatives and the more participatory democratic ways to forge and pursue them?" One answer is that like disadvantaged "people themselves, we [people of the G8 world] can do battle with anti-development or underdevelopment of development as it affects all sorts of 'minority' peoples. However, on further inspection these disadvantaged minorities turn out to be the majority...Ethnic, national, linguistic, racial, social sectoral, age, vocational and other minorities are all subject to the inequity and inefficiency of economic development. Adding them all up, they surely constitute a numerical majority both globally and nationally."[1]

Postmodernist development critic Arturo Escobar also acknowledges that development continues to be desired by many, but counterposes development to various groups' desire for self-definition.

And yet, despite the recognition of its demise, the imaginary of development—still without viable alternatives although somewhat weakened by the recent crisis—continues to hold sway. If at the level of social movement theory new social orders are clearly imaginable, in the arena of development—which to a great extent determines the economic and political practices necessary to bring about new orders—the picture is blurred, adumbrating a future society where only "basic needs" are met, that is a "developed" or quasi-developed society. But to arrive at this society (assuming that it were possible) would entail that all the fuss about plurality, difference, and autonomy—notions central to social movement discourse, as is argued below—would have been in vain.[2]

It needs to be said that people who are both pro-development and pro-plurality can be found in academic life and also in other settings, such as trade unions, community groups, and in religious organizations that value social justice and human freedom. People who participate in groups focused on self-help, individual healing, and psychotherapy usually favour development too, if only the individual kind. Groups that are perpetually left out or pushed out of their societies know what it is to seek development that will enable them to be equal to, but still somewhat separate from, their neighbours. It is clear that there are still very large constituencies who favour development.

As the years pass in postmodern times (and also in my life), there is a temptation to become nostalgic about the past and to see the limitations of our experience as blessings in disguise or even virtues. In this way people trivialize both their own experience and the hopes of their children for development and self-expression. Now that that post-World War II social order has been largely disassembled, there is a tendency to look back at the 1950s as not so bad after all, as a golden age, in fact, when people were better taken care of than they are today. For me, there is the temptation to excuse the harsh treatment that post-World War II society meted out to my father and to our family as a whole, now that I am middle aged and living at a considerable distance from my childhood home. I also have a growing tendency to perceive the ebullient excess that characterized Long Island's post-World War II economic growth as somehow worthy of celebration. One trip to one of the island's very numerous shopping centres will dispel this view.

Rostow himself still supports the ideas he espoused a half century ago. Rostow survived many of his critics and in 1998 published a book that reiterated his previous optimistic prognoses, with some qualifications. In *The Great Population Spike and After: Reflections on the 21st Century*, Rostow writes approvingly of people who are "relative optimists about the prospects for the world economy over the next century." These optimists "foresee the achievement, no doubt with many vicissitudes and setbacks, of a plateau of more or less universal affluence, achieved at different times for different nations, as a possible and statistically more likely outcome of industrial civilization than either a great, convulsive global crisis and decline or an early and purposive adoption of a no-growth, income redistribution strategy."[3]

The unremorseful apostle of growth devotes some paragraphs to dismissing the view of how the U.S. and the world should develop presented in the influential 1972 book *The Limits to Growth*. Rostow dismisses the arguments presented by Donella Meadows, Dennis Meadows, Jorgen Randers, and William W. Behrens III in *The Limits to Growth* as unrealistic and naive.[4] So even at the end of the twentieth century, the split between nay sayers to growth and those who seek growth above all is still a critical divide in discussions about allocation of the world's resources. It it therefore still necessary to keep resisting growth oriented development that occurs without diligent attention to distribution of resources, human rights, and sustainability.

The negative consequences of post-World War War II growth oriented development are still limiting the choices available to most people in North and South America and will continue to do so for an unpredictable period to come. These consequences are material realities that cannot be mitigated through nostalgic recollections of the 1950s or through postmodernist discourse that symbolically dethrones growth oriented development while leaving it squarely in the drivers' seats of business and government. It is important to name a few of these ongoing consequences before proceeding to sketch the outlines of a new, more adequate development theory.

First of all, capitalist development in North America at mid-century repressed people's needs to have differences accepted and their human rights respected. My own family's special problems and differences were never acknowledged by any authority. Other families lived with the strain of trying to conceal marital infidelity and breakdown. In suburban communities and small towns, divorce was seen as an evil almost as great as Communism. Divorce was one of the stigmas that prevented liberal Democrat Adlai Stevenson from winning the presidency in 1952.

During the 1970s, 1980s, and even to the present day, the people who never fit in have been crawling out from under the rug with stories about psychological stress, physical assaults, and humiliating discrimination.

Some of the other, more strictly economic failures of development described in Chapters One and Three are still evident on the streets of cities and rural communities in the Americas today. North America's transportation system for people and goods continues to be one of the most conspicuous of those failures. Computerization of just about everything has not seemed to reduce the number of trips made by automobiles and trucks; in fact the opposite seems to be the case.

Robert Caro's thousand page chronicle about the hubris of Robert Moses stresses over and over that Moses' overbuilding will lead finally to an apocalyptic gridlock on the road that will lock up the New York area from stem to stern.

> The problem was so immense now that it was difficult to comprehend its dimensions. How come to grips in one's imagination with a situation in which a mighty expressway, a gigantic superhighway of dimensions almost unknown to history, could be opened in one month, and be filled to absolute capacity the next, in which expressways opened in 1952 were by 1955 carrying the traffic load that had been forecast for 1985, in which, in this city

and metropolitan area already congested to the breaking point, every indicator—auto registrations, commuting trips per day—was increasing in
more than arithmetical, *in almost geometrical*, progression?[5]

There is still no policy or political force in place which can guarantee the nonoc-
currence of a state of total vehicular paralysis. In fact, since the 1950s, there has
been nothing but tinkering—through measures such as emission controls—with
the system that assigns a higher priority to the needs of trucks, cars and their drivers than to just about everything else.

In cities like Sao Paulo or Mexico City, the traffic is as heavy as it is in the largest urban centres in the United State and Canada, but the traffic jams are less mon-
umental and easier to unravel because their scale is smaller. There are no limited
access roads of the MacDonald Cartier, 401 type in these cities, and there may
never be any. In this aspect of economic development, the less developed urban
centres of the world may be more fortunate and, indeed, more "developed" in the
postmodern sense than their North American counterparts.

The explosive growth of megacities, called "world city states" by Ricardo
Petrella, is part and parcel of the truck and car economy which has flourished in
most parts of the world for the past half century. It is doubtful that most of the
world's cities—including smallish "large" cities such as Monterrey, Mexico, or
Belo Horizonte, Brazil—are going to thin out or become significantly smaller in
future. There is no indication that a massive return to rural areas in any country of
the world would aid economic development; it would probably prove disastrous,
given the way most rural economies are currently structured. Nor do I as an individual commentator hold any brief for a "back to nature" movement; a city person
since my earliest years, to this day I feel most at home when I am downtown. Yet
no observer of world demographic patterns denies that the growth of megacities is
a disturbing trend. Somehow the trend toward a world of big cities flanked by
roads filled with refugees on their weary way to these cities has to be reversed.

The fact that many large downtowns in the United States are not economic
development success stories and are in fact just barely viable is acknowledged even
by Walt Rostow in *The Great Population Spike and After*. In this book, Rostow also
indirectly articulates one of the main theses of *Reshaping the World for the 21st
Century*: that underdevelopment is a problem in the world's wealthiest countries
as well as in the nations of the third world. Rostow asserts first of all that there
needs to be "the bringing about of a systematic and substantive process of decline
in the social pathology of the inner city."[6] He voices a fear that the United States
will "turn inward" and fail to play its part "at the critical margin" if the urban
problem is not solved.[7] Rostow also admits that "in fact, the underdevelopment of
American inner cities has a great deal in common with underdevelopment abroad.
The major difference—more important than initial income per capita—is the
greater weakness of the families in the American inner cities."[8]

Rostow also makes a tacit admission that the theory of growth is not adequate and that another, more inclusive perspective is required. "But there is something missing here if we are to draw citizens into a sustained effort of this kind. The missing element is vision."[9] In his proposal for how to overhaul life in the teeming downtowns, Rostow seems to draw on the ideas of Paulo Freire or of the *Limits to Growth* authors. "What is needed are institutions created by a partnership between the community as a whole and those who live in the inner city. In time, these institutions ought to be run entirely by men and women of the inner city. Only thus will the sense of neo-colonial dependence be broken and the people of the inner city gain a sense that control of their own destiny is possible."[10] In fact, two conflicting views of development co-exist in the *Great Population Spike*, but the contradiction goes unacknowledged. The old cold warrior gives a nod to the fact that his old categories do not apply to the current era, but seems unable to bring himself to say so.

Now that the dominant post-World War II development models —based on Keynsian capitalism and Communism respectively—have been pulled apart by globalization, there is a need for development theory or theories that will overcome the deficiencies of earlier viewpoints. First and foremost as a theoretical issue is the question of how development capital will be accumulated to eliminate poverty and accomplish other kinds of development in third world countries and in deprived areas of the developed world such as inner cities and Indian reserves. This question, which has plagued every less developed society and has never been satisfactorily answered was not squarely faced by W.W. Rostow in his writing about the growth. Rostow's colleague, University of Glasgow economist A.K. Cairncross did directly ask the question: where will the money be found? Capitalism never has come up with a satisfactory answer to this question. The claim that profits from growth would someone find their way—in the form start-up aid or job programs—to less developed countries, inner cities, and Indian reserves has proved illusory. Communist governments tried to answer the question by redistributing capital in their societies, sometimes by force. This seizure of assets was so unpopular with people who experienced it and with those people's allies in the world's wealthiest countries that it set up a scenario of counter-revolution against the expropriating government. In this post-Communist, egregiously globalized era, the question "where will the money come from?" sounds tiresome and the questioner, querulous. Still, it needs to be answered.

The issue of capital accumulation is by no means the only important one. The questions posed in Chapter One: "who controls capital and the development funded by it?" and "who benefits?" are equally weighty. There has to be recognition of the reality, strongly voiced by Andre Gunder Frank and some other dependency thinkers in the 1960s and 1970s, that market oriented economics is not a self-sufficient discipline. The market does not allocate resources wisely, justly, or at all evenly. The key role of human intention and agency in economic development needs to be stressed instead. Stories about how groups of people decide to do things and then accomplish them are needed in economics as much or more as diagrams of growth curves and cycles.

The perceptions of liberation theology or a like-minded school of thought are required in any account of how development happens, in other words. Constant attention is needed to the fact that the world is ruled not just by material necessity or the unstoppable force of the market; human initiative also shapes events on our planet. It is ironic that this emphasis on human capabilities is needed at the same time as a strong campaign for environmental protection and for human moderation in exploitation of natural resources. People everywhere need to be reminded that they can be powerful because the preaching of the world's small group of globalizers that resignation to globalization is required of everyone has met with great success. In fact, globalization has managed to generate an aura of "untouchability" for itself. The natural world has never acquired this air of inviolability, partly because globalizers are some of the chief extractors of natural resources and partly because "nature" really is open and unprotected (though not undefended, at least in the animal kingdom). In the long run—or, at the end of the day, in globalization talk—the natural world is the possessor of a unique and inexorable force which is totally absent from globalization. Yet few people want to acknowledge or think about that. Despite the imperative to leave much of the natural world unplundered, human beings still need to be reminded that they can accomplish something substantial.

The abbreviation I use for the economic development theory needed by the people in both the developed world and the third word is "Marxism, plus human rights and sustainability." With this abbreviation, I try to suggest the great importance that should still be attached to the accumulation and distribution of capital; political rights and the need to let nature be are, however, equally important and cannot be shuffled aside for the sake of immediate material gain.

My abbreviation does have real meaning, but it does not convey the great complexity and capacity to differentiate among a multiplicity of situations that will be required of a development theory or theories in the future. It is doubtful that an adequate theory will be as simple or as dogmatic as V.I. Lenin's model of imperialism or W.W. Rostow's sketch of growth oriented capitalism, or as simple as my own "Marxism plus human rights plus sustainability." In our post-modern Western world, just about everyone has "been there" and "done that." Ambiguity and irony are much easier to come by than simple belief. Dogmatic expression of any kind has become as popular as a remaindered Chairman Mao jacket. On a 1999 trip to New York, Bernardo Bertolucci, the director of a number of great political films, commented on this cultural shift. "Politics was completely in the veins of the cinema of the sixties and seventies…Today, politics itself, since the fall of the Berlin Wall…has lost that kind of fantastic priority and excitement."[11]

Recognition of the need for a sophisticated, unemotional discourse about politics and development is evident in a 1999 manifesto on global poverty issued by the Canadian Council for International Cooperation (CCIC). The manifesto, *In Common*, includes 10 distinct points that covered a variety of bases: sustainable development, human rights, an equitable global economic order, gender equity, protection of children, peace building, food security, corporate social responsibility, foreign aid, and citizen participation.[12] *In Common* presents a great deal of detailed information but few general statements or theoretical analysis. One of its subtitles, "Make it Happen," suggests that there is little new left to say on the matter of global poverty; what matters is to do something.

The detachment, irony and even cynicism that characterize much of the talk about social issues in the U.S., Canada, and Europe may be absent from theoretical political discussions in less developed nations that are still struggling to rid themselves of widespread poverty and build some self-reliant economic strength. Societies where a drastic overhaul is needed to achieve a measure of equity may be designated as potentially revolutionary; revolutions have seldom been powered by irony. Instead, plain speaking ideas and slogans, such as "Bread and Land" (Russia) and "Liberty, Equality, and Fraternity" (France) have been the order of the day.

Some recent revolutions and rebellions in this hemisphere have displayed the capacity to combine postmodern skepticism and even self-deprecating humour with enthusiastic commitment to social change. Two noteworthy cases in this regard are the Sandinistas in Nicaragua and the Zapatistas in Mexico. The 1979 Sandinista Revolution was a "nicer," more self-doubting, and less dogmatic revolution than the 1959 Cuban revolution. One intellectual wellspring for this postmodern revolution in Central America was liberation theology, a body of thought that did not exist in 1959; it later came to appreciated by Fidel Castro, whose conversations with the liberation theologian Frei Betto were published as the book *Fidel and Religion. Conversations with Frei Betto*. Subcomandante Marcos and the Zapatistas likewise have taken some inspiration from liberation theology and have showed a capacity for critical reflection on their own actions. Marcos himself often sounds more like Hamlet in a ski mask than like Emiliano Zapata. It may be argued that the price of these two movements' lack of dogmatism has been abysmal failure. The Sandinistas lost power in 1990, and the Zapatistas never had it in the first place. Still the possibility can't be dismissed that a postmodern—dedicated but self-doubting—revolutionary approach could be successful at some future point.

A development theory that seeks justice as well as efficient production will also have to take into account the needs and desires of individual people. Development starts with a personal wish for fulfillment; individuals will not find satisfaction in a development process that pushes aside their concerns for the sake of an abstract greater good. This insight about the personal nature of development was one of my first clear perceptions about politics, and I have never found a reason to discard it. This was why I never felt inclined to join one of the many Communist, Maoist, or Trotskyist groups that sprung up in Toronto and other North American cities during the 1960s and 1970s. Bethinho, who, as a youth, was drawn to Maoism in Brazil, seems to have had similar reaction. In a 1996 CBC radio interview, he talked about how he "started seeing the reality…people were not Maoists. They [people] were working and struggling for their rights, normal rights…Then, little by little, I discovered that my friends were crazy, and I was crazy too."[13]

I have brought individuals like myself, Bethinho, Marion Boyd, Andre Gunder Frank, and even the fictional George Bailey into this book in order to suggest the importance of individual needs and initiatives in development. These characters have been presented only in brief sketches because this book is about broad social issues and is not a biography or autobiography. Robert Caro's method in *The Power Broker* is the polar opposite of my thumbnail sketch approach to individual portraits. His book is *both* a biography and an evaluation of twentieth century development in the New York area. Caro attributes so much power to Moses and describes Moses' deeds so exhaustively that, by the end of the book, the reader feels convinced that one man singlehandedly ruined Manhattan and Long Island. This emphasis on personal power is typical of analysis done at the centre or right of the political spectrum. In contrast, left or progressive thinkers have often erred by neglecting the role of personal agency in political change. My approach is to assign an important but not dominating role to individuals.

An adequate development theory starts from the individual but goes on to point out the needs of the community, and the importance of caring for and taking responsibility for other community members. This was the emphasis of Brazil's Campaign Against Hunger and Misery, which pointed out that people should not be so heartless that they deny bread to hungry children and adults; in fact, the bread should be freely offered. Caring also has provided the energy for Toronto's Out of the Cold and other community programs that offer overnight shelter to the homeless. The contrast of caring community to heartless capitalism was also the theme of "It's a Wonderful Life." Without this "caring" part of economic development theory, the theory has no value whatever. Caring is just the start of doing good economics, however. Political action and long term national planning are also required. The criterion of "caring" needs detailed elaboration before it can be effectively used in a political or business arena. Otherwise politicians might, and frequently do, express the certitude that tough denial of immediate benefits is the best way to show caring for the hungry.

In the long run, some statement of principles is needed in order to indicate the kind of relationships an adequate economic development theory seeks among humans, and between humans and the natural world. The world does not lack such statements of principles, but these have usually been seen as political ideals rather than economic goals. The link between human rights and the operation of national and world markets needs to be made much more directly.

There are numerous codes that put forward the ideal of humanity living in fellowship and also in harmony with the natural world. There is the "justice, liberty, and democracy" of the Mexican revolution and the Zapatistas. The EZLN also has eleven fundamental demands: for work, land, housing, food, health, education, independence, freedom, democracy, justice, and peace.[14] IBASE tips its hat to solidarity, participation, and diversity, as well as to the 18th century ideals of liberty and equality. The U.S. Bill of Rights is one of the world's more comprehensive and well enforced statements of individual civil rights. The problem with the U.S. code, from the viewpoint of an economic analyst, is that it does not link the notion of rights to peoples' needs for work, food, and housing. The Universal Declaration of Human Rights is one of the few government sanctioned codes that states the rights to food, clothing, housing and medical care as basic human rights. Endowing the Universal Declaration of Human Rights with some teeth would be a good first step toward enforcement of economic rights for all people.

An adequate development theory for the future will include elements that pertain to both the developed world and the countries of the third world. There will also be important differences, however, in the analysis and action needed in the first and third worlds. These differences will be most conspicuous in discussions about how capital for various kinds of production will be accumulated and how decisions about its spending will be made. The shortage of capital available to meet people's basic needs is more dire in the third world than in the developed world, especially in the world's poorest countries, a number of which are in Africa. In the developed world, capital is often misapplied rather than completely missing. It should be noted that misapplication of capital occurs frequently in third world countries too, even in countries where cash is least available.

The matter of how capital may be accumulated in third world countries, which did not experience nationally controlled industrialization in either the nineteenth or twentieth centuries, has not been adequately addressed by growth oriented capitalist theory, by Marxism, by Leninism, or even by the most militant third world governments, such as Cuba's. Still the third world's need for capital to satisfy basic human needs has not disappeared. Since the huge clouds of the debt crisis rolled onto the world horizon in the early 1980s, peoples' awareness has grown that a lot of capital for third world development could be freed up by reducing third world debts or by forgiving them completely. At first this was a subversive notion promoted mainly by some third world leaders who figured that debt relief was not a favour, but instead simple justice owed to their countries. At a later date, debt forgiveness came to be an important plank in the development programs promoted by NGOs and church organizations in both the first and third worlds. By the mid-1990s, debt forgiveness was being advocated by the governments of the G8 nations and by some of the world's chief spokes people for the status quo. On the eve of 1999 G8 summit in Germany, the archbishop of Canterbury and the president of the World Bank issued a joint statement on debt relief. "Several hundred millions of these poor [people] live in countries where crushing debt stands in the way of lasting poverty reduction. How did we get here, and what can we do to reduce burdensome debt in the poorest countries?"[15] Relief of debt for developed countries such as Canada and the United States, or even for economically weighty third world nations such as Mexico and Brazil, has not been mentioned in G8 discussions. The need for relief—not "forgiveness"—is expressed with reference only to the world's poorest countries such as Mozambique.

Steps toward relief taken by the G8 in 1996 and 1999 are clearly more similar to bankruptcy proceedings than to debt cancellation.

The conditions for relief are stringent, and the amount and type of debt to be relieved, quite limited. The fact that the debt relief plan was hatched within the G8 instead of a more inclusive organization such as the United Nations indicates the plan's terms were dictated by creditor nations rather than discussed as a matter that strongly affects the whole world's welfare. The 1999 plan calls for the cancellation of $15 billion of the $130 billion owed by the world's poor nations.[16] This measure could be financed through the sale of close to 10 percent of the International Monetary Fund's gold reserves. A further $50 billion in trade debts backed by government guarantees and $20 billion in soft development assistance loans could also be considered, in coordination with the debtor nations' plans for economic reforms.[17] The Archbishop of Canterbury and the President of the World Bank agree debt relief must be conditional. "Relief must be provided only when there is common agreement that freed resources will, and can, be used wisely and productively...Strict accountability at every level will increase confidence that the poor will really benefit from debt relief."[18]

Many of the world's churches and other NGOs complained that the 1999 debt relief measures were much too stingy. Oxfam issued a statement pointing out that, even with the new provisions, Mozambique would still be paying twice as much every year for debt payments as for primary education. Oxfam's measured response to the G8 leaders' carefully measured proposal did not take into account another less practical, but not impossible, approach to the problem of how third world debt can be set aside in order to free up capital for the development needs of the world's poor countries. This approach would entail a calculation by former colonies' of the costs of political and economic imperialism to their economies over the course of a century or so. Some pundits have suggested that black people in the Americas could bring a lawsuit for the damages caused by slavery; the settlement in such a suit would be unimaginable. Why couldn't former colonies bring suits for the loss of natural resources, loss of life, and mental suffering caused by colonialism and neo-colonialism? Another method might be the use of an international war crimes tribunal to assess damages caused by the murder of millions of aboriginal people during the course of settling the Western hemisphere. A great advantage to this way of thinking about and acting on debt cancellation is that it would put those who usually do the asking of questions in the witness box for interrogation. Another is that it would show that debts are owed from the developed world to the third world and not just visa-versa. A third good point is that, by treating one of the world's biggest problems as a matter for litigation, it could help prevent outbreaks of regional war or domestic unrest. Many NGOs would probably cringe at the thought of leaving this political matter to be settled by legal arguments, but it cannot be denied that legal arguments are usually less destructive than guns.

This lawsuit strategy should not be quickly dismissed as a daydream. Who would have thought that legal action could be used to catch Chile's 1970s and 1980s dictator to justice? Who would have thought that a war crimes tribunal could make a sentence of death stick to some of Rwanda's genocidal murderers? How many people believed that Holocaust victims' money could be recovered from Swiss banks? Recent events seem to indicate that the rule of law is becoming more genuinely international. The world cannot yet tell how many old crimes and debts may still be unearthed and brought to public attention.

Another eminently arguable position on international debt is that its cancellation should not depend on the good behaviour of the governments in countries where the debt is lifted. A lack of conditionality in debt cancellation, while wrong headed in some respects, is only simple justice from the viewpoint of debtor nations. Most of these countries did lose a lot of wealth during the colonial period and feel that the world owes them something for what was taken. Many third world leaders also believe that the bankers who proffered them loans so willingly in the 1970s now owe their debtors at least as much as visa versa. It is true that debt cancellation for human rights violating or spendthrift third world governments does not seem just or even sensible.

Still, it must be asked whether it would it be just to award damages to a grievor and then refuse to turn it over unless the grievor spends it wisely. The same issue about the wisdom of generating new money for dictatorial or cruel third world governments arose during discussions of the NIEO during the 1970s. Why pay more for copper or bauxite if an unjust ruler will keep the revenues from reaching the people who most need it? I believe that the correct answer in that case was that the higher price was merited whether or not the government that would benefit from the price was clearly "deserving." In the current discussion of world debt there is likewise a pressing need to show the world that third world governments are not deadbeats that need a break, but instead creditors in their own right.

The establishment of an fund or bank for ongoing concessional loans to third world development projects is needed as a complement to or element of an adequate debt relief plan. What third world governments want and need is a bank that looks after their best interests and where they wield some real power—a Bailey Savings and Loan for the world, you might say if you wanted to be whimsical. What is needed is an International Development Association (IDA) with a new name, provisions for long-term funding, and a governing body located in the

United Nations or some international organization other than the World Bank. The International Fund for Agricultural Development (IFAD) launched in 1978 was intended to be such an agency, but there was not enough oil revenue available to make it a significant presence globally.

These days there is no pot of money anywhere that seems to be a feasible source of cash for the reborn IDA-IFAD. Provision of foreign aid funds continues to sag. One possibility favoured by lots of NGOs and by the Global Governance Commission is a tax on foreign exchange transactions, commonly known as the Tobin tax. This eminently sensible form of taxation would dampen down the speculation that leads to the jitters and crises such as those that swept across Asia, Latin America, and Russia in 1997 and 1998. The money such a tax would provide for third world development would be a nice, big bonus. The Tobin tax, however, appears nowhere on any G8 agenda for economic reform.

Leaders gathered at the 1999 G8 meeting in Germany rejected even proposals for regulation of hedge funds and for capital controls. Instead they favoured status quo oriented measures such as provision of programs for rapid IMF and World Bank support of needy people in any future crisis. "The world has proved crazy of late," French President Jacques Chirac told the media. "We are taking steps to create a world that is more stable, more generous and more courageous."[19] His words would have been more convincing if the G8 had moved toward imposition of the Tobin tax. It should be remembered, however, that a personal income tax seemed a chimera not long ago, but continues in effect in countries around the world despite the efforts of anti-tax governments in the U.S. and Canada.

Using National Resources

Third world efforts to achieve national development based on the of using local resources are as important as the transfer of money from the developed world either as aid or debt relief. A nation without revenue-generating enterprises over which its nation and people have some control will be tied to the wearying treadmill of economic dependency in perpetuity. A national development strategy of this kind requires at least two thrusts—one focused on building a manufacturing sector and one geared to agricultural development. The problems associated with this kind of two pronged development obviously vary according to the size of the country and the degree of development already achieved. The problems of development also differ according to the disposition of the third world government: committed to a fair distribution of wealth, indifferent to glaring social injustices, or somewhere in between. Brazil's dilemmas are clearly quite different from Nicaragua's, yet the two countries do share a number of characteristics; they are both underdeveloped in the sense that large numbers of people in both countries are poor and lack basic health and educational services.

Every economy in the world can benefit from building its capacity to manufacture (and perhaps export) some fully finished goods. The assembly of computer components or sewing of clothing in an export processing zone does not count as manufacturing because these activities provide only meager wages and do nothing else to benefit the domestic economy. The making of handicrafts for sale at home or for export is a borderline case; whether or not it qualifies as manufacturing depends on the volume of goods produced and the kind of system set up to merchandise the crafts.

Import substitution also qualifies as manufacturing; one big limitation of import substitution is that is has very often been initiated by companies based outside the host country. Efforts by governments to control multinational corporations operating within their countries were common in the 1960s and 1970s; in the 1990s, these nationalistic strictures have in 99 percent of countries given way to shamelessly eager invitations for corporate investment. In the era of globalization, corporations want people to believe that their triumph over nationalistic restrictions is total and without any end, and they have largely sold this version of our planet's evolution to the world. Still, unexpected events have a way of changing history's course every so often, and the day for national controls over investment capital may come again; indeed those days have never gone in countries such as Cuba. Another possibility is for supranational restrictions on the activities of multinational corporations initiated by an international organization such as the United Nations or by people's organizations, that is, trade unions or NGOs based both in the developed world and the third world.

The kind of manufacturing cited most often and most fondly by third world advocates is small scale (but not tiny) production of consumer goods mainly for the local and regional market; the furniture making business in Caracas, Venezuela, was, for instance, named as an exemplary enterprise by Robert Gwynne in his 1985 book *Industrialization and Urbanization in Latin America*. Though such enterprises are praiseworthy, they cannot serve as the foundation for a national economic development strategy. Gwynne suggests that these modestly capitalized companies could play important economic roles if they gained access to larger supplies of capital; a scenario to make capital accumulation possible is needed.

Agricultural development is the other *sine qua non* for third world countries. Rostow asserted that a rise in agricultural productivity and income was an essential precondition for capitalistic industrialization. Military expansion was the only alternative to agricultural productivity named by Rostow in his 1960s article "Leading Sectors and the Takeoff." Most third world oriented economists would probably agree with Rostow that a high priority should be assigned to agriculture, but their reasons for that opinion might be quite different. The most pressing reason for paying attention to agriculture, especially in third world countries, is that no country can afford to give up production some of its own food supplies. The ability to produce its own sustenance puts a community or a nation squarely on the road to self-reliance. The desire for self-reliance is what fuels the demand of Chiapas *campesinos* to hold on to their *ejido* based system of corn production. In this situation or other comparable ones, where subsistence production is barely tolerated as a poor relative of cash crops, subsistence crop producers need to hold firmly onto their traditional role in national economies.

In many countries, there can and should be another, more ambitious role for agriculture beyond the production of food for production at home. Should it be the generation of foreign exchange through cash crop exports controlled by multi-national corporations like Del Monte and Dole? During the 1970s and 1980s, this question was answered resoundingly in the affirmative by the governments of Mexico and numerous other third world countries. Falling commodity prices during the 1980s and 1990s and the failure to share national resources equitably made this strategy a failure. Now it may be remembered that there are other possible roles for agriculture: the generation of nationally controlled revenues that can be put in the pockets of agricultural owners and labourers. These monies can then in turn be used to purchase manufactured goods produced through import substitution or some other means. Many third world governments have tried to implement this kind of strategy, usually with very limited success. It is still one of the only routes to prosperity that seems open to small, less developed economies.

International aid agencies, governments in both the developed and less developed world, and third world revolutionary organizations have struggled with the question of how to make agriculture produce more revenue for a greater number of people. Leftists have argued that agrarian reform is a sine qua non for such a positive change, but leftists have not found a satisfactory way to overcome the objection of John Kenneth Galbraith to this strategy, which was cited in Chapter Three. "The world is composed of many different kinds of people, but those who own land are not so different—whether they live in China, Persia, Mississippi, or Quebec—that they will meet and happily vote themselves out of its possession." Economists on the right have argued vehemently that large scale production of cash crops is the way for less developed countries to go, but they have not been able to counter the objection that such production does nothing to help the majority, and particularly not landless peasants, who labour on large plantations for meager wages. Falling commodity prices have also exerted a steady drag on third world agriculture.

During the 1960s and 1970s, many aid agencies, NGOs, third world governments, and even some dependency theorists tried to come up with a "third way" to do agricultural development, a strategy that would support some of the least affluent without touching the prerogatives of the most affluent. The result of these efforts was the "basic needs" approach to economic development described in Chapter Two, which enjoyed a vogue during the 1970s but declined in popularity thereafter. The basic needs approach was not necessarily tied to rural areas, but it most often was seen as a method of rural development. In its heyday, it was disliked by dependency theorists like Andre Gunder Frank because it skirted the problems of land distribution and fair world prices. (The dislike was felt despite the fact that basic needs thinking was inspired, at least in some respects, by dependency theory.) Basic needs is still rejected by progressive peoples' organizations that aim for thorough, radical change in their countries' rural sectors. Brazil's *Sem Terra* (MST) has been conducting an international petition campaign against a "basic needs" type rural development program mounted in Brazil by the World Bank in the late 1990s. Under this *Alivio de la Pobreza* (Poverty Alleviation) program for small producers, $150 million was loaned to Brazil in 1998 for the purpose of purchasing land. The ultimate goal is to lend up to $1 billion for this purpose. MST representative Ramos Figuereido criticized the poverty alleviation scheme on a number of grounds at a public meeting in Toronto. The program would increase the country's foreign debt, he said, and serve to enrich the landholding class. Landless *campesinos* would buy from landowners with World Bank credit at a price set by the owners themselves. These new properties owners would probably lose their new land very soon, according to Figuereido, because the program does not provide technical assistance or credit for the production process.[20] MST demands instead an agrarian reform process that would provide poor *campesinos* with adequate amounts of land, credit, and technical assistance.

The critics of the basic needs approach do not include only groups and analysts who may be identified with the traditional left. Post-modernists like Arturo Escobar also dislike it because it seems to level down the aspirations of the world's people to the lowest possible level. If everyone has a roof and four walls, a source of clean water, a way to grow some food, and a way to become literate, then it can be said that their basic needs are met, after all. Yet is goal of "basic needs for all" is finally not very ennobling or even satisfying to the complex beings who walk the earth on two legs and are also capable of writing songs and poetry.

Despite the beating it has taken from all sides in the development debate, there is still some legitimate role for basic needs oriented projects in Latin American and other areas of the third world. The World Bank and other aid analysts who fashioned basic needs were smart in the way that they took ideas that had their origins in the third world and translated them into the development parlance of the developed world's capital cities. These analysts introduced a degree of compatibility into objectives that were opposite to each other in many ways; this route, the one always taken by liberal reformers, very often has some achievements to claim. Swedish development analyst Bjorn Hettne has described the successful aspects of the World Bank approach: In the World Bank version of basic needs, "redistribution and growth were treated as complementary rather than contradictory elements of a new development strategy...the BNA [basic needs approach] thus reached a wide acceptance ranging from World Bank economists, who enriched their growth models with social indicators, to global reformers, who inflated the BNA into a future programme not only for the 'underdeveloped' but also for the 'overdeveloped'."[21]

Beyond opening room for compromise between owners and the dispossessed on some agricultural development issues, there is still a great need to satisfy peasants just demands for land to work, for an adequate subsistence income, and for surplus income to spend or else invest in new production. Calls for social revolution in the countryside that were issued in the 1960s and earlier years were stilled during the 1980s because they seemed futile, not because social revolutions had been accomplished. Then in the 1990s, the calls in Brazil, Mexico, and some other Latin American countries were heard again, issued by a new generation, but no less urgent than before.

There is reason to believe that the countryside will be a space where future radical social changes will occur in Latin America, because this hemisphere's poorest people are its landless peasants, who possess nothing and have to work like beasts (as the young Frank Capra discovered even as far away as Sicily). These dispossessed people will not stop trying to change their situations. Governments that are interested in self-reliant economic development will also try to make changes in the countryside in order to improve agricultural production and make country life more attractive to *campesinos* who are potential migrants to the great cities. Some of the truths of Maoist theory need to be resurrected and reformulated in a twenty-first century idiom; the goal of this reformulation will be to describe how agriculture may benefit rural workers and their nation as a whole.

Radical social change is already happening in the rural areas of Mexico and Brazil. The Zapatistas and *Sem Terra* are launching bold initiatives that both depict to the national and international media how much they want radical social change and also are sometimes effective in accomplishing that change. U.S. sociologist James Petras, who has written a number of books on Latin American revolutionary movements, has called *Sem Terra* "the most dynamic rural social movement in Latin America."[22] The two movements can be considered not only dynamic, but also revolutionary in a postmodern sense that requires careful definition and attention to detail. They are revolutionary because, though they do not aim to overthrow their national governments, they intend to change how their societies operate in very profound ways. The absence of ambition to topple the central government may come from a realization that it just can't be done; the lack of interest in taking over the nation's capital might also reflect an astute awareness that the power of most governments, and especially those in less developed countries, has greatly waned during the past twenty-five years. *Sem Terra* and the Zapatistas have not proposed national strategies for agriculture that they would like to see implemented. Instead the two have shown strong determination to protect the lands of Chiapas' indigenous people and to obtain land for Brazil's landless *campesinos*. Both organization have made it clear that they have a lot of other goals too.

An aspect of both organizations that may be termed revolutionary is their law breaking and limited use of force to obtain their goals. The Zapatistas possess a very small stock of unsophisticated arms and used them to stage one local rebellion. They needed armed muscle to draw attention to their demands, and retained this tiny amount of muscle indefinitely. The only force used by *Sem Terra* is the occupation of land, a tactic used by non-violent protestors all over the world. A difference between a *Sem Terra* occupation and many other sit-ins is that people under the *Sem Terra* banners intend to occupy the land permanently, while most sit-ins are for a day or a week. *Sem Terra* occupations have been contested so forcefully by Brazilian authorities that its members might be forgiven if they ask themselves whether they need some equipment to defend themselves.

Despite their similarities, the Zapatistas and *Sem Terra* are easy to distinguish from each other in style and methods. Although they have roots in Chiapas, the Zapatistas display an urban sophistication and at times a tinge of self-deprecating melancholy that is uniquely theirs. (Some might say that the melancholy is a Mexican cultural characteristic.) They and their allies also have had access to computer technology that does not yet seem to be part of *Sem Terra's* informational arsenal. A trademark of *Sem Terra* that is evident in the bearing of at least some of its members is an eager belief in and love for their peoples' struggle. MST representative Ramos Figuereido radiates an optimism and a certainty of victory that seemed more characteristic of the 1960s than of the present. "You cannot make the sun rise, but you can see it rise if you get up early," said Figuererido at a 1999 meeting. "The future belongs to us, and that is why we get up early…Only those who love will struggle. Only those who struggle will triumph." This presentation was emboldening, even to spectators who were middle aged and/or inclined to skepticism.

What about North America?

This text has reported on the ways North American governments and corporations underdeveloped their own societies, and then transferred the same underdeveloping strategies to the countries of the third world. It is not the task of this book to propose how the U.S. and/or Canadian governments might set about the daunting task of somewhat decapitalizing the strongest sectors of societies and infusing capital and other resources into neglected areas. This process might be even harder than developing the underdeveloped areas of the third world. A viewpoint about how the largest parts of the economy might be made smaller and the most deprived parts might be strengthened will have to be done in another book or by another writer.

Still a few possibilities need to be proposed. It seems very unlikely that effective movements for social change in the U.S. will be led by either industrial or agricultural workers—the sectors designated as the chief instigators of social revolution by Marx and Mao respectively. Instead the more likely movers and shakers are those who remain dispossessed, even in the midst of lavish consumption. In the 1960s, African-Americans effected important changes in the U.S. that benefitted them and also the country as a whole. The time was ripe because the federal government was on their side (at least in a limited way), and the feudal

South was ripe for dissolution. In the 1990s, poverty and isolation remain the lot of many black communities in Harlem and other inner cities. Events like the Los Angeles riot of 1992, the New York demonstrations of 1999, the 2001 unrest in Cincinnati, the O.J. Simpson trial, and the Million Man March make it clear much still needs to be done to build an equitable society. Even Walt Rostow admitted in his 1998 book that economic development has not occurred in U.S. inner cities.

African-Americans who have not made a good life for themselves in the U.S. are not the only Americans still suffering from seemingly endless underdevelopment. A new class of poor and underprivileged has become larger and more visible during the 1990s—single parent families who were hurt by the 1996 welfare law, the mentally ill who make their homes on the street, and people who have been hit by changes to public housing legislation. It seems unlikely that any movement of dispossessed people will be led by the Democratic or Republican parties. An agglomeration of church people—who provided a lot of the energy and guts for the civil rights movements—NGO supporters, and other dissatisfied people seems a more likely alternative for a successful leadership.

The goal of such a movement of the dispossessed cannot be only to provide a bit more money for inner cities or Indian reserves. This more generous provision of money to the poor, which was tried in the 1960s, did result in some positive changes, but not enough to redress the imbalance between the most well off and the least well off in the country. Measures to initiate truly self-reliant development are needed instead.

In Canada, the situation is quite different from that in the U.S. The casualties of Canada's semi-industrialized, dependent economy are similar to those who may be found in U.S. cities and rural areas—the impoverished aboriginal nations, the people of colour, the single parent families, the homeless. Canadians' way out of their current fix will have to be very different from the course taken by Americans, because the course of Canada's economic development does not resemble that of the U.S. It may be argued that the whole of the Canadian economy—and not just parts of it as in the U.S.—has failed to achieve a measure of self-reliance. The course of social activism in Canada will be easy to distinguish from that of the U.S. because at least some Canadian trade unions retain a militancy that has been hard to detect in the U.S. trade union movement in recent years. Canadian trade unions have spearheaded the protests against globalizing provincial governments, and it seems likely that they will continue to do so.

A final word needs to be said about the economic and political realignments needed to achieve economic development for all the peoples of this hemisphere. Chapter Six asserted the need for a shift in global alliances and for changes in international governance. The collapse of the Soviet Union and the weakness of the third world since the start of the debt crisis in the early 1980s have increased the urgency for such a regrouping. The number of governments expressing views different from U.S. government and corporate spokespeople has been very drastically reduced during the past decade. A new group of middle powers, with Canada as a leading presence among them, could make a difference in how international decisions are made. Though Canada has been tied more closely than ever before to the U.S. since the start of the free trade regime, the tie has caused more bickering and tension than friendship. Continuing trade disputes could cause some separation between the northern two North American nations. There is still room to manoeuver on this and other international fronts.

Where Do the Ducks Go?

This book has tried to present a vision of how economic development could change for the better in this hemisphere. The vision is made out of my studies, my personal experience, and my political activism. My vision also allows for the presenter's self-doubt and for a sense of humour. I would like to end an anecdote about life on the road, which is also where the book began. "One day George Bailey ran into a duck while he was on his way to the beach. 'Doggone it, duck, have you seen the girl from Ipanema?' 'No George,' said the duck, 'I haven't had a glimpse of her, but I've been searching because I'd like to ask her to lend me a dime for a cup of coffee.' 'Well then,' said George, 'let's get going before old Potter catches us.' So they got going and continued on the road."

NOTES
1. Gunder Frank, "Underdevelopment of Development," *Scandanavian Journal of Development Alternatives*, Vol. 10, no. 3 (September 1991), p. 61.
2. Arturo Escobar, "Imagining a Post-Development Era? Critical Thought, Development and Social Movements," *Social Text*, 31/31, p. 21.
3. W.W. Rostow, *The Great Population Spike and After. Reflections on the 21st Century* (New York: Oxford University Press, 1998), p. 136.
4. Ibid. p. 134.
5. Robert A. Caro, *The Power Broker. Robert Moses and the Fall of New York*, (New York: Alfred A. Knopf, 1974), p. 914.
6. Rostow, *Spike*, p. 157.
7. Ibid., p. 158.
8. Ibid., p. 168.
9. Ibid.. p. 177.
10. Ibid., p. 170.
11. *The Globe and Mail*, 20 May 1999, C2.
12. Canadian Council for International Cooperation, *In Common*, 1999.
13. Interview with Robert Carty on *This Morning*, 8 February 1998.
14. Dan LaBotz, *Democracy in Mexico. Peasant Rebellion and Political Reform* (Boston: South End Press, 1995), p. 41.
15. *The Globe and Mail*, 17 June 1999, A21.
16. *International Herald Tribune*, 19-20 June, 1999, 1.
17. *The New York Times*, 19 June 1999, A1.
18. *The Globe and Mail*, 17 June 1999, A21.
19. *The New York Times*, 19 June 1999, A8.
20. Ramos Figuereido at a public meeting at Bloor St. United Church, Toronto, 18 April 1999.
21. Bjorn Hettne, *Development theory and the Three worlds* (New York: Longman Scientific and Technical, 1990), p. 168.
22. James Petras, "Land Occupations in Brazil," *Links. International Journal of Socialist Renewal* 10 (March to July 1998): 111-17.

INDEX

COFFEE WITH PLEASURE
Just Java and World Trade

Laure Waridel
Foreword by Maude Barlow
Photographs by Éric St-Pierre

This book looks at the fair-trade movement by examining the issues surrounding the production and trading of coffee.

Using Mexico as an example, part one describes the conventional coffee trade, tracing the coffee bean's journey from the tree, through the hands of several intermediaries in both the North and South, to its final destination as a cup of coffee. Part two presents the fair trade concept through the example of the Mexican peasant organization which was one of the first to embrace the fair trade system, and which was also a pioneer in the production of organic coffee. The third part explores the situation of fair-trade in North America, and provides comprehensive sources and references for anyone who wants to get involved, at any level.

Legions of people who produce our coffee suffer abysmally low wages because of absurdly low prices. Solving this problem, by buying with conscience, would cost coffee drinkers almost nothing...To read *Coffee With Pleasure* is to know that we can change the world in simple, meaningful ways now. —*Paul Hawken, author of* The Ecology of Commerce *and* The Next Economy

You hold in your hands a rare treasure...a book about hope, life and ethics. It is the story of a cause and of a movement and it builds a bridge of promise to tomorrow for millions of workers and their families around the world. —*Maude Barlow, Council of Canadians*

LAURE WARIDEL is a researcher with the POLIS Project on Ecological Governance and a columnist with Radio-Canada. She was co-founder of Équiterre, a Montreal-based organizaton that promotes ecological and socially responsible choices.

192 pages, photographs
Paperback ISBN: 1-55164-190-9 $19.99
Hardcover ISBN: 1-55164-191-7 $48.99

GREEN GUERRILLAS
Environmental Conflicts and Initiatives in Latin America and the Caribbean
Helen Collinson, editor

Leading environmental activists, from both sides of the Atlantic highlight the struggles and initiatives of indigenous communities in the Ecuadorian Amazon, in Argentina, in Haiti, in Puerto Rico, in Salvador, and in Honduras.

Challenges conventional stereotypes about the region's environmental crisis demonstrating both the diversity and dilemmas of local struggles. —*Marcus Colchester, World Rainforest Movement*

Provocative and wide-ranging. Portrays the complex face of grassroots environmental politics in Latin America. —*Marianne Schmink, Co-Director of the Tropical Conservation and Development Program*

Documents numerous examples of how closely human rights violations are intertwined with threats to creation. —*United Church Observer*

250 pages, index
Paperback ISBN: 1-55164-066-X $23.99
Hardcover ISBN: 1-55164-067-8 $52.99

FROM THE GROUND UP
Essays on Grassroots and Workplace Democracy
C. George Benello
Len Krimerman, Frank Lindenfeld, Carol Korty, Julian Benello, editors
Foreword by Dimitrios Roussopoulos

In this collection of classic essays, C.George Benello persuasively argues that modern social movements need to rise to the challenge of spearheading a radical reorganization of society based on the principles of decentralization, community control, and participatory democracy.

Where the utopian confronts the practical, Benello is perhaps most creative…a valuable contribution to creating a new politics. —*Z Magazine*

An enjoyable read that contains a wide range of provoking possibilities to ponder and a greatly appreciated reminder of the wider efforts for community and economic democracy. —*Humanist in Canada*

251 pages, index
Paperback ISBN: 1-895431-32-8 $19.99
Hardcover ISBN: 1-895431-33-6 $48.99

JUST DOING IT
Popular Collective Action in the Americas
Gene Desfor, Deborah Barndt and Barbara Rahder, editors

Massive protests have disrupted global summit meetings from Seattle to Quebec City and from Gothenburg to Genoa. These demonstrations let the world know that resistance to globalization remains strong and vibrant. Not as clearly heard, though, are accounts of local communities organizing popular collective actions to resist those same institutions and policies of globalization.

Focusing on four countries—Mexico, Guatemala, United States, and Canada—and with the understanding that acts of resistance begin with the individual and move to communities, to cities, to regions and to nation-states, the narratives in this volume tell of peoples' collective struggles for environmental, economic and social justice.

They deal with: indigenous peoples struggles against violence and coercion in Guatemala; Guatemalan refugees mobilizing in exile; environmental education for sustainable agriculture in Mexico; organizing waste pickers of Mexico; the resistence efforts to better working conditions of telemarketing operators; improving seniors housing; and the ways people of color have taken community actions to change oppressive environments through grassroots organizing, education and community planning in New York City.

> These poignant, inspiring stories of communities taking action and successfully resisting corporate agendas reveal the strength and creativity of people living on the margins, from Santiago Atitlán in Guatemala to Vancouver, Canada. —*Leonie Sandercock, author of* Making the Invisible Visible

Apart from the editors, contributors include: Galit Wolfensohn, Egla Martinez-Salazar, Cindy McCulligh, Sheelagh Davis, W. Alexander Long, Emily Chan, Sarah Koch-Schulte, and Emilie K. Adin.

GENE DESFOR, DEBORAH BARNDT, and BARBARA RAHDER, teach in the Faculty of Environmental Studies at York University.

224 pages, photographs
Paperback ISBN: 1-55164-200-X $24.99
Hardcover ISBN: 1-55164-201-8 $53.99

BOOKS of RELATED INTEREST from

BLACK ROSE BOOKS

Commonwealth of Life, *by Peter Brown*
Canada and Radical Social Change, *Dimitrios Roussopoulos, editor*
Culture and Social Change, *Colin Leys, Marguerite Mendell, editors*
Decentralizing Power: On Paul Goodman, *Taylor Stoehr, editor*
Defending the Earth, *by Murray Bookchin*
Designing Utopia, *by Michael Lang*
Dissidence: Essays Against the Mainstream, *by Dimitrios Roussopoulos*
Fighting for Hope, *by Joan Newman Kuyek*
First Person Plural, *by David Smith*
Fugitive Writings, *by Peter Kropotkin*
Legacy of the New Left, *by Dimitrios Roussopoulos*
Nationalism and Culture, *by Rudolf Rocker*
Perspectives on Power, *by Noam Chomsky*
Previews and Premises, *by Alvin Toffler*
Public Place, *by Dimitrios Roussopoulos*
Rethinking Camelot, *by Noam Chomsky*
Words of A Rebel, *by Peter Kropotkin*
Year 501, *by Noam Chomsky*

send for a free catalogue of all our titles
BLACK ROSE BOOKS
C.P. 1258, Succ. Place du Parc
Montréal, Québec H3W 2R3 Canada
or visit our web site at: http://www.web.net/blackrosebooks

To order books:
In Canada: (tel) 1-800-565-9523 (fax) 1-800-221-9985
email: utpbooks@utpress.utoronto.ca
In United States: (tel) 1-800-283-3572 (fax) 1-651-917-6406
In Europe: (tel) London 44 (0)20 8986-4854 (fax) 44 (0)20 8533-5821
email: order@centralbooks.com

Printed by the workers of
MARC VEILLEUX IMPRIMEUR INC.
Boucherville, Québec
for Black Rose Books Ltd.